Domestic Violence in Context

Domestic Violence in Context

An Assessment of Community Attitudes

Robert T. Sigler
University of Alabama

Lexington Books
D.C. Heath and Company/Lexington, Massachusetts/Toronto

Library of Congress Cataloging-in-Publication Data

Sigler, Robert T.
  Domestic violence in context : an assessment of community
attitudes / Robert T. Sigler.
    p.   cm.
  Bibliography: p.
  ISBN 0–669–20936–8 (alk. paper)
    1. Family violence—United States. 2. Wife abuse—United States.
3. Child abuse—United States. 4. Aged—United States—Abuse of.
I. Title.
HQ809.3.U5S59   1989
362.82'92—dc20   89–33788
                                        CIP

Published simultaneously in Canada
Printed in the United States of America
Casebound International Standard Book Number: 0–669–20936–8
Library of Congress Catalog Card Number: 89–33788

The paper used in this publication meets the minimum requirements of
American National Standard for Information Sciences—Permanence of
Paper for Printed Library Materials, ANSI Z39.48–1984. ∞™

Year and number of this printing:

89 90 91 92 10 9 8 7 6 5 4 3 2 1

Contents

List of Figures and Tables

Figures

Tables

Acknowledgments

The author is indebted to the many students who have assisted in the collection and coding of data in both of the studies reported here and in a number of studies conducted in the past. The attention of these students to detail and commitment to quality in the conduct of research is an essential factor in the success of my efforts. Mark Houge, in particular, is to be commended for his efforts in supervision and quality control during the collection of the data in three of the four studies reported. He will do well as he pursues his own career.

The contributions of Beverly Curry, my wife, are sufficiently substantial that she can claim much of the credit for the quality of the manuscript. In addition to a critical reading of the seemingly unending series of drafts, she maintained a supportive and inquiring dialogue throughout the development, implementation, analysis, and manuscript preparation stages of the project which prevented errors and improved quality throughout.

Introduction:
The Scope of Domestic Abuse

T he interest in domestic abuse, at least in domestic violence, has been extensive in recent years. This interest can be attributed in part to changing cultural values and in part to social activists who seek reform in the manner in which society and its institutions respond to women who are abused by men, to children who are abused by their parents, and to elders who are abused by their children. In particular, the activists have acted to raise social consciousness about the severity and scope of the behavior. Because it is dramatic, visible, provable, and capable of generating great sympathy, violence has been the focus of much attention in the area of domestic abuse. Violence in the use of extreme physical force, in the use of women to satisfy the sexual needs of their abusers, and in the use of children to satisfy the sexual needs of adults with or without the use of physical force has captured public attention and has produced increased public concern for the victims of these forms of domestic abuse in the United States.

This attention has generated an expanded area of research. This research has been victim centered and has tended to focus on the use of physical force (violence) and on sexual abuse. The linkage between activism and research appears to have been firm, and much research appears to provide support for activist positions. As a result, the present level of knowledge is limited and, to some extent, potentially misleading.

Historical Perspective

Historically, the United States has been characterized as a violent nation. The use of violence to obtain legitimate ends has been endorsed or at least tolerated through most of its history. Movies and novels promote the concept that the use of violence to defeat the Indians, to control the rustlers, to prevent the homesteaders from settling the range, and to rescue the fair maiden in a hail of righteous gunfire and mayhem is an honorable way to proceed. Many contemporary movies hold to this pattern, with such characters as Dirty Harry,

Action Jackson, and Rambo, spreading mayhem and violence as they fight for right and for the American way of life.

The acceptability of violence in the domestic context predates the settlement of the United States. Throughout history, men have been held responsible for their women and children. With this responsibility, men were given power. That is, men historically have had the power to use force to control the behavior of their dependents and were expected to use so-called reasonable force in the exercise of their responsibilities. At times, reasonable force has included death and has typically included beatings and deprivation of food and other resources.

While reform efforts have been present since the Middle Ages, the unwillingness of society to intervene in family affairs remained firm until quite recently. The use of physical force in domestic settings has been broadly publicized, and public concern about the extent and severity of the problem has increased. It has been suggested that the acceptance of violence in the domestic context has declined. However, it is possible that acceptance of domestic violence has always been low and that what is changing is the public's unwillingness to allow social institutions to intervene in domestic affairs.

Contemporary interest in this phenomenon has been increasing as activists successfully present for public review dramatic cases of domestic abuse. It is possible that these presentations distort reality by presenting dramatic cases in order to win support. It also is possible that in the process, they direct attention away from other forms of abuse that may be pervasive and damaging to the victims. In any event, the contemporary move to criminalize domestic violence and to provide resources for women and children who are abused is presently enjoying considerable success in changing the law and in persuading agencies to allocate additional resources for the amelioration of this social problem.

Types of Abuse

Domestic abuse has tended to be classified in terms of the type of victim or target of the abuse. Contemporary interest in domestic abuse has emerged in stages, beginning with a growing concern for severely abused wives who were trapped in violent domestic situations with no means for successfully removing themselves and their children to a safer, less abusive environment. Shortly after the public became aware of the plight of the abused wife, the movement for children's rights increased in prominence, focusing on the plight of severely physically abused and sexually abused children. More recently, public attention has been directed toward the plight of the elderly.

Spouse abuse takes many forms. Although much public attention has been given to wife beating, with limited attention directed toward sexual abuse, women can be abused in a number of ways. If the definition of abuse includes behaviors that harm the target, then neglect, psychological and emotional abuse, and nonviolent sexual abuse also occur. The extent and nature of these forms of abuse have not been a focus of concern and generally have not been estimated or examined other than as collateral issues in cases of severe physical abuse. It is also possible for men to be targets of all these forms of abuse in the domestic environment.

While a great deal of research has examined spouse abuse, there are no accurate assessments of the extent and nature of this phenomenon. The research that does exist tends to be distorted in several ways and constitutes one of the problems that this book addresses.

A similar situation exists for child abuse. Research has examined the use of physical force and the use of children for the sexual gratification of adults. If the focus of research is on the cause of the behavior, it is possible that these two behaviors are completely different (one abuse, the other the manifestation of a psychological disturbance that produces harm to the child). If the focus is on the impact of the behaviors, it is possible that they both are aspects of a common form of behavior, abuse.

In the case of children, there appears to be continued tolerance of the use of physical force in the context of discipline. Like wives, children also can be harmed through neglect and through the use of psychologically damaging behavior. As is the case in spouse abuse, these other forms of abuse have received relatively little attention.

Abuse of the elderly, or elder abuse, is a newly emerging field. There has been a focus on the use of abusive force; however, some attention appears to be directed toward other forms of abuse, including neglect, psychological abuse, and financial abuse. The increased use of nursing homes to provide basic care for the elderly and the potential for abuse in these institutions have influenced research in this field and have possibly introduced some confusion in public perceptions of elder abuse.

The area of domestic abuse is still an unclear configuration. Although the volume of research has been formidable, much of the research has been limited to the more visible forms of abuse and has tended to focus on the harm to victims and to the victim's perspective of the abusive situation.

Definition of the Problem

Two problems are identified in this book: (1) the social problem that can be loosely termed *domestic abuse* (not domestic violence) and (2) the weaknesses of activist-driven research. The two are related somewhat: it is difficult to seek an understanding of a social problem without being motivated to some extent by the problem itself. However, high-quality, objective research can be accomplished if adequate care is taken to approach the design task from a research perspective, rather than from an activist perspective.

Domestic abuse is a legitimate target both for research and social concern and for attempts to develop successful social intervention programs that are generated by legitimate social concern. The fact that it is highly likely that there will be some form of social intervention increases the need to conduct comprehensive, high-quality research. It is not sufficient to develop valid information. The development of valid information with a limited focus on only one aspect of the phenomenon introduces a consistent bias and, if pursued exclusively to emphasize that dimension, is not professional, regardless of the legitimacy of the cause.

Research in the area of domestic abuse is subject to criticism on this basis. Much of the research has met professional standards in that it has used accepted research methods and designs for the discipline in which the researcher is based. However, it has tended to focus consistently on the more visible severe forms and cases of abuse. There is also a consistent focus on the more sympathetic victims. The victims who provide the basis for most research tend to be women, and at times a denial that men can be victims of abuse is implicit, if not explicit, in the research designs and supporting arguments.

More recent research has tended to extend this problem, rather than to reduce it. It is common for an imbalance to exist in an emerging field as initial parameters are located and evaluated. At some point, the dimensions of the phenomenon tend to emerge, and debate about definitions begins. Although some researchers have begun to examine noncentral, nonactivist perspectives, others have continued to measure physical force. In some studies, these enhanced measures seem to be designed to inflate the volume of behavior that can be included in the general class, rather than to establish clear parameters or to increase understanding of the nature of the relationships of interest.

There is a need to begin the process of comprehensively examining domestic abuse. This will not be accomplished in a single massive research project. As has been the case to date, domestic abuse will remain an area or a set of areas of research interest. That interest must be expanded to include projects designed to identify the parameters that can be expected to provide the basis for a conceptual framework that is explanatory in nature. Once domestic abuse has been tentatively defined in theoretical terms, research can focus on the many contextual variables that influence the development and implementation of abusive interactions and on the various coping skills presently in use.

Focus of the Book

This book examines the definitions in use by the general public, with attention to both the placement of domestic violence in the broader context of general violence in the perceptions of the subjects and the denotative definitions in use by the public. It is designed to present the findings of research on public perceptions of domestic abuse and the placement of domestic violence in the broader context of violence. Context for these findings is provided in the first four chapters. Chapters 1 through 3 focus on the types of abuse as discussed in the literature: spouse abuse, child abuse, and elder abuse. This three-chapter review is designed to be representative rather than comprehensive and includes commentary concerning gaps in the literature. The review is an attempt to present a non-data-based, logically structured framework that can be used as a starting point. The models are superficial and limited and should remain so until additional data provide a basis for a more elaborate model. The fourth chapter briefly summarizes the wealth of information presently available regarding violence in America.

The remaining three chapters address the study itself. The first of these, chapter 5, provides detailed information regarding the research design. Chapter 6 presents the analysis and findings and will be of primary interest to many readers. The final chapter examines in detail the need for additional research in the area of domestic abuse, with comments concerning research potential in the area of violence.

The book also contains an expanded bibliography. While this bibliography does not include all of the references in this area, an attempt was made to compile as comprehensive a bibliography as possible. No assertions are made about the quality of the entries, and the omission of an entry does not indicate a negative judgment—it simply means that a particular citation was not identified.

1
Spouse Abuse

S pouse abuse was one of the first areas of domestic violence to come to the public's attention. The resulting scrutiny led to wide-ranging changes in the written law and in the operation of the justice system. As is the case with other forms of domestic violence, spouse abuse has dimensions that do not include violence. And as is the case with all forms of domestic violence, defining spouse abuse is a difficult and confusing task.

Spouse abuse typically is characterized in terms of male abuse of the women with whom they live and includes common law marriages and other relatively permanent living arrangements as well as conventional marriages. Little attention is paid to cases in which males are mistreated by their mates or to cases in which reciprocal mistreatment occurs. Although it is probable that instances of male mistreatment are relatively rare, the potential for reciprocal abuse may be greater than presently anticipated. Studies that measure the simple use of force tend to indicate that both husbands and wives use physical force at relatively high rates (Straus, Gelles & Steinmetz 1980).

Spouse abuse also can include acts of neglect, psychological abuse, and financial abuse. To some extent, spouse abuse is occurring now because of changing social values. Acts that are challenged today were accepted behavior throughout much of Western history.

Historical Perspective

Throughout written history, women have been subordinate to men. Written records indicate that women were subordinate to men in Mesopotamia, Greece, Egypt, Rome, and early England (Bullough 1974). The first written codes defining a woman's status appeared in Rome. The Roman law of marriage made wives absolutely subject to their husbands' wishes and charged the husbands with a responsibility to rule over their wives (O'Faolain & Martines 1974). These laws were liberalized over time, but the decline of Rome and the rise of Christianity reestablished the older Roman and Jewish values

(Okun 1986). The role of women in relation to men is defined by the religions of the West (Christianity and Judaism) in terms of obedience and submission. It has been suggested that one of the effects of religion has been to reinforce the subjugation of women (Daly 1978; Dobash & Dobash 1979; Wilson 1978). These values were perpetuated through the patriarchal system of male dominance in families and through inheritance and transmission of wealth through the male line or through the husbands of the daughters (Brownmiller 1975; Dobash & Dobash 1979).

The economic inequality of women has been strongly incorporated in both European and New World law (Clark & Lewis 1977). The first written laws were constructed during the reign of Romulus in Rome (Okun 1986). All authority was vested in the male head of the family, and women were possessions of their husbands. In English common law, this was expressed in the principle of coverture, which established a condition in which a wife had no legal existence outside of her relationship with her husband. During the course of her marriage, a woman ceased to have a legal existence as an individual (Okun 1986). To some extent, a wife became the property of the husband to do with as he wished. In the United States, before the law was reformed, all property of a woman was controlled by her husband.

When reform did begin to appear in the 1800s, the protection offered tended to be protection of a wife's assets from a husband who abandoned her. Before this reform, the husband could return to the marriage if the wife acquired property, could use that property, and then could abandon her again. Only in the latter part of the 1800s was the wife's right to control her own property recognized in the law, if not in practice (Dobash & Dobash 1979).

The assertion that women were perceived as property can best be seen in the construction of the rape laws of England and the United States. Rape was originally perceived as an act against the husband or father of the victim. The proper disposition of a case of rape was the payment of compensation to the male owner for the damage done to his property (Clark & Lewis 1977). This failure to distinguish the female victim's rights from those of the husband/ father introduced confusion in the early definitions of rape, confusion that continues today (Brownmiller 1975). In addition, wives did not have the right to refuse their husbands, who could assert their conjugal rights by force, a right that remained in force until the 1970s.

Men also were responsible for the behavior of their women and were expected to control them. If women committed crimes, men were held accountable for the damage. As the dominant sex, men were expected to discipline their women. In the exercise of this discipline, men also were expected to use reasonable physical force. *Reasonable physical force* was defined as including black eyes and broken noses (Dobash & Dobash 1979).

The law of chastisement of early Rome set the pattern for subsequent standards. Laws of chastisement were adopted in many settings, such as t.. rule-of-thumb laws, so named because one of the rules in English law specified that a man could beat his wife with a rod or switch as long as it was no thicker than his thumb (Dobash & Dobash 1979). Well into the 1600s in many areas of Europe, including England, a man legally could kill his wife (Okun 1986). Community approval of the practice of the use of force by husbands to discipline wives continued uninterrupted into the nineteenth century (Okun 1986).

There is a tendency to perceive the movement for reform of these laws and conditions as a contemporary one. In fact, reform has been a fairly continuous process for over one hundred years. John Stuart Mill (1870) in the United States and Frances Cobbe (1878) in England wrote about the abuse of women and advocated reform. In England, reform took the form of legislative initiatives, which included severe beatings as grounds for divorce, a ban on selling wives and daughters into prostitution, and a ban on keeping wives locked up (Martin 1976). In the United States, reform occurred initially in case law, rather than in the legislature. North Carolina, followed closely by Alabama and Massachusetts, overturned the right of chastisement privilege of husbands. The decisions were carefully phrased to limit the extent to which the courts could intrude into marital affairs (Eisenberg & Micklow 1976). Legislation began to appear in 1883, and by 1910, thirty-five of the forty-six states had passed reform legislation that classified beating one's wife as assault (Dobash & Dobash 1979).

The visibility of wife battering declined after the beginning of women's suffrage in the 1920s and did not become salient again until the 1970s, when pressure began to develop to force the justice system to treat wife beating as a criminal offense. Although the feminist movement was not concerned with domestic affairs in the early years of its most recent resurgence, as women's roles changed and women became more involved in women's issues domestic violence became a topic of concern (Okun 1986). Attention was focused on practices of the justice system that effectively made wife beating a nonenforced offense in all but the most extreme cases.

Dimensions of Spouse Abuse

The only dimension of spouse abuse that has received careful scrutiny has been abuse involving the use of force. This tendency to conceive of spouse abuse in terms of physical force is so pervasive that spouse abuse often appears to be defined in terms of violent behavior in which the wife is the victim and the husband is the abuser. Variations from this theme include cases in which the wife abuses the husband and cases in which the abuse is reciprocal but still framed in terms of violence (Shupe, Stacey & Hazlewood 1987).

The dimensions of other types of domestic abuse tend to be broadly defined and include a number of nonviolent behaviors. It is not that there are no other forms of spouse abuse, it is just that the dimension of violence tends to be dominant. In addition to violence, spouse abuse can be psychological or emotional abuse, sexual abuse, or neglect (economic abuse).

Violence is the act that catches attention. Although it is difficult to build a case for intervention in private domestic disputes when the issue is denial of recognition, access to financial resources, or use of derogative language, the presence of bruises or broken bones provides a basis for public sympathy and justice-system intervention. This appears to be true more often for spouse abuse than for other types of abuse. Numerous studies have focused on the battered wife and have examined the battering situation carefully, with only peripheral attention given to other aspects of domestic abuse. Unlike other forms of domestic violence, such as child abuse, there does not appear to be a threshold of mitigating circumstances identified in the literature. That is, any intentional physical contact (and in some cases, attempted use of force) can be identified as *physical abuse.*

There is a tendency to focus on those cases and examples in which the abuse is outrageously severe, perhaps because the public will respond to severe physical damage. It appears that many who conduct research in this area are pursuing social reform agendas and thus focus on approaches that provide information that maximizes the potential for success in the political arena. Criminal justice agencies have responded to this pressure and focus on processing all cases in which it appears that physical force has been used, regardless of the severity of the abuse and regardless of the wishes of the victim.

Any use of force with intent to do harm is legally classified as *assault,* regardless of the marital status of the parties involved. This tends to be the standard applied to situations of domestic violence in which a husband is the aggressor and the wife is the victim (Shupe, Stacey & Hazlewood 1987). Although the adoption and degree of effective enforcement of this position vary from police agency to police agency, most police departments have reviewed their policies and have adopted policies that provide more protection for the battered wife. In short, the argument that husbands have a right or a responsibility to control and to discipline their wives is no longer an adequate defense for the husband who abuses his wife through physical force.

One form of domestic sexual abuse that has been identified as inappropriate is forced marital intercourse (Sigler & Haygood 1988). Although there appears to be some agreement that this behavior is inappropriate, there is a great deal of unwillingness to treat this behavior as a legal matter. It is argued that rape laws do not apply when the behavior occurs between spouses. Evidence suggests that the general public is less likely to endorse the criminalization of forced intercourse when a relationship exists between the parties involved, with the number of people endorsing criminalization declining as the degree of relationship increases (Sigler & Haygood 1988). The public is less likely to support legislation to control forced intercourse when the parties are married or living together than when they are dating or when they have no relationship.

Forced marital intercourse lies at the intersection of physical abuse and sexual abuse, and wives can be sexually abused without the use of force. Traditionally, women have been expected to submit to the desires of their husbands. Women have gained considerable freedom and control over their destinies during the past century, but it is possible that the belief that a wife has a duty to submit sexually to her husband unless she is ill still prevails (note the continuing popularity of headache jokes). *Sexual abuse* can occur if a wife is forced to submit to sexual intercourse with her husband when she does not wish to, even if physical force is not the form of coercion used.

Considerable disagreement exists among us about the acceptability of various forms of sexual behavior. As long as the behavior is consensual and occurs in private, society generally does not have an interest. When a consensus does not exist between partners and one partner forces the other to participate in behaviors offensive to him or her, spousal sexual abuse occurs. In some cases, physical force is used to gain compliance; in others, nonphysical forms of coercion are used. When nonphysical means are used, the behavior frequently falls at the intersection of psychological abuse and sexual abuse.

Psychological abuse and emotional abuse are difficult to identify, particularly if intent is a component of the definition. The identification of factors that cause psychological or emotional damage and factors that serve as buffers to protect mental health are uncertain at best and appear to be highly individualized. Acts that cause damage to one person may not cause damage to another. If skilled professionals cannot identify damaging behavior, it may be unreasonable to hold spouses accountable for the damage they may cause.

When the effects of specific behavior cannot be identified, then the intent of the actor becomes important in determining abuse, and intent can be difficult to establish. This fact provides those men and women who intend to abuse their spouses with an effective defense and reduces the ability of victims to gain assistance in their efforts to defend themselves. It is difficult to differentiate between those actions that are offensive but not damaging and those actions that are intended to and do cause serious psychological damage. It is possible that a person may do unpleasant things to his or her spouse in anger or because of a defective personality without intending to or without being aware that he or she is causing serious damage to the spouse. The difficulty of recognizing, describing in understandable terms, and treating this type of abuse probably assures that it will continue to be ignored to some extent.

Neglect, primarily financial abuse, tends to be abuse in which wives generally are the victims. It is probable that this behavior is defined as acceptable except in its most extreme forms, such as starvation by denial of food for the wife. Men have traditionally controlled the financial resources of the family, including until the beginning of this century their wives' resources. In many families, the husband continues to be the primary breadwinner and controller of family resources. Although in many families the wife is responsible for budgeting and purchasing, it is still common for the husband to make the important financial decisions. The family partnership is becoming more common, but there continues to be widespread support for male-dominated families.

In a family in which the husband dominates and controls the financial resources, the potential for neglect exists. This type of neglect can range from the subtle denial of access to the resources needed to maintain basic health, appearance, and self-esteem to the denial of access to life-maintaining resources, such as food and medical attention. This type of abuse can aggravate other types of abuse by creating a situation in which the wife is completely subordinate to the husband's wishes and lacks the resources needed to flee the abusive situation.

This form of abuse is likely to be ignored, as it is unlikely that the public would endorse efforts to interfere in a family's private financial affairs. There are no statutes controlling this behavior, and there is general acceptance of the right of the husband to control the allocation of family resources, particularly when he is the sole or primary breadwinner.

Prevalence of Spouse Abuse

The prevalence of domestic violence tends to be underestimated by the general public. The term *assault and battery* brings to mind barroom fights and disputes between neighbors. Empirical studies have found, however, that from 11 percent to 52 percent of all assaults occur in the family (Boudouris 1971) and that between 5 percent and 11 percent of all assaults reported to the police involve spouse battering (Gelles 1972). It has been suggested that these figures are misleading because domestic violence is more likely to be underreported than other types of assault. Several studies of battered women indicate that less than 1 percent of all wife beatings are reported to the police and that up to half of those women who demonstrate histories of violence victimization have filed a complaint with the police (Dobash & Dobash 1977–78; Gelles 1972; Steinmetz 1977–78). About 80 percent of the responses to calls to police regarding domestic disturbances involve legally married spouses, and 32 percent involve the use of physical force (Bard & Zacker 1974). Domestic calls are also dangerous to police. About 22 percent of police murders and 28 percent of assaults on police occur during responses to domestic disturbances (Fields 1977–78).

Several studies have attempted to measure the incidence of the use of force in domestic settings. The most comprehensive of these found that 26 percent of all couples surveyed had experienced at least one incidence of domestic violence in the past year and that 28 percent had experienced at least one incidence of domestic violence during their relationship (Straus, Gelles & Steinmetz 1980). Both acts by males and acts by females were included, and violence included attempts to use force. Projections from the results of this study indicate that from 1.8 million to 3.6 million women are battered in the United States each year, and nearly 5.5 million conjugal assaults occur each year (Straus, Gelles & Steinmetz 1980; Straus 1977–78; Steinmetz 1977b).

The same researchers have conducted studies of college students in an attempt to measure the amount of domestic violence that occurs in families. Of the subjects in one study, 16 percent reported that an act of violence had occurred between their parents during their senior year in high school (Straus 1974). In a second study, the students reported that they had observed the use of violence between their parents at some time (Steinmetz 1977b).

Estimates of the relative rates of the use of force by sex vary greatly. Dobash and Dobash (1979) reported a ratio of men to women of 66:1 (data for this study were collected in Scotland), Levinger (1974) reported 13:1, Martin (1976) reported from 4:1 to 20:1, and O'Brien (1974) reported about 5:1. In their comprehensive study, Straus, Gelles, and Steinmetz (1980) found that in 49 percent of the cases reporting the use of physical force, the force was mutual; in 27 percent, the use of force was exclusively male; and in 24 percent, it was exclusively female.

To some extent, these differences can be attributed to the lack of a clear definition of the term *violence*. In some studies, any act of physical force or attempted physical force was counted as violence; in others, physical harm had to result; and in others, serious force was the standard. As a result, it is difficult to compare results across studies.

Spousal assaults tend to be more violent than other forms of assault. They account for 12 percent of assaults producing serious injury, 16 percent of all assaults requiring medical attention, and 18 percent of all assaults causing the victim to miss work (Gaquin 1977–78). Murders in which a spouse is the victim account for 12 percent to 18 percent of all murders reported to police (Fields 1977–78), with over 40 percent of all females murdered dying at the hands of their husbands (Dobash & Dobash 1977–78) and 10 percent of all males murdered dying at the hands of their wives (Mowat 1966). In spousal murders, wives are the victims in 52 percent of the cases (Dobash & Dobash 1977–78). Husbands are more likely to have precipitated their murders (60 percent of the husbands as compared with 9 percent of the wives) by initiating the violence and/or by routinely battering their wives (Dobash & Dobash 1977–78).

Limited information is available concerning the prevalence of marital rape. Studies of clients of shelters have found that more than one-third of the clients (abused wives) said that they had been raped by the men with whom they were living at the time the rape occurred (Finkelhor & Yllo 1983). One survey of the general population found that 14 percent of the women reported a sexual assault, 12 percent reported being forced to have sexual intercourse, and 2 percent being forced to participate in other types of sexual behavior (Russel 1984). Researchers in Boston collected similar data and discovered that 10 percent of the women reported that their partners had used physical force to have sex with them (Finkelhor & Yllo 1983). In both of these studies, it was found that women were more likely to be sexually assaulted by their partners than by strangers.

While statistical data are available for the types of abuse that involve the use of physical force, no information is readily available regarding the incidence of other types of abuse. Those studies that do consider the collateral issues in domestic violence tend to fail to report incidence rates for psychological abuse, emotional abuse, and neglect. In fact, most researchers who report on these factors tend to present case histories rather than quantifiable data.

Legal Dimensions

Much of the discussion of legal issues in the area of spouse abuse focuses on the legal rights or lack of rights for women. Historically, women have not had independent legal status. As discussed earlier, the law has viewed women as property or as children. Women were not perceived as competent to make contracts or to protect themselves. While there has been a tendency to assign blame to the legal system for this plight, it should be noted that the law and its enforcement by the criminal-justice system tend to reflect contemporary social values (Paterson 1979).

In the past, before marriage a woman was under the control of her father or legal guardian, and after marriage she was under the control of her husband. This lack of legal status lasted well into the twentieth century (Blackstone 1966). The husband had legal right to sexual access and could use force to exercise this right (Martin 1982). Although legal reform in this area has been under way for over one hundred years, progress has been slow, with many legal rights recently becoming available to women.

Parker (1985) has identified three themes to be considered in any attempt to understand the relationship between battered women and the law: (1) the ideology of privacy, (2) the gap between the written law and contemporary practice, and (3) the complexity and lack of integration of existing legal remedies. Regarding the first theme, British law held the home to be a private place. Acts occurring in the privacy of the home were generally held to be of no interest to the public. As long as the couple continued to live together in a common home, the husband could not be ordered to change his behavior or be ordered to equitably distribute family resources (Kidd 1982; Pahl 1980). Regarding the second theme, for a number of reasons the justice system traditionally has been unwilling to intrude in domestic affairs. Battered women have experienced difficulty in persuading police and the courts to intervene with actions designed to control their husbands. Regarding the third theme, the laws that exist are complex and at times might appear to the resourceless woman to be contradictory and unenforceable. The laws regarding property, divorce, custody, financial obligations, and criminal culpability are separate acts, rather than integrated codes focusing on the problems encountered in domestic violence. Although new domestic violence statutes have reduced this confusion and have increased integration in the jurisdictions in which they have been adopted, an attorney is still an essential requirement for successfully negotiating the system.

Many of the remedies available to the abused wife are civil remedies, even in states in which family protection (domestic abuse) legislation has been adopted. In addition to divorce proceedings, some form of nonmolestation order (peace bond) is available in all jurisdictions. Most states also provide for orders for payment of attorney's fees, and some provide for orders for support and for restrictions on the disposition of family property. In the absence of family protection legislation, these latter options are usually difficult to achieve (Boylan et al. 1982).

Use of criminal remedies has been limited in jurisdictions that have not implemented reform. Violation of a civil order is a criminal offense. All jurisdictions have some form of assault and/or battery, disturbing the peace, disorderly conduct, trespassing, and malicious mischief statutes. However, it is difficult to maintain an action when the wife is the sole witness and the remedy is usually a relatively small fine. In poor families, a fine may punish the wife and children as much or more than the husband by depriving them of needed financial assistance.

About one in six wives are assaulted by their husbands (Schulman 1979; Straus & Gelles 1986). It has been suggested that police share cultural values that define actions occurring in the family as private. As a result, police have tended to use their discretion and to avoid processing cases of domestic violence (Rokeach, Miller & Snyder 1971; Dutton 1987). The use of discretion is an essential part of police work. Discretion keeps the justice system's work load manageable and permits minor indiscretions to pass with limited investment of justice system resources. Discretion can lead to inequity when its use is based on prejudice, bias, or inaccurate perceptions. In the area of spouse abuse, the results have been a systematic underenforcement of the law. Police officers have been unlikely to arrest an assaulter when the victim is his wife (Dobash & Dobash 1979).

When violence occurs, police tend to arrest the attacker, regardless of the circumstances, *except* in cases of domestic violence. One study found that 75 percent of assault cases involving unrelated people were resolved with an arrest, while only 16 percent of cases of assault involving family members resulted in an arrest. Assaults against spouses were more likely to be charged as misdemeanors (Field & Field 1973).

The perception of domestic violence as a misdemeanor rather than as a felony restricts police behavior. Police can make an arrest when they believe that a felony has occurred but must witness the act or must have a warrant in order arrest someone accused of a misdemeanor. Thus, police tend to perceive themselves as barred from making an arrest in domestic-violence cases (Paterson 1979).

Domestic violence cases have received low priority in police departments. Domestic violence calls tend to be screened out first when the work load becomes so great that all calls cannot be answered and a screening process is instituted (Dobash & Dobash 1979). Police have been unwilling to arrest a husband when an incident is characterized as domestic. There has been a tendency to encourage the wife to forgive and to submit; that is, the wife victim has been encouraged to withdraw her complaint unless the physical damage is severe or the husband refuses to modify his behavior in the presence of police (Dobash & Dobash 1979).

With the emergence of an awareness of the need for shelters for battered women, proponents moved aggressively to change the orientation of police agencies toward violent husbands. Many police agencies have responded with new guidelines, additional training, and new policies designed to increase the likelihood that violent husbands will be controlled. These efforts have been reinforced in many instances by special legislation designed to control domestic violence.

Problems have been encountered when wife victims turn to the courts for assistance. In many cases, the wife is referred to the courts by police; at the time of the incident, the wife is instructed by police to go to the prosecutor's office and file a complaint if she wants police to arrest her husband. On the filing of a complaint, the prosecutor can, but does not always, issue an arrest warrant for the husband. There is a tendency on the part of the prosecutor to treat such matters as civil rather than criminal matters. The process is difficult and acts to reduce the availability of the courts to the wife victim (Dobash & Dobash 1979).

The effect of this orientation can be seen in the results of attempts to seek redress. In Washington, D.C., in 1966, over 7,500 women attempted to file complaints against their husbands. Only 200 of these women were successful in their attempts to file a formal complaint (Field & Field 1973).

Both the police and the prosecution have used informal dispositions in domestic-abuse cases. In Tuscaloosa, Alabama, police officers have issued mock divorces in an attempt to resolve incidents of persistent spouse abuse. Similar techniques have been used in Washington, D.C. Prosecutors conduct informal hearings, threaten arrests, and prepare mock written divorce proceedings in an attempt to settle the dispute without formally processing the complaint (Field & Field 1973). When formal action is taken, it tends to take the form of a peace bond. When cases are taken to court and successfully prosecuted, the penalties exercised tend to be fines, suspended sentences, and probation (Dobash & Dobash 1979).

Representatives for various components of the justice system state that the formal processing of domestic-violence cases is difficult. Battered spouses frequently have been living with the violence for some time. When assistance is requested, the environment to which police respond is generally hostile, thus presenting a danger to police officers and a condition in which demands are made in anger for intervention. When the situation is under control, victims often change their orientation and withdraw their complaints and their cooperation (Frost, Lucianovic & Cox 1977).

It also has been noted that recantation can occur under stress. Witnesses have expressed fear of retaliation (Cannavale 1976), and recanting wives are often accompanied by their husbands when they come to the prosecutor's office to withdraw complaints (Lerman 1983). Police and prosecutors have expressed hesitancy to invest resources in efforts involving domestic violence because of the volume of cases and the difficulties in processing cases against the victim's wishes. Many of the reform statutes provide for continued formal action in cases involving recantation. Prosecutors also have expressed the belief that intervention causes more harm than good (Subin 1973) and that domestic violence is victim precipitated (Miller 1969).

In the late 1970s and early 1980s, changing community attitudes were reflected in the emergence of reform in the form of changed laws and changed justice-system procedures. These changes in the justice system were not entirely voluntary. Three lawsuits were central to the rapidly growing success of the abused-wife reform efforts. Lawsuits were brought before the courts in Los Angeles and Oakland, California and in New York City alleging that police were not affording women the full protection of the law (Paterson 1979). These suits ultimately were resolved with consent decrees in which the plaintiffs agreed to terms that provided support for the advocates promoting change.

Since 1975, most states have passed legislation to provide protection and services for battered wives. These statutes usually provide civil and criminal remedies for abused family members. Many require accurate record keeping of incidents of domestic violence and define the responsibilities of various criminal-justice agencies. Most provide for shelters and related services (Lerman, Landis & Goldzweig 1983).

Under many of the new statutes, victims can file for protection orders or special injunctions, which can be issued on an emergency basis. These orders are designed to protect the wife from abuse and harassment by ordering support, awarding custody, and prohibiting contact with the family by the offender (Lerman 1983). A violation of a protection order is a criminal offense, usually a misdemeanor or contempt of court. Although most states rely on existing assault-and-battery statutes to control domestic violence, a few have enacted statutes making domestic violence a specific offense and have expanded police powers in making arrests (Lerman, Landis & Goldzweig 1983).

Having been made aware of the problem, many criminal-justice agencies are developing new and expanded services for victims of domestic violence. Early in the reform effort, some prosecutors developed approaches that utilized enhanced application of traditional remedies, such as informal hearings and peace bonds, coupled with arbitration, education, and referral to counseling or other treatment programs (Parnas 1973; Field & Field 1973). The use of arbitration and referral was sharply criticized by advocates of reform and generally was abandoned (Eisenberg & Micklow 1976; Lerman 1983).

The movement to provide protection for battered wives began as a grass-roots organization. In the beginning, the movement was essentially a sanctuary movement, with sympathetic organizers finding places for abused wives and their children in private homes. The shelter movement developed slowly but gathered speed as the reformers began to use the media effectively to focus attention on the problem through the presentation of particularly severe cases. By the 1980s, there were over six hundred shelters in the United States (Martin 1983). Workshops and seminars emerged, and as public awareness increased, state legislatures began to provide funding for shelters and to examine and strengthen the laws regarding protective orders. Legal suits brought against police resulted in consent decrees, which set a new law-enforcement standard that was rapidly adopted by many police departments.

The new policies were reflected in law by the middle 1980s, as legislation emerged that required police officers to treat domestic violence as violence rather than as a domestic matter (Martin 1983). This was followed by the development of programs to enhance the prosecution of cases of domestic violence and the emergence of domestic-violence statutes that provide for active prosecution and provide the abused wife with a range of civil remedies that can be used to protect her interests and the interests of her children. While the adoption of these reforms has not been universal, it is certainly widespread.

Victim Characteristics

There are a number of characteristics common to women who are victims of abuse. Abused women are more likely to have come from families that encouraged passivity and controlled emotions. They tend to isolate themselves socially, assume responsibility for the abusive situation, cooperate, and do not fight back (Star 1982). Battered women have low self-esteem and negative self-concepts (Dobash & Dobash 1977–78). They feel helpless and inadequate (Martin 1983; Walker 1979). These traits act to keep a woman in an abusive situation from which she might otherwise flee.

While the range in age for battered women in most studies includes both the very young and the very old, the average age varies from about twenty-six years of age to thirty-seven years of age, depending on the study (Okun 1986). Gelles (1972) found that the most violence occurs among couples between forty-two and fifty years of age, and O'Brien (1974) found that about two-thirds of those respondents reporting abuse had been married from thirteen to thirty-seven years. There is no consistent relationship between other demographic variables and victims. The results from most studies tend to be weak and contradictory from study to study for factors such as race, religion, social class, income, and education.

Pregnancy appears to be related to the frequency of abuse, with pregnancy increasing the incidence of violence (Gelles 1977; Carlson 1977; Rounsville 1978). Battered women are also more likely to have been raised in violent families, with estimates ranging from 23 percent to 68 percent for abused women who are daughters of abused women (Carlson 1977; Eisenberg & Micklow 1976; Gayford 1975; Gelles 1972; Pagelow 1981; Roy 1977; Star 1982).

A diagnostic category, the battered woman syndrome, has been developed and includes many of the factors identified with battered wives in most studies (Walker 1979). It identifies a set of factors associated with emotional disturbance that occurs in women with a history of being battered. The study from which this model was developed found that there are no personality characteristics common to battered women, but that there are a number of characteristics common to batters. There are common background factors for battered women that reduce the ability of these women to withdraw from a battering situation. These background experiences are psychologically damaging and are sufficiently persistent to be labeled as a psychological disorder.

Although it is true that men are often victims of domestic violence, little or no research has focused on this phenomenon. As a result, there are no profiles of battered men. In addition to the cultural biases regarding manhood, it is probable that men, who often tend to control family income, have more freedom in leaving a negative situation. Men, on the average, are also better equipped physically to protect themselves from a physical attack.

Offender Characteristics

Although a great deal has been written about men who batter, much of the data has come from women victims, rather than from the men themselves.

Like the women whom they abuse, male offenders demonstrate a number of psychological patterns. They have low self-esteem and negative self-concepts (Dobash & Dobash 1977–78). They feel helpless, inadequate, and ashamed (Martin 1983; Walker 1979).

Like their victims, abusers also come from violent homes (Shupe, Stacey & Hazlewood 1987), and there is no consistent relationship between demographic variables and offenders. Race, religion, social class, income, and education are not consistently related to being a batterer. Occupational status and unemployment have been linked with income and, to some extent, social class. Although most studies find domestic violence at all economic and class levels, there tends to be slightly more violence among blue-collar workers and the poor. Unemployment has consistently been found to be related to domestic violence. Unemployed and underemployed men are more likely to engage in spouse battering (Okun 1986). Wife beaters tend to have been abused as children, to have poor communication skills, to have poor impulse control, and to be traditional in orientation and domineering in manner (Shupe, Stacey & Hazlewood 1987).

In many cases, violent women act in self-defense. They are being attacked or abused by their husbands and are seeking to defend themselves or to end the abusive session; however, there are a substantial number of instances in which the woman is the instigator of the violence. In some cases, the woman is seen as the instigator even if she does not land the first blow. These women are characterized as having difficulty controlling their impulses. A verbal argument escalates until one partner resorts to the use of physical force. In some cases, the wife is the aggressor and the husband is passive. These women account for only about one in ten violent women, and they share the characteristics of other batterers (Shupe, Stacey & Hazlewood 1987).

Situational Factors

It has been noted that almost half of all domestic violence involves both partners and that these men and women tend to share a number of personality and background factors. It also should be noted that even when the victim is passive, violence is an interactive process and, in most cases, this interaction is repetitive. While precipitating factors are not causes, factors that create stress in the lives of the participants tend to bring on episodes of violence. Sexual jealousy and financial problems are the two most common precipitating factors (Bard & Zacker 1971; Carlson 1977; Dobash & Dobash 1979).

Relationships in which battering occurs tend to be unstable. The wives in from 66 percent to 88 percent of the cases have left their husbands one or more times (Dobash & Dobash 1979; Eisenberg & Micklow 1976; Hilberman & Munson 1977–78). Virtually all studies have found a link between alcohol consumption and domestic violence. Violent families tend to be pathological in a number of ways (Okun 1986).

Summary

In spite of the attention directed toward spouse abuse, there is still a great deal of confusion about what constitutes spouse abuse, the dynamics of spouse abuse, and the causes of spouse abuse. There is a tendency to perceive spouse abuse as the use of violence by husbands toward their wives. It appears, however, that family violence between spouses can be mutual.

Spouse abuse also can take other forms. Psychological and emotional damage can occur in situations in which no physical abuse is present. Spouses can be sexually abused without the use of force, and spouses can be neglected through denial of access to family resources. Relatively little attention has been directed toward spouse abuse that does not involve the use of force; nonviolent forms of abuse have been treated as collateral issues in situations in which physical abuse occurs. It is possible that this condition exists because nonviolent forms of abuse are more difficult to identify, because there is a lower level of public interest in these forms of abuse, because these forms do not fit the present reform agenda being advanced by activists, and because these acts are less likely to be identified as abuse or as legitimate areas of public interest.

Historically, the behaviors presently identified as sufficiently unacceptable to warrant justice system intervention have been perceived as acceptable and expected behaviors. Throughout history, women have been identified as subordinate to men. In most cases, they have had no legal identity outside of their roles as daughters or wives. Men were expected to control and to discipline their women, and reasonable force was an accepted technique. This perspective was not challenged until the beginning of the twentieth century, and it is possible that many still support the concept of male dominance, if not the use of force and the role of discipline.

The excessive use of force by some men provided a focal point for advocates of reform in the laws regarding the resources available to battered wives. Attempts to increase public awareness of the plight of the severely abused wife have been relatively successful. Reform legislation has been adopted by most states, and the justice system, for the most part, has changed its orientation from avoiding interference in private family affairs to one of increasing the prosecution rate for husbands who batter their wives.

These changes are based on perceptions of community attitude and focus on the use of force in marital relationships. While such changes may have followed a necessary path for reform, the lack of attention to other forms and dimensions of spouse abuse must be corrected. Spouse abuse is both a contemporary social problem and a legitimate area of interest for social-science researchers, not only those with an interest in violence, but also those with an interest in deviance, criminalization, and the family.

References

Bard, M., and Zacker, J. 1971. The prevention of family violence: Dilemmas of community intervention. *Journal of Marriage and the Family* (11): 677–82.
———. 1974. Assaultiveness and alcohol use in family disputes. *Criminology* 12(3): 293–92.
Blackstone, W. 1966. *Commentaries on the law of England.* Dobbs Ferry, N.Y.: Oceana.
Boudouris, J. 1971. Homicide and the family. *Journal of Marriage and the Family* 33(11): 667–76.
Boylan, A.M.; Schulman, J.; Williams, A.; and Woods, L. 1982. *Legal advocacy for battered women.* New York: National Center for Women and Family Law.
Brownmiller, S. 1975. *Against our will: Men, women, and rape.* New York: Simon and Schuster.
Bullough, V.L. 1974. *The subordinate sex: A history of attitudes toward women.* Baltimore: Penguin.
Cannavale, F. 1976. *Witness cooperation.* New York: Lexington Press.
Carlson, B.E. 1977. Battered women and their assailants. *Social Work* 22(6): 445–60.
Clark, S.M., and Lewis, D.J. 1977. *Rape: The price of coercive sexuality.* Toronto: Women's Educational Press.
Cobbe, F.P. 1878. Wife torture in England. *Contemporary Review* (April): 55–57.
Daly, M. 1978. *Gyn-ecology: The metaethics of radical feminism.* Boston: Beacon Press.
Dobash, R.E., and Dobash, R. 1977–78. Wives: The "appropriate victim." *Victimology* 2(3/4): 426–42.
———. 1979. *Violence against wives: A case against the patriarchy.* New York: Free Press.
Dutton, D.G. 1987. *The domestic asssault of women.* Boston: Allyn and Bacon.
Eisenberg, S., and Micklow, P. 1976. The assaulted wife: "Catch 22" revisited. *Woman's Rights Law Reporter* 3(1): 138–60.
Field, M.H., and Field, H.F. 1973. Marital violence and the criminal process: Neither justice or peace. *Social Science Review* 47(2): 221–40.
Fields, M.D. 1977–78. Wife beating: Facts and figures. *Victimology* 2(3/4): 643–47.
Finkelhor, D., and Yllo, K. 1983. Rape in marriage: A sociological view. In *The dark side of families,* ed. D. Finkelhor, R.J. Gelles, G.T. Hotaling, and M.A. Straus. Beverly Hills, Calif.: Sage Publications.
Forst, B.; Lucianovic, J.; and Cox, S. 1977. *What happens after arrest?* Washington, D.C.: Institute of Law and Social Research.
Gaquin, D.A. 1977–78. Spouse abuse data: Data from the National Crime Survey. *Victimology* 2(3/4): 632–43.
Gayford, J.J. 1975. Wife battering: A preliminary survey of one-hundred cases. *British Medical Journal* 30(1): 194–7.

Gelles, R.J. 1972. *The violent home.* Beverly Hills, Calif.: Sage Publications.

————. 1977. Violence and pregnancy: A note on the extent of the problem and needed services. *Family Coordinator* 24(1): 81–86.

Hilberman, E.C., and Munson, K. 1977–78. Sixty battered women. *Victimology* 2(3/4): 460–71.

Kidd, T. 1982. Social security and the family. In *Sex differences in Britain,* ed. I. Reid and E. Wormald. London: Grant McIntyre.

Lerman, L.G. 1983. Legal help for battered women. In *Abuse of women: Legislation, reporting, and prevention,* ed. J. Costa. Lexington, Mass.: Lexington Books.

Lerman, L.G.; Landis, L.; and Goldzweig, S. 1983. State legislation on domestic violence. In *Abuse of women: Legislation, reporting, and prevention,* ed. J. Costa. Lexington, Mass.: Lexington Books.

Levinger, G. 1974. Sources of marital dissatisfaction among applicants for divorce. In *Violence in the family,* ed. S. Steinmetz and M. Straus. New York: Harper and Row.

Martin, D. 1982. Wife beating: A product of sociosexual development: In *Women's sexual experience: Explorations of the dark content,* ed. M. Kirkpatrick. New York: Plenum.

————. 1983. *Battered wives.* New York: Pocket Books.

Martin, P. 1976. *A marital therapy manual.* New York: Brunner/Mazel.

Mill, J.S. 1870. *The subjection of women.* New York: D. Appleton.

Miller, F. 1969. *Prosecution: The decision to charge a suspect with crime.* Boston: Little, Brown.

Mowat, R.R. 1966. *Morbid jealousy and murder.* London: Tavistock.

O'Brien, J. 1974. Violence in divorce-prone families. In *Violence in the family,* ed. S. Steinmetz and M. Straus. New York: Harper and Row.

O'Faolain, J., and Martines, L., eds. 1974. *Not in God's image: Women in history.* Glasgow: Fontana/Collins.

Okun, L. 1986. *Woman abuse.* Albany, N.Y.: Suny Press.

Pagelow, M.D. 1981. *Woman battering: Victims and their experiences.* Beverly Hills, Calif.: Sage Publications.

Pahl, J. 1980. Patterns of money management in marriage. *Journal of Social Policy* 9(3): 323–35.

Parker, S. 1985. The legal background. In *Private violence and public policy: The needs of battered women and the response of the public services,* ed. J. Pahl. Boston: Routledge and Kegan Paul.

Parnas, R. 1973. Prosecutorial and judicial handling of family violence. *Criminal Law Bulletin* 9(4): 733–69.

Paterson, E.J. 1979. How the legal system responds to battered women. In *Battered women,* ed. D.M. Moore. Beverly Hills, Calif.: Sage Publications.

Rokeach, M.; Miller, M.G.; and Snyder, J.A. 1971. The value gap between police and policed. *Journal of Social Issues* 27(2): 155–71.

Rounsville, B.J. 1978. Battered wives: Barriers to identification and treatment. *American Journal of Orthopsychiatry* 48(3): 487–94.

Roy, M., ed. 1977. *Battered women.* New York: Van Nostrand Reinhold.

Russell, D.E.H. 1979. *Sexual exploitation: Rape, child sexual abuse, and workplace harassment.* Beverly Hills, Calif.: Sage Publications.

Schulman, M. 1979. *A survey of spousal violence against women in Kentucky.* Washington, D.C.: U.S. Department of Justice.

Shupe, A.; Stacey, W.A.; and Hazlewood, L.R. 1987. *Violent men, violent couples.* Lexington, Mass.: Lexington Books.

Sigler, R., and Haygood, D. 1988. The criminalization of forced marital intercourse. *Marriage and Family Review* 16(2): 121–30.

Star, B. 1982. Characteristics of family violence. In *The many faces of violence,* ed. J.P. Flanzer. Springfield, Ill.: Charles C. Thomas.

Steinmetz, S. 1977. The use of force in resolving family conflict: The training ground for abuse. *Family Coordinator* 26(1): 19–26.

———. 1977–78. The battered husband syndrome. *Victimology* 2(3/4): 499–509.

Straus, M.A. 1974. Leveling, civility, and violence in the family. *Journal of Marriage and the Family* 36(February): 13–30.

———. 1977–78. Wife beating: How common and why. *Victimology* 2(3–4): 443–59.

Straus, M.A., and Gelles, R.J. 1986. Societal change in family violence from 1975 to 1985 as revealed by two national surveys. *Journal of Marriage and the Family* 48(August): 465–79.

Straus, M.A.; Gelles, R.J.; and Steinmetz, S. 1980. *Behind closed doors: Violence in the American family.* Garden City, N.Y.: Anchor.

Subin, H. 1973. *Criminal justice in the metropolitan court.* New York: DaCapo Press.

Walker, L. 1979. *The battered woman.* New York: Harper and Row.

Wilson, J. 1978. *Religion in American society: The effective presence.* Englewood Cliffs, N.J.: Prentice-Hall.

2
Child Abuse

The second area of focus in this examination of domestic violence is child abuse. Child abuse is more difficult to address than spouse abuse. Parents have a duty to their children, yet they have few restrictions on the manner in which they choose to raise their children. In matters of discipline, religious instruction, style of living, and support, parents are permitted to apply their own values.

Only in extreme situations will the court intervene in the family's affairs. In regard to children, the court will intervene in three areas: neglect, sexual abuse, and violence. As is the case with other areas of abuse, the neglect must be extreme before the justice system will intervene. In cases of neglect, there generally is physical evidence of neglect or there is abandonment, which justifies the court's intervention. In the area of physical violence, even when the use of physical force is extreme the parent may be able to argue successfully that the physical force is a matter of discipline rather than a case of abuse. Sexual abuse is difficult to prosecute. When child sexual abuse occurs in the family, the parties deny its occurrence; in addition, the child victim frequently is not a credible witness.

Historical Perspective

The power that parents today wield over their children pales in comparison to the powers parents exercised in the past. Historically, parents virtually have held the power of life and death in regard to their children. Even infanticide was accepted as an appropriate behavior, and the killing of unwanted legitimate as well as illegitimate children continued into the nineteenth century (Mause 1974). In France, the statutes specified a number of conditions under which a father had the right to kill his adult son or daughter (Marvick 1974). Consistently throughout history, female children have been more vulnerable to this fate than male children. In addition to risk of life, boys and girls were sold into slavery or abandoned if economic conditions were poor for the family (Mause 1974).

Child-rearing practices also placed children at risk. Normal child-rearing practices included swaddling or wrapping the infant so tightly in bandages that the child could not move and could be placed conveniently anywhere, thus making the child-care task much simpler. Washing was believed to be an unhealthy practice (Robertson 1974). Standards of child care were different, reflecting less care for the welfare of children then is generally accepted today.

This difference in perspective regarding the use of children can also be seen in relation to sex. The use of children for sexual purposes is well documented. The prostitution of both boys and girls has been fairly common. Children were introduced to sexual exploitation in the home by adults, both relatives and friends (Mause 1974). The values regarding sexual activity were considerably different in early Europe than they are now. At that time, children were considered to be sexually mature at an earlier age than is accepted today, and sexual access to children was not universally condemned. These values from early European history, recorded in diaries and in literature, are still held by some people today.

Discipline was also severe in earlier times. Severe beatings were accepted as appropriate methods of control, and children who were apprenticed at an early age (as young as seven years of age) were expected to obey their masters. Apprentices also might be denied food if their work was not satisfactory and might be chained if they ran away. When reform efforts arose during the Renaissance period, an attempt was made to encourage adults to use lighter sticks and whips rather than clubs when beating their children and to strike the body rather than the head. Beatings and severe whippings continued to be accepted practice through the nineteenth century (Mause 1974). Commonly accepted practices easily would be classified as child abuse by today's standards, even though "spare the rod and spoil the child" is still commonly accepted as a truism by many of today's adults.

The orientation of society toward children changed slowly. Early in history, children were treated as small adults. The fifteenth and sixteenth centuries brought the beginning of recognition that children had individual personalities and needed special care and attention. By the seventeenth century, children were dressed differently than adults, and harsh treatment of children was criticized (Aries 1962). By the late nineteenth century, a new concept of childhood emerged and held that children must be safeguarded and properly prepared for adulthood (Hobbes 1972). In the United States, under pressure from advocates for children, the juvenile court emerged, and society accepted the responsibility for assuring a safe and correct upbringing for all children (Platt 1969). It should be noted that at the same time, discipline was stressed as an essential ingredient in child rearing and the use of physical force in this context was to be anticipated rather than criticized (Bremmer 1970).

Public interest in protecting neglected and abused children did not emerge until late in the nineteenth century. The first recognized case of public intervention occurred when neighbors reported the abuse of a young girl named Mary Ellen. When friends of Mary Ellen sought to intervene in her behalf in 1874 after finding her chained to her bed, undernourished and apparently physically abused, they discovered that such treatment of a child was not a violation of the law. Advocates for Mary Ellen captured public attention by seeking assistance for the child through enforcement of laws designed to protect animals from abuse and utilized the assistance of the Society for the Prevention of Cruelty to Animals (McCrea 1910).

Responsibility for child abuse cases was added to the jurisdiction of the newly organized juvenile and family courts, which began to emerge at the turn of the century. The primary function of these courts was to control delinquents, and their secondary emphasis was on protecting the interests of children who came under their authority. Traditionally, the juvenile court has hesitated to extend its broad powers to exert control and discipline over abusing adults. In most jurisdictions, adults who abuse children must be charged with an offense in the adult courts. As a result, the appropriateness of the referral of child victims to the juvenile court has been argued, based on the assertion that the court will damage, rather than assist, child victims because of its basic orientation (Flexner & Balwin 1914).

Public acceptance of child abuse as a social problem was slow to develop. It was 1962 before a national survey of the prevalence of child battering was reported, appearing in the *Journal of the American Medical Association*. The report introduced the battered-child syndrome and produced a movement toward public awareness and public concern (Kempe 1962). The feminist movement, in raising public awareness of the plight of women in the home, developed an environment receptive to the pleas of those who sought to place boundaries around those behaviors that are unacceptable when directed toward children.

Dimensions of Child Abuse

Child abuse includes physical abuse, sexual abuse, psychological abuse, neglect, and abandonment. Each of these reflects damage to the child; some reflect acts of commission, and others reflect acts of omission.

Neglect and *abandonment* are acts of omission. The adults responsible for the child fail to provide the things needed for the child's healthy development. Neglect cannot be defined clearly, as there are no standards available that address the minimal needs of growing children. In addition, some parents who provide few resources would provide more if they had the means to do so. In terms of the care and support provided for children, cultural and class values frequently come into conflict, and questions are raised concerning the proportion of family resources that should be allocated to meet specific family needs. Poor families are subject to criticism when they choose to allocate resources to an expensive color television and cable service rather than to clothes or food items defined as healthy by the system dominating middle-class citizens. A more sensitive issue is the use of resources for adult entertainment, particularly when the entertainment involves alcohol. Although some degree of consensus on these issues has been identified among middle-class mothers, working-class mothers, and social workers (Polansky 1978), lack of resources and the perspectives of the poor have not been assessed. Child neglect may be more prevalent than abuse, but it receives less attention (Wolock 1984).

There are times when the line between neglect and abandonment is not clearly drawn. Generally, leaving children alone in the home unattended for relatively short periods of time when the adult intends to return is characterized as neglect. Such incidents of neglect occur when the responsible adults leave their children alone in order to pursue recreation, to shop, to conduct family business, or to work. Although abandonment is often defined as leaving an infant on the steps of an orphanage or leaving children to fend for themselves indefinitely, the above examples of short-term periods when children are left unattended have been and can be classified as abandonment. This use of this classification serves as a legal tool that can be used to provide the justice system with the leverage needed to intervene in a child's behalf.

Neglect and abandonment are types of abuse that can be viewed as class offenses. Low-income families are more apt to be involved in these behaviors. These types of abuse are class based because they reflect economic limitations, rather than the intent of the adults involved. Families with adequate or abundant financial resources are not required to make the choices about allocation of resources that low-income families are forced to make. If affluent adults neglect their children, the neglect may take the form of abundant resources but little personal attention, causing emotional neglect.

The financial aspect of neglect can be best illustrated by considering the nature of the problems with baby-sitting encountered by families of different resource levels. For affluent families, a problem arises as the oldest child reaches his or her teens. This child believes that he or she is old enough to be left alone, but the parent insists on hiring a baby-sitter. For girls, it is possible that the transition from having a baby-sitter to being a baby-sitter occurs within the same month or, in some cases, overlaps. The girl may be taking care of other children in limited circumstances before she is allowed to stay alone in her own home. For poor families, the issue is reversed. There is economic pressure to define the children as capable of caring for themselves at as early an age as possible in order to conserve family resources. In short, if a baby-sitter is paid, there is no money left for recreation, even if that only means transportation costs. As a result, a preteen may be left to care for his or her younger brothers and sisters. This does not reflect a lack of care as much as it reflects a lack of money.

When the system seeks to intervene in such a case, there are no clear solutions. Conventional wisdom holds that it is better to leave children in a home in which they are loved even if they are neglected if the neglect is not life-threatening or likely to impair their health seriously. Even when their health may be affected by the lack of an adequate diet, the social-service system and the justice system lack viable options, such as adequate alternative homes for placement. Thus, only severe cases of neglect can be addressed effectively.

Child psychological abuse is the exposure of a child by an adult to experiences that can cause psychological or emotional distress. Psychological abuse is more difficult to address than other types of abuse because of such issues as intent, level of knowledge, difficulty of diagnosis, and difficulty of obtaining proof. Psychological damage can occur even when the adults in the child's environment have no intention of abusing the child. The adults are meeting their own needs or are doing things that they think are right. In some cases, not only do they lack intent to do harm, but they will argue that no harm is occurring or likely to occur as a result of their acts and that they are doing the best that they can do with the resources available.

This stance should not be surprising, given the general level of knowledge presently available even to well-educated adults. The dynamics of maturation, particularly mental maturation, are not well understood. This field of study, as is the case with much of the social sciences, is characterized by disagreement among the many theoretical perspectives advanced by competing competent social scientists.

Psychological damage is difficult to diagnose. Distinguishing between those children who are behaviorally disturbed and those who are psychologically disturbed is complex and expensive. It is easier to diagnose unacceptable behavior as characterizing delinquency or poor behavioral adjustment than to intervene in a child's behalf or to seek an expensive psychological evaluation. As a result, the psychological damage is usually severe before the system responds. Even when a psychological pathology is identified, it is difficult to determine a clear cause or to apportion the blame among the many elements in the environment that could have contributed to the child's mental state.

As a result, it is virtually impossible to prove in a court of law that a parent has psychologically abused his or her child, and parents can mount effective defenses against social-service intervention and/or justice-system intervention. Psychological and emotional abuse of children is a cause for concern, but the potential for effective intervention is very low; thus, psychological abuse is a neglected area.

Child sexual abuse is the exposure of a child by an adult to any experience designed to or reasonably expected to produce sexual stimulation in either party. This form of abuse is also difficult to process. There is often no physical evidence of the abuse, the victim is not a reliable witness, and there is usually a denial of the situation by the child victim and by other children and adults in the environment. In most cases, physical force is not used when sexual abuse of children occurs in the home. Enticement, persuasion, bribary, and verbal intimidation usually suffice in a situation in which the child victim does not fully appreciate the implications of the acts in which he or she is asked to participate. As a result, investigators can do as much or more damage to the victim than the offender if they are not carefully trained and properly oriented. At times, the child victim is not aware that something wrong has occurred until relatives or investigators become disturbed in the child's presence.

The sexual act is as much a violation of contemporary moral values as it is a violation of the child's health and well-being. As a result, when cases are successfully prosecuted, the punishments are severe. However, cases rarely are successfully prosecuted. Adult abusers frequently do not see themselves as being in the wrong. Some argue that parents have a right to use their children; others see sexual acts in general as permissible behavior and no one else's business; some see society (nosy neighbors and social workers) as wrongfully interfering in family matters.

In these cases and in cases in which the offender acknowledges the wrongness of the act, the act is denied, not only by the offender, but by others in the family. Denial results from embarrassement, a desire to protect the child from social labeling, fear of the offender, fear of the penalty that might be assessed, loss of family income and/or stature in the community, placement of blame on the child victim, expressed regret combined with promises of reform by the offender, and unwillingness to accept the reality of the offense. Frequently, a complaining adult will regret statements made to police and will recant his or her testimony. In these cases, the adults will bring pressure on the child to recant his or her statements, sometimes with no more pressure than the need to protect Daddy (or some other relative) from a "bad" justice system.

Although the justice system acts affirmatively when successful prosecutions are completed, such occurrences are rare. In an unknown number of cases, the offense remains a family matter for the same reasons that adults and children frequently recant. The affair remains a family matter, with outsiders (such as social workers, police, neighbors, and other relatives) excluded unless the abuse is severe. *Severe* tends to mean the use of physical force, the involvement of an infant victim, or the long-term, persistent nature of the abuse. At times, the abuse becomes known because of a family fight or as an act against the offender for reasons other than his sexual abuse of the child victim. The offender's abusive behavior may be reported to punish him for other acts such as spouse abuse or lack of fidelity.

Prosecutions also are hampered by the difficulties involved in obtaining convincing testimony from child victims. Children are easily intimidated, not only by the offender and other family members, but also by the justice system and the court. Child witnesses frequently lack the confident manner that convinces juries, and they also are easily influenced. In cases involving sexual abuse, the adults in the child's environment are frequently too uncomfortable to discuss explicit sexual behavior with the child, cannot risk damaging the child further by engaging in sexually explicit interrogation, or cannot risk charges of or actually coaching the child to report behavior that has not occurred. Children can become confused about what really occurred and can report abuse that did not take place. The occasional divorce or custody action in which one parent coaches a child to claim sexual abuse by the other parent is more than sufficient to allow the average defense attorney to introduce doubt about the child's testimony. Although child sexual abuse is dramatic and the occasional cases that are provable are used effectively to promote public concern about child abuse, this form of child abuse is not an area in which successful intervention can be maintained.

The remaining area of abuse, *child physical abuse,* is the form of child abuse that is most often the focus of successful intervention efforts; however, it defies precise definition. The definition of physical child abuse contains subjective components because of the lack of consensus about the extent to which adults can use physical force to discipline their children. This lack of agreement about what constitutes reasonable force makes precise definition impossible.

In view of this, the best definition possible is that *child physical abuse* is the direction of excessive physical force toward a child. As a practical matter, only extreme use of physical force is included. Even with this limitation of definition, physical abuse is more amenable to intervention than other types of abuse. Because the abuse must be extreme, it leaves physical traces that can be introduced as evidence and that are difficult to deny. Intervention can be maintained even if the key witnesses recant. The abuse cannot be concealed, as bruises are visible and broken bones, bad sprains, and burns must be treated. The offender cannot deny the damage, but denial can be maintained if the damage can be successfully blamed on another cause. However, if there is a consistent pattern of so-called accidents, system interest can be justified, and intervention can be initiated and sustained.

Prevalence of Child Abuse

The incidence of child abuse in the United States is difficult to assess. Much of the behavior that could be classified as child abuse is hidden and known only to the actors in the situation. A national report stated that 631 children died in 1974 due to abuse (Kadushim 1978). This number seems small for a nation the size of the United States and seems suspect, especially when one considers that in 1973, 41,104 cases of child abuse were reported for the ten largest states alone (Cohen & Sussman 1975) and that this number of reported abuses does not take into account the large number of cases that undoubtedly went unreported because of hesitancy to report. It is probable that many deaths caused by child abuse were officially attributed to other causes, such as accidental death. In general, it is probable that only cases of abuse severe enough to require treatment in the emergency room of a hospital were reported.

There is a hesitancy on the part of health-care providers to report all cases that are suspect because of potential liability and because of the risk that a vigorous program of reporting abuse to authorities would cause parents to withhold treatment from their children because of fear of investigation and possible prosecution (Fontana & Besharov 1977). One estimate suggests that about 5 percent of all cases involving injured children treated by health-care providers involve a case of child abuse (Gelles 1985). Neglect is so infrequently reported that there are no figures reflecting its incidence (Kadushim 1978).

Underreporting is influenced by the fact that a natural parent is the most likely abuser. Two different studies have focused on family abuse. In one, it was found that 55 percent of those who abuse children were fathers and that 68 percent of those who neglect children were mothers (American Humane Society 1978); in the other study, 50 percent of the abuse was attributed to mothers and stepmothers, while fathers were held accountable for 40 percent (Gil 1979).

Sexual abuse of children also is underreported, possibly for the same reasons. Incidences of sexual abuse of this type have been estimated at from fifty thousand to seventy-five thousand incidents per year (DeFrancis 1965). In a three-year study of cases of sexual abuse in New York City, DeFrancis (1979) found that 27 percent of the abusers were members of the child's own household and another 11 percent did not live in the household but were closely related. In addition, 37 percent were friends or acquaintances, and only 25 percent of the offenders were classified as strangers. Most of the incidents occurred in or around the home, with very few occurring in public places. In incest cases, the father is usually the offender, and the mother is usually aware of the abuse, even though she is not likely to be the complainant (Conte 1984; Furness 1984).

Incest may be a fairly prevalent form of abuse. A study of college students discovered that over 19 percent of the women and 8 percent of the men had been sexually abused as children. Male victims were most often abused by acquaintances (girls, 33 percent; boys, 53 percent); however, the most frequent abuser of female victims was a family member (43 percent) (Finkelhor 1979). A study of patients hospitalized for psychiatric problems found that 37.5 percent of the nonpsychotic female subjects, 10 percent of the psychotic female subjects, and 8 percent of the male subjects had been sexually abused as children (Emslie 1983).

The psychological damage that occurs in cases of incest is extensive (Finkelhor 1985). Nevertheless, incest is difficult to prosecute because the only witness is frequently the child victim, who may be traumatized by the need to testify and who may not be an effective witness (Berliner 1984).

Treatment programs for victims and for offenders have met with limited success. Children of battered women who sought help from a shelter experienced less future battering because many of the women left their battering husbands (Giles-Sims 1985), with similar results found for respite programs that separated children from abusing parents for a short period of time. Other studies have found behavioral marital counseling, the use of informal helping networks (Ballew 1985), small group short-term counseling (Barth 1983; Breton 1977; Magura 1982; Wollert 1982), multidisciplinary teams (Hoorwitz 1983; Kristal & Tucker 1975; Mouzakitis 1985), skill-deficit training (Scott 1974), safety programs (Comfort 1985), and sex-education programs for children successful in prevention of abuse. Attempts to predict or identify potential abusers have met with limited success (McMurtry 1985; Wolf 1985).

Legal Dimensions

As has been indicated earlier, the legal dimensions of child abuse are confused at best. The most visible and most controllable aspect of child abuse is physical abuse. Physical abuse leaves physical traces that can be observed and that can be introduced as evidence in trials. However, physical force can be used in the context of discipline. The characterization of the use of force as discipline and the absence of a general consensus, or for that matter even a body of knowledge, regarding appropriate methods of disciplining children create a condition in which the courts are hesitant to move aggressively to control the use of force against children. In essence, discipline is an effective defense against the charge of physical child abuse.

From a historical perspective, children were not legally protected until quite recently. Roman law gave fathers virtually absolute authority over their children. Fathers could sell, abandon, offer in sacrifice, devour, kill, or otherwise dispose of their children (Bybee 1979; Bowling 1977).

This lack of children's rights was fairly universal and did not change until the nineteenth century, with early intervention designed to control the exploitation of children in the workplace. The French Declaration of the Rights of Man treated children as a subcategory of persons without full human rights, and the United Nations Universal Declaration of Human Rights did not include a provision for children (Boulding 1977). The English Poor Law Amendment Act of 1868 was the first legislation that sought to control parents. It held parents accountable for their children's health and provided for the punishment of parents who failed to care adequately for their children (Adams et al. 1971). Attempts to implement this bill provided the instances of the use of discipline as a defense in cases charging abuse.

In the United States, early concern with the plight of children was frustrated by a lack of legal status for children. Child advocates captured attention with the case of Mary Ellen, discussed earlier (McCrea 1910). Church workers who sought to remove the child from the home had to bring their action through the Society for the Prevention of Cruelty to Animals, as no statutes existed protecting children. Public attention to the fact that animals were better protected than children led to the establishment of the Society for the Prevention of Cruelty to Children in 1871 and to the passage of the first children's charter in 1889 (Wilderson 1973). This charter provided for the removal of children from threatening situations, allowed children to give testimony in court against their parents, and provided for the establishment of departments to attend to the welfare of children and to administer the act.

The issue of children's rights became confused with the emergence of the juvenile and family court movement. The child-saver movement sought to improve the treatment of children by removing them from the jurisdiction of the adult criminal-justice system (Platt 1969). Two agencies became responsible for children with problems. Welfare agencies had responsibility for providing financial support and, with the courts, for arranging adoptions and determining custody. The newly established family courts operated under the *parens patrie* philosophy, which vested the court with both parental rights and parental responsibilities for the wards of the court. The court acted *in loco parentis,* or in the place of the parents. Children were held to have diminished capacity and thus diminished responsibility for their acts. The courts were to act in a parental manner to discipline and to protect children. These courts frequently were responsible for all matters regarding children; thus, child offenders were mixed with child victims.

The distinction between the two groups faded over time, and by the 1950s, the family court was under attack as an abuser of children. It was held that the courts were making decisions not in the best interests of children and that children and their parents were unable to protect the children from the court because these children did not have the same basic rights held by adults and that could be used for protection. Various attempts to remove or separate children who were wards of the court because their behavior was criminal from those children whose behavior was adolescent misbehavior and from those children who were victims met with only limited success. In some cases, the children in need of supervision (CHINS), minors in need of supervision (MINS), and persons in need of supervision (PINS) movements were locally popular, but although they were nationally debated, they were not nationally adopted until the legal rights of children were established by the courts.

In the 1960s, a series of cases were heard by the Supreme Court regarding children's rights. In 1966 in *Kent v. United States,* 383 U.S. 541, the Court noted that there was a discrepancy between the theoretical purpose and the actual performance of some juvenile courts and suggested some changes. It did not rule in such a manner as to encourage fundamental change in the juvenile-court process. In 1967, the Court held *In re Gault,* 387 U.S. 1, that if the juvenile court was going to deal with children as adults, then the children must be given most of the rights of adults charged with crimes. The juvenile-justice system accepted the second half of this conditional statement, and the juvenile court became more legalistic in its approach. In 1979 in *Tinker v. Des Moines School District,* 393 U.S. 503, the Supreme Court held that children are persons under the Constitution.

From 1967 to 1970, twenty-seven states and two territories passed amendments to change their statutes regarding the rights of children. Most of these statutes went beyond the criminal-rights issue and included civil-rights issues and addressed the reporting of abuse. These changes included the requirement that certain professionals report suspected cases of abuse, expanded the definitions of what could be considered reportable abuse, designated social-service agencies as responsible for processing abuse complaints, and established central registries for recording abuse complaints (DeFrancis & Lucht 1974).

The debate regarding rights for children focuses on the need to protect children who have limited capacity to make correct decisions regarding their own welfare and the need to allow children adequate protections from those who would abuse them. Those who propose a bill of rights for children argue that children should be recognized as persons for legal purposes (Foster 1974) and advocate the protection of all civil rights of children with all of the constitutional protections available to adults (Farson 1979). Others propose that the rights to nurturance (the rights to life, food, clothing, shelter, education, and proper moral standards), rather than rights to self-determination, should be the focus of efforts to protect children (Coughlin 1979; Forer 1979).

Victim Characteristics

As is discussed in the following section, the world of abnormal rearing (WAR) cycle is common in cases of child abuse (Bowling 1977). As such, the primary characteristic of child victims may be that they are born to parents who were abused as children. Child temperament also has been identified as a factor in child abuse. Personality conflicts can occur between parents and their children, and some children are difficult to raise (Newberger & Bourne 1985). All studies indicate that child victims are emotionally and/or psychologically damaged as a result of being abused (Smetana 1984; Carlson 1977; Polansky 1978).

A number of other studies have focused on the characteristics of the child victims of abuse. An early study found that 75 percent of children who were abused were under the age of thirteen and that about half were under seven years of age. The children were not unusual in terms of intelligence, physical disability, or mental pathology. They did display patterns of hostility, destructiveness, and fear directed toward their abusers, were hyperactive, and displayed depression (Merrill 1962).

Another study found that the self-concepts of abused children were affected. Abused children tended to see themselves as "bad." The same study first identified the link between abused children and abusing parents by demonstrating that many abusing parents were abused when they were children (Young 1964).

A study that compared abused children with nonabused children found no difference in terms of physical health but did find that abused children tended to have more scars and deformities. Abused children who had been removed from their homes demonstrated better health than abused children who had remained in their homes. Abused children were more likely to be classified as mentally retarded, have poor impulse control, and demonstrate atypical anger responses (Elmer 1967).

The characteristics of child sexual offenders have been controversial in that some researchers have suggested that the child victims are at fault. Victim perception theories suggest that the abuse occurs because the victims are masochistic and seek to be abused (Shainess 1977) or that the victims have characteristics or behaviors that trigger the abuse (Block & Sinnott 1979; Finkelhor 1979; Steinmetz 1977; Watkins 1982). It has been noted that at times one child in the family is chosen as the target of abuse and that these targeted children tend to have deformities and scars, mental retardation, low self-concepts, low impulse control, and high levels of anger (Elmer 1967; Friedrick & Boriskin 1976). Another study concluded that there are children at high risk for abuse. These children have physical or social defects that could make them targets, such as low intelligence or having been conceived out of wedlock (Browning & Boatman 1977). Age also has been noted as a factor, with first-born or older females overrepresented among abused children (Tormes 1968), as are those from a large family in which the parents married young (Specktor 1979).

In the first study of children who had participated in sexual relations with adults, the researchers concluded that the children were hyperactive, physically normal, pleasant, personable, and generally attracted to adults and that the children were very cooperative or took an active role in the sexual exchange (Bender & Abram 1937). This position was advanced occasionally when female victims were evaluated from the psychoanalytic perspective (Sloane & Karpinski 1942). However, the argument is rejected by opponents, who argue that seductiveness is one of the consequences of being sexually abused. The child is conditioned to be seductive during repetitive sexual encounters with the abusing adult (Cantwell 1981; DeYoung 1984; Swan 1985; DeYoung 1982).

Most studies of victims of domestic sexual abuse have been based on small samples because of the limited number of identified cases available for study. Although a number of factors have been identified in these studies, caution in generalization of the findings is prudent. Girls are more apt to be victims than boys, and when complaints are registered for abused males, the abuser tends to be male (Finkelhor 1979; Rush 1980). A recent study based on a large sample of cases found that sexually abused children were behaviorally or emotionally disturbed and did not find support for the factors identified in the Finkelhor (1979) and Rush (1980) studies (Vander Mey & Neff 1986). A second recent large study found that girls raised in high-income homes were more apt to be abused than girls from low-income families (Russell 1986).

Some consideration must be given to the possibility that characteristics of abused children are the results of, rather than cause of, the abuse. Physical characteristics such as scars, personality characteristics such as hostility and low-self concept, and impaired functioning at both physical and intellectual levels could be caused by a pattern of abuse that produces both physical and mental damage.

Offender Characteristics

It is difficult to separate the types of abusers by type of abuse. They appear to be similar; in fact, in most cases a person who abuses his or her children will also abuse his or her spouse and others in the family environment (Gayford 1975; Hilberman & Munson 1977; Scott 1974; Walker 1979).

While few data sets are available, most researchers suggest that abusers come from all social, economic, racial, and ethnic backgrounds. At least one study suggests that there appears to be more abuse among low-income groups (Newberger & Bourne 1985), yet it should be noted that more affluent families have the resources necessary to resist labeling. Newberger and Bourne identify three other factors that tend to be associated with the child-abuse situation: (1) abusing families tend to be social isolates, make little contact with neighbors, and move frequently; (2) abusing families are under social stress, and abuse increases as the stress increases; and (3) child abuse tends to be intergenerational in nature—those who abuse their children tend to have been abused themselves as children. This last factor has been widely accepted.

Most studies suggest that parents who abuse their children have character and personality problems. The parents who abuses their children usually see these children as instigators. The abused child is seen as different, selfish, duller than other children, brighter than other children, sickly, defiant, defective, fussy, deviant, or different in some way. Studies have found that abusive parents do not differ from nonabusive parents in terms of social or ethnic background or in terms of specific personality types (Steele 1975; DeFrancis 1965; Philbrick 1960).

Abusing parents are emotionally insecure and reluctant to accept help from others. They maintain an aggressive barrier toward society and professionals and are assertive, have a poorly directed sense of anger, and are defensive as a way of dealing with their feelings of inadequacy. These adults are seen as unable to feel pleasure and as socially isolated from the community and the family (Steele 1975), but they tend to be protected by the nonabusing parent (Nurse 1964). These characteristics are identified with or held to be caused by early childhood experiences that produced abnormal development. The abusive parent tends to place his or her needs before those of the child and demonstrates an irresponsible and impulsive behavior. At times, role reversal occurs, with the child assuming parental responsibilities and attitudes and the parent appearing more childlike (Philbrick 1960).

A number of researchers have focused on the personality traits of abusing parents (DeFrancis 1963; Meyer 1985; Philbrick 1960; Steele 1975; Storkey 1985; Susman 1985; Nurse 1964). Their work indicates that abusive personalities are immature, dependent, and antisocial and have unmet emotional needs that they go to extremes to satisfy. Other studies contradict these findings (Plotkin 1982; Steele & Pollock 1968). At best, the data in this area are limited; much of the research is based on case histories or limited samples.

One study that attempted to identify types of abusers did focus on personality types (Flammang 1970). Ten personality/behavioral factors were identified, and five were present in a large percentage of the cases: (1) the abuser was rigid, with severe value systems (present in 60 percent–70 percent of the cases); (2) the abuser was a strict disciplinarian (present in 30 percent of the cases); (3) the abuser exhibited mental or emotional deviation (present in 48 percent of the cases); (4) the abuser was under life stress (present in over 62 percent of the cases); and (5) the abuser was a neglected and abused child (present in 35.2 percent of the cases).

Abusing parents tend to have been abused as children with sufficient regularity to be identified as participants in the WAR cycle, or the world of abnormal rearing (Helfer n.d.). The abused child grows up to abuse his or her own children in the same way that he or she was abused. The cycle is a process of learned behavior (Bakan 1971). Some role reversal occurs, with the parent demanding that the child meet his or her needs, rather than the parent meeting the child's needs. The abused child acts more mature than other children and takes care of the adult. When the child is abused or disciplined with violence, he or she accepts the use of violence as an appropriate means of accomplishing goals, or as behavior that makes other people comply with the abuser's wishes.

A number of researchers have suggested that child abuse can be understood only from the interactionist perspective, which asserts that the characteristics of the child, the characteristics of the abuser, and the characteristics of the situation interact to produce abuse (Berger 1980; Smith 1984; Zimrin 1984). Others have focused on the presence of environmental stress, such as the loss of a job or the lack of financial resources, as a mediating factor (Barth 1983; Ostbloom 1980).

Summary

The perpetrators of child abuse are frequently the child's own parents. This familial relationship generally confuses the issues. Parents have a duty to raise their children to adulthood. In the process, they are expected to define values and to exert control over their children. Precisely what a parent is to provide and what constitutes discipline are unclear, with parents given considerable latitude in the range of behaviors that even if not acceptable, are beyond the legitimate interests of society. These parental rights can be asserted when a parent is charged with abusing his or her child.

Child abuse includes physical abuse, sexual abuse, psychological abuse, neglect, and abandonment. All of these with the exception of sexual abuse are difficult to define outside of parental rights and financial circumstances, and all are difficult to prove in court. Most cases that are pursued successfully involve physical abuse because this type of abuse, when severe, leaves physical evidence that is difficult to deny.

Historically, children have had little status in society. They had no rights and were seen as the property of their parents. The parents could treat their children any way they saw fit. Children's rights began to emerge during the Renaissance period and were expressed in the British so-called poor laws, resulting in restrictions on the power of parents and identification of basic parental responsibilities. Children still had only limited legal rights until the 1960s and 1970s, when in the United States the children's rights movement was reflected in court decisions and legislation that expanded the rights of children.

The prevalence of child abuse cannot be determined. Much of the behavior that constitutes child abuse occurs in the privacy of the home and is not reported. The figures that are reported represent just the tip of what is probably a substantial iceberg. Because child abuse will continue to be a family matter, it is unlikely that there will ever be an accurate accounting of the incidence of this behavior.

A number of studies have evaluated the characteristics of both abusers and their victims. A number of personality factors have been associated with both victims and offenders. Many of the factors identified with offenders could result from abuse rather than cause abuse. The one factor that appears to be fairly constant is the intergenerational nature of child abuse. Child abusers tend to have been victims of child abuse. These learned patterns are passed on from generation to generation.

References

Adams, P.; Berg, L.; Berger, N.; Duane, M.; Neill, A.S.; and Ollendorff, R. 1971. *Children's rights: Toward the liberation of the child.* New York: Praeger.

American Humane Society. 1978. *National analysis of official child neglect and abuse reporting.* Washington, D.C.: Government Printing Office.

Aries, P. 1962. *Centuries of childhood.* Trans. R. Baldick. New York: Alfred A. Knopf.

Bakan, D. 1971. *Slaughter of the innocents: A study of the battered-child phenomenon.* Boston: Beacon Press.

Ballew, J.R. 1985. Role of natural helpers in preventing child abuse and neglect. *Social Work* 30(1): 37–41.

Barth, R.P. 1983. The contribution of stress to child abuse. *Social Services Review* 57(5): 477–89.

Bender, L., and Abram, B. 1937. The reaction of children to sexual relations with adults. *Journal of American Orthopsychiatry* 16(6): 500–18.

Berger, A. 1980. The child abusing family . . . parent-related characteristics. *American Journal of Family Therapy* 8(1): 53–66.

Berliner, L. 1984. The testimony of the child victim of sexual assault. *Journal of Social Issues* 40(1): 125–47.

Block, M.R., and Sinnott, J.D. 1979. *The battered elder syndrome: An exploratory study.* College Park: University of Maryland Press.

Boulding, E. 1977. A "children's rights." *Society* 15(1): 39–43.

Bowling, D. 1977. *An attitudinal study of child abuse in Tuscaloosa, Alabama.* Master's thesis, University of Alabama.

Bremmer, R.H. 1970. *Children and youth in America: A documentary history.* Cambridge: Harvard University Press.

Breton, M. 1977. Nurturing abused and abusive mothers: The hairdressing group. *Social Work with Groups* 2(2): 161–78.

Browning, D.H., and Boatman, B. 1977. Incest: Children at risk. *American Journal of Psychiatry* 134(1): 69–72.

Bybee, R. 1979. Violence toward youth. *Journal of Social Issues* 35(1): 1–14.

Cantwell, H.B. 1981. Sexual abuse of children in Denver, 1979: Reviewed with implications for pediatric intervention and possible prevention. *Child Abuse and Neglect* 8(1) 75–85.

Carlson, B.E. 1977. Battered women and their assailants. *Social Work* 22(5): 455–60.

Cohen, S.J., and Sussman, A. 1975. The incidence of child abuse in the United States. *Child Welfare* 54(6): 432–43.

Comfort, R. 1985. Sex, strangers and safety. *Child Welfare* 64(6): 541–45.

Conte, J. 1984. Progress in treating the sexual abuse of children. *Social Work* 29(3): 258–63.

Coughlin, B.J. 1979. The rights of children. In *Children's rights: Contemporary perspectives,* ed. P.A. Vardin and I.N. Brody. New York: Teachers College Press.

DeFrancis, V. 1963. *Child abuse: Preview of a nationwide survey.* Denver: American Humane Association, Children's Division.

———. 1965. *Protecting the child victims of sex crimes committed by adults.* Denver: American Humane Association, Children's Division.

DeFrancis, V., and Lucht, J.D. 1974. *Child abuse legislation in the 1970s.* Denver: American Humane Association, Children's Division.

DeYoung, M. 1982. Innocent seducer or innocently seduced? The role of the child incest victim. *Journal of Clinical Child Psychology* 11(1): 56–60.

———. 1984. Counterphobic behavior in multiple molested children. *Child Welfare* 63(5): 333–39.

Elmer, E. 1967. Developmental characteristics of abused children. *Pediatrics* 40(4): 596–609.

Emslie, G.J. 1983. Incest reported by children and adolescents hospitalized for severe psychiatric problems. *American Journal of Psychiatry* 140(6): 708–11.

Farson, R. 1979. The children's rights movement. In *The future of children and juvenile justice,* ed. L.T. Empry. Charlottesville: University of Virginia Press.

Finkelhor, D. 1979. *Sexually victimized children.* New York: Free Press.

———. 1985. Sexual abuse and physical abuse: Some critical differences. In *Unhappy families,* ed. E.H. Newberger and R.B. Bourne. Littleton, Mass.: PSG.

Flammang, C.J. 1970. *The police and the underprotected child.* Springfield, Ill.: Charles C. Thomas.

Flexner, B., and Balwin, R.N. 1914. *Juvenile courts and probation.* New York: Century Press.

Fontana, V.J., and Besharov, D.J. 1977. *The maltreated child.* Springfield, Ill.: Charles C. Thomas.

Forer, L.G. 1979. Rights of children: The legal vacuum. In *Children's rights: Contemporary perspectives,* ed. P.A. Vardin and I.N. Brody. New York: Teachers College Press.

Foster, H.H. 1974. *"Bill of rights" for children.* Springfield, Ill.: Charles C. Thomas.

Friedrick, W.N. and J.A. Bonsilin. 1976. The role of the child in abuse. *American Journal of Orthopsychiatry* 46(6): 580–90.

Furness, T. 1984. Organizing a therapeutic approach to intrafamily child sexual abuse. *Journal of Adolescence* 7: 309–17.

Gayford, J. 1975. Battered wives. *Medicine and Science Law* 15(2): 237–45.

Gelles, R.J. 1985. Family violence: What we know and can do. In *Unhappy families,* ed. E.H. Newberger and R.B. Bourne. Littleton, Mass.: PSG.

Gil, D.G. 1979. Violence against children. In *Child abuse and violence,* ed. D.G. Gil. New York: AMS Press.

Giles-Sims, J. 1985. A longitudinal study of the battered children of battered wives. *Family Relations* 34(2): 205–10.

Helfer, R. n.d. *The diagnostic process and treatment programs.* Washington, D.C.: Department of Health, Education, and Welfare.

Hilberman, E., and Munson, M. 1977. Sixty battered women. *Victimology* 2(1/2): 460–71.

Hobbes, T. 1972. The citizen. In *Man and citizen,* ed. T.S.K. Scott-Craig and B. Gert. Gloucester, Mass.: Peter Smith.

Hoorwitz, A.N. 1983. Guidelines for treating father-daughter incest. *Social Casework* 64(5): 515–24.

Kadushim, A. 1978. Neglect—Is it neglected too often? In *Child abuse and neglect: Issues on innovation and implementation,* vol. 1, ed. M.L. Lauderdale. Washington, D.C.: Government Printing Office.

Kempe, C.H. 1962. The battered child syndrome. *Journal of the American Medical Association* 191(1): 17–24.

Kristal, H.F., and Tucker, F. 1975. Managing child abuse cases. *Social Work* 20(3): 392–95.

McCrea, R.C. 1910. Societies for the prevention of cruelty to children. In *Preventive treatment of neglected children,* ed. H.H. Hart. New York: Russell Sage.

McMurtry, S.C. 1985. Secondary prevention of child maltreatment: A review. *Social Work* 30(1): 42–48.

Magura, S. 1982. Clients view outcome of child protective services. *Social Casework* 63(5): 522–31.

Marvick, E.W. 1974. Nature versus nurture: Patterns and trends in seventeenth-century French child rearing. In *The history of childhood,* ed. L. de Mause. New York: Psychohistory Press.

Mause, L. de 1974. *The history of childhood.* New York: Psychohistory Press.

Merrill, E.J. 1962. Physical abuse of children—An agency study. In *Protecting the battered child,* Denver: American Humane Association, Children's Division.

Meyer, L. 1985. Battered wives, dead husbands. *Student Lawyer* 6(7): 46–51.

Mouzakitis, C.M. 1985. A multidisciplinary approach to treating child neglect. *Social Casework* 66(2): 218–24.

Newberger, E.H., and Bourne, R. 1985. *Unhappy families: Clinical and research perspectives on family violence.* Littleton, Mass.: PSG.

Nurse, S.M. 1964. Familial patterns of parents who abuse their children. *Smith College Studies in Social Work* 35(1): 11–25.

Ostbloom, N. 1980. A model for conceptualizing child abuse causation and intervention. *Social Casework* 61(1): 164–72.

Philbrick, E. 1960. *Treating parental pathology.* Denver: American Humane Association, Children's Division.

Platt, A. 1969. *The child savers.* Chicago: Chicago University Press.

Plotkin, R.C. 1982. Utility of a measure of aggression in differentiating abusing parents from other parents who are experiencing familial disturbance. *Journal of Clinical Psychology* 38(6): 607–10.

Polanksky, N.A. 1978. Assessing adequacy of child caring: An urban scale. *Child Welfare* 57(4): 439–49.

Robertson, P. 1974. Home as a nest: Middle-class childhood in nineteenth-century Europe. In *The history of childhood,* ed. L. de Mause. New York: Psychohistory Press.

Rush, F. 1980. *The best-kept secret: Sexual abuse of children.* New York: McGraw-Hill.

Russell, D.E. 1986. *The secret trauma: Incest in the lives of girls and women.* New York: Basic Books.

Scott, P. 1974. Battered wives. *British Journal of Psychiatry* 125: 433–41.

Shainess, N. 1977. Psychological aspects of wife beating. In *Battered women: A psy-*

chosociological study of domestic violence, ed. M. Roy. New York: Van Nostrand Reinhold.

Sloane, P., and Karpinski, E. 1942. Effects of incest on the participants. *American Journal of Orthopsychiatry* 12(5): 666–73.

Smetana, J.G. 1984. Abused, neglected, and nonmaltreated children's conceptions of moral and social-conventional transgressions. *Child Development* 55(2): 277–87.

Smith, S.L. 1984. Significant research findings in the etiology of child abuse. *Social Casework* 65(3): 337–46.

Specktor, P. 1979. *Incest: Confronting the silent crime.* Minneapolis: Minesota Program for Victims of Sexual Abuse.

Steele, B. 1975. *Working with abusive parents.* Washington, D.C.: Department of Health, Education, and Welfare.

Steele, B., and Pollock, C.B. 1968. A psychiatric study of parents who abuse infants and small children. In *The battered child,* ed. R.E. Helfer and C.H. Kempe. Chicago: University of Chicago Press.

Steinmetz, S.K. 1977. *The cycle of violence: Assertive, aggressive, and abusive family interaction.* New York: Praeger.

Storkey, C. 1985. Personal worth, self-esteem, anomie, hostility, and irrational thinking of abusive mothers. *Journal of Clinical Psychology* 41: 414–21.

Susman, E.J. 1985. Child-rearing patterns in depressed, abusive, and normal mothers. *American Journal of Orthopsychiatry* 55(2): 237–51.

Swan, R.W. (1985). The child as active participant in child abuse. *Clinical Social Work Journal* 13(1): 62–77.

Tormes, Y. 1968. *Child victims of incest.* Denver: American Humane Association, Children's Division.

Vander, Mey, B.J., and Neff, R.L. 1986. *Incest as child abuse.* New York: Praeger.

Walker, L.E. 1979. *The battered woman.* New York: Harper and Row.

Watkins, C.R. 1982. *Victims, aggressors, and the family secret: An exploration into family violence.* St. Paul: Minnesota Department of Public Welfare.

Wilderson, A.E. 1973. *The rights of children.* Philadelphia: Temple Press.

Wolf, D.A. 1985. Child-abusive parents: An empirical review and analyses. *Psychology Bulletin* 97(4): 462–82.

Wollert, R.W. 1982. Self-help groups for sexually abusive families. *Prevention in Humane Services* 1(1): 99–109.

Wolock, I. 1984. Child maltreatment as a social problem: The neglect of neglect. *American Journal of Orthopsychiatry* 54(4): 530–43.

Young, L. 1964. *Wednesday's child.* New York: McGraw-Hill.

Zimrin, H. 1984. Child abuse . . . encounter between needs and personality traits within the family. *American Journal of Family Therapy* 12(1): 37–47.

3
Elder Abuse

Elder abuse is, in many senses, more difficult to examine than other forms of domestic violence. Much of the abuse directed toward elders is not violent, and much of it is not domestic. It has been suggested that the elderly tend to be more likely to be victims of both traditional criminal activity (or at least tend to experience high levels of fear of victimization) and the full range of frauds, including those that are illegal and those that are legal but of questionable morality. Elders can be institutionalized against their wishes, and the level of care in institutions that provide substandard care in order to increase profits can be characterized as abuse.

In the case of the elderly, neglect can be lack of attention and might be a matter of differences in expectations, held by the actors, in the level of attention due an elderly parent by an adult child. Elders may perceive themselves as abused not because of a failure on the part of their children to provide services at an accepted identified level, but because the level of care they receive is less than the level they expect. This is not to suggest that elder abuse does not occur—it does; however, it is less clear and broader in scope than other forms of abuse.

Elder abuse frequently extends beyond the home. Although the various dimensions of elder abuse are discussed below, this chapter focuses on the domestic dimensions of elder abuse.

Historical Perspective

Little has been written about the historical development of elder abuse. Since elder abuse is the most recently emerging focus of interest in the area of domestic abuse, it has not been subjected to the level of scrutiny directed toward child abuse and spouse abuse. In fact, concern for the elderly in the context of abuse may have emerged from studies of spouse and child abuse, which led to a broader examination of the problem within the context of domestic violence (Gelles 1987). Social values have been changing, and less emphasis has been placed on family and individual responsibility and more emphasis on social or public responsibility, including responsibility for the elderly.

Unlike the orientation toward women and children, the change in society's orientation toward the elderly has not been consistently in the direction of reform. Throughout history and across many cultures, the elderly have been respected and revered. They have enjoyed a protected status and have been objects of devotion and respect in literature and custom (Stearns 1986).

At the same time that the elderly have been the objects of respect and devotion, they have represented authority. This has generated conflict. Intergenerational conflict is a theme that occurs repeatedly throughout history in both literature and custom (Reinharz 1986). Stearns (1986) suggests that orientation toward this conflict varies and identifies three shifts in concern about intergenerational conflict. Concern about intergenerational conflict was high during the seventeenth and eighteenth centuries, declined during the nineteenth and twentieth centuries, and appears to be increasing now, indicating the beginning of a new cycle.

Violence directed toward elders appears to vary in stages that correspond with the cycles of concern regarding intergenerational conflict. During the sixteenth, seventeenth, and eighteenth centuries, elders were frequent victims. Older women were the common targets of witchcraft trials, and at times, older men were the most frequent murder victims. During this period, the elders controlled the economic resources of the family, with independence for adult children coming with the parents' deaths.

This pattern of dependence changed during the Industrial Revolution, which provided opportunities for adult children to become independent and changed patterns of family wealth such that during the nineteenth and twentieth centuries, the elderly became dependent on their children. During this period, there was relatively little reported elder abuse.

At the present, the pattern is changing once more, and the elderly are gaining some independence from their adult children because of resources provided by increased national productivity, which has produced savings and pensions. Along with these changes, there is an increased level of concern about intergenerational conflict and elder abuse. It is possible that there are few or no changes in behavior and that changing levels of abuse can be attributed to changing levels of concern. In other words, there is more perceived abuse and conflict because society is more concerned and is paying more attention to relations between elders and their younger relatives (Stearns 1986).

It is also possible that elder abuse is newly emerging because the elderly as a group are, to some extent, newly emerging. It is only recently that improved levels of health care have extended the life expectancy of men and women to the point that there is a large elderly population. As a result, the proportion of elderly in our population has increased and will continue to increase. As the age of our population increases, the dependency ratio (the proportion of those who are dependent as a function of those who can provide care) increases. Adults today face an increasing number of elder relatives for whom they can be expected to provide care (Steinmetz 1983). Adult children can expect their parents to be with them for long periods of time, thus any established commitments or patterns can be anticipated to continue. In essence, there are more potential elders who will be dependent for a longer period of time, causing care givers to avoid establishing patterns of support.

The results of changing demographic characteristics and social values can be seen in the development and growth of institutions for the elderly. Prior to the development of these institutions, the elderly were cared for by family members (Mercer 1983). The shift from personal responsibility to social responsibility began to emerge during the Elizabethan period in England (Randall 1965). When the family could not care for family members such as the elderly, care was provided by the government. Attempts in England in the early 1900s to modify the English poor laws to provide for a separate agency to care for the elderly were not successful (Douglas & Hickey 1983).

The use of public homes or asylums to care for those who could not care for themselves and who were not cared for by their families was brought to the American colonies and was expanded with a form of relief called outdoor relief, which made payments of families who had limited resources to care for a disabled or senile family member. After the American Revolution, the use of alms houses was increased as the preferred approach to charitable aid. This increasing use of alms houses was the beginning of the use of long-term institutions to care for those who were unable to care for themselves (Cohen 1974; Randall 1965). The same forces that created the child-saver movement and the settlement-house movement pressed for a better way to meet the needs of the elderly, but the use of institutions for the elderly and the mentally ill continued until quite recently and even included the housing of the elderly in mental institutions (Regan 1983; Randall 1965).

Changing economic structures led to changes in family structure, with fewer multigenerational homes and reduced care of the elderly by their children. The advent of Social Security provided greater financial security for those over sixty-five years of age. The impact of the Social Security Act included the growing availability of private residential facilities designed to provide care based on Social Security income (Stathopoulus 1983). Nursing homes became more prevalent and tended to be widely used as an appropriate option for those elderly unable to care for themselves (Randall 1965). The growing acceptance of the nursing home has both lessened and increased pressures on adult children. An acceptable option is available in the form of nursing/retirement homes, but the growing tales of elder abuse in nursing homes causes hesitation in exercising this option, and for many, feelings of guilt are associated with the use of nursing homes.

Dimensions of Elder Abuse

Elder abuse has several dimensions other than that of domestic violence, which is the focus of this chapter. These areas are reviewed briefly before abuse that occurs in the context of the family is examined.

The elderly have been identified as particularly vulnerable to crime and criminals. A review of crime statistics and the results of victimology studies indicates that the elderly are no more likely than younger citizens to be victims of ordinary criminal activities such as assault, robbery, and burglary (Finley 1983; Hindelang 1976; Antunes et al. 1977). Other studies indicate that the elderly suffer no more physically and financially than other age groups, nor do they suffer more psychologically than other groups (Cook et al. 1978). It does appear, however, that the elderly do demonstrate greater fear of being victimized than other groups (Hahn 1976; McAdoo 1979; Sundeen & Mathieu 1976). It has been suggested that this increased fear distorts the victimization findings in that fear causes potential victims (in this case the elderly) to restrict their activities to avoid victimization; thus, crime rates are lower at the expense of personal freedom (Ling & Sengstock 1983).

There is limited evidence to support the contention that senior citizens are more vulnerable to fraud schemes than younger citizens (Braungart et al. 1979). The elderly, whose life spans have included a more trusting time, have financial resources, are often lonely, are not accustomed to managing fixed incomes, and seek to expand their wealth in order to have something to leave to their children. As a result, they fall prey to work-at-home schemes, securities frauds, franchise frauds, commodities frauds, medical quackery, land frauds, home-improvement frauds, funeral-plan frauds, pension frauds, and insurance frauds (Pepper 1983). Most of these types of fraud have legal counterparts, and at times it is difficult to draw the line between activities that are outright frauds and those that are legal but take advantage of the unwary elder.

One area of fraud to which the elderly are particularly vulnerable is fraud concerning nursing homes. Although many nursing homes are well-operated care providers, there are some that operate at substandard levels and use inappropriate practices. Much of the fraud occurring in the operation of nursing homes is directed at federal and state agencies, rather than at the elderly patient (Halamandaris 1983). Medicaid abuse includes inflating costs by billing for services and employees that in actuality have not been provided. There is a direct cost to the patient in that if these services are needed and not being provided, the patient's needs are not being met. In addition, patient accounts can be billed inappropriately, and in some cases, patient assets are used inappropriately by the nursing home or its staff (Halamandaris 1983).

Patients in nursing homes can be exposed to several types of abuse. There are instances in which the elderly in nursing homes have been exposed to violence, psychological abuse, neglect, and sexual abuse. In addition to these direct forms of abuse, the nursing-home process itself can be abusing in that the decision to enter a nursing home may not be voluntary. Social-service-agency employees, relatives, or custodians may decide that it is in the best interests of the older person to be placed in a nursing home. To older persons who are involuntarily committed, this may be an act of neglect, a denial of their right to determine their own futures, a reduction in freedom, or implied/imposed helplessness; in short, the involuntary commitment can be psychological abuse. When this is coupled with the loss of control of their assets, the elderly are further abused. This increased dependency makes them more vulnerable to unapproved use of their assets, which can range from the use of assets to pay the costs of unwanted maintenance to outright appropriation of assets by custodians.

Even when admission is voluntary, there are unanticipated consequences of institutionalization. Many patients experience difficulty adjusting to the radical change in life-style that occurs (Wolk & Reingold 1975; Bourestom & Pastalon 1981), producing passivity and withdrawal from the outside world (Kasl 1972) that is complicated by the tendency of some institutional staff members to treat the residents as dependent and sick, promoting the infantilization of the elderly (Gresham 1976). The residents lose control over their lives, the freedom to make choices about basic living patterns, and privacy.

This produces in them feelings of helplessness (Schultz & Aderman 1973) and fosters learned helplessness (Mercer & Kane 1979), which can lead to withdrawal, depression, and early death (Schultz & Aderman1974).

In the case of elders, neglect and abuse can be self-neglect and self-abuse (Quinn & Tomita 1986). This form of behavior can range from choosing not to purchase needed resources in order to conserve their children's inheritance or to maintain their wealth to failure to follow basic habits and customs that promote good health and a clean living environment. This can lead to or be caused by depression, despondency, and a failure to thrive.

There are instances in which the elder remains in the home of a relative. Reasons for this may lie in the values of the participants or in financial constraints. At times, values are in conflict when the elder expects greater care and attention from his or her adult children than the children expect or are able to deliver. In some cases, the children feel a need to provide the care, yet either do not wish to provide it or resent the elder's presence. Simultaneously, the children may experience guilt at the thought of placing the elder in a nursing home. For many families, the period between the increased dependency of the elder and the decision to place the elder in a nursing home is a traumatic period for all involved.

Kosberg (1983) has developed a comprehensive list of activities that constitute elder abuse. The list includes physical abuse, psychological abuse, material abuse, and violation of rights. Block and Sinnott (1979) have a similar list that includes poor residential environment; Douglas and colleagues (1980) add two categories of neglect; and O'Malley and colleagues (1979) add sexual abuse. Johnson (1986) summarized the forms of abuse identified in twenty-one studies of elder abuse and developed a complex definition of elder abuse. Her comprehensive list includes abuse, neglect, active neglect, passive neglect, physical abuse, physical neglect, psychological abuse, psychological neglect, verbal/emotional abuse, material abuse, medical abuse, exploitation, and violation of rights. This diversity of definitions produces confusing results in the literature.

Physical violence includes the use of physical force against the victim, in this case the elderly parent or resident of a nursing home. With advancing age, the elderly lose the physical ability to defend themselves from physical attack by relatively youthful and physically active caretaker relatives or institutional employees. Acts of violence against the elder can range from mild slaps to severe beatings that produce bruises and broken bones.

Physical abuse can include acts that are not acts of direct violence. Acts such as denial of food, medical care, or personal care can be characterized as neglect or as physical abuse, depending on the intent of the actor. If these acts reflect a lack of concern for the needs of the elderly by health-care providers, then neglect occurs. To the extent that the acts reflect an intent to harm, control, or punish the elder, they constitute abuse, which can be characterized as physical abuse.

Neglect of the elderly is similar to and at the same time different from the neglect of children. In both cases, there is a condition of dependency that can be and often is managed by the families of those who need the attention. In both cases, this family obligation at times is not satisfied in a manner consistent with contemporary values, and in both cases when this occurs, those who have not met their obligations are sanctioned by society.

The difference lies in the strength of the respective obligations. There is fairly universal agreement that parents have a duty to provide the basic necessities of life for their children. While there is considerable disagreement about the absolute levels of resources that should be allocated to children and exactly what constitutes neglect, there is a consensus that suggests that parents are expected to be responsible for meeting the needs of their children. This consensus does not appear to exist regarding the responsibilities of adult children toward their elderly parents.

Our values in this regard have been changing over the years. During the first quarter of the twentieth century, when the elders of today were born, and in the ensuing decades during which they matured and gained their values, the family's obligation to support its elderly members was generally accepted; however, during the lifetime of these elders, traditional values began to change. Today, many people still hold the belief that the family has a responsibility for providing the basic necessities for its elders, but this belief is a matter of personal values rather than one that is adhered to and reinforced by society as a whole. Thus, those who do take elderly parents into their homes may be commended, but those who do not are not criticized if an acceptable alternative, such as a nursing-home placement, is provided.

Most of the supportive services received by the elderly are provided by family members. It has been estimated that up to 80 percent of long-term care provided to elders is provided by family members (Hudson 1986). Providing services, particularly to an impaired elder, can place a burden on the adult children. This caretaker burden includes physical, financial, psychological, and emotional problems experienced by the adult children because they are providing services to an elder (George 1986). Social norms of reciprocity and solidarity place demands on caretakers, which creates demands for commitments that are difficult for them, thus producing stress. These norms are somewhat contradictory (balanced exchange v. provision of resources based on the family member's needs) and can enhance the potential for stress when the needs are great.

Neglect has been identified as active and passive (Cicirelli 1986). *Active neglect* is the refusal or failure to fulfill a caretaking obligation and includes a conscious and intentional attempt to inflict physical or emotional distress on the elder. *Passive neglect* includes the same behaviors without the *intent* to do harm. Neglect is relatively invisible, as it occurs in private, but it tends to be the most common form of abuse (Steuer & Austin 1980).

The changing financial resources available to the elderly may enhance the conflict between values of solidarity and reciprocity. Social Security has given most elders the financial resources to meet their own basic needs; however, there is ample room for confusion of expectations in this area. It is probable that most elders hold expectations for nurturance from their family members, expectations that are greater than the expectations held by their adult children for the level of care the children feel they should be expected to provide. Children who are aware of these differences may experience guilt, and as a result, they take more responsibility for their elders than they feel is necessary or want to take, producing a situation in which resentment, neglect, and abuse can develop. Guilt can increase avoidance-producing behavior, which elders consider to be neglect.

There is no clear definition or even a set of reasonable parameters for identifying neglect of elders. The best that can be said at this point is that the perception of neglect occurs when the elder receives less assistance or attention from his or her children than he or she expects. Avoidance or lack of attention can cause a threat to physical health of the elder when the case is extreme and the financial resources are not adequate to provide the basic necessities of life, including food, shelter, and adequate health care.

However, from this perspective, neglect probably produces psychological damage more frequently than it produces physical damage or a health threat. The apparent withdrawal of love, the feeling of abandonment, and the sense of helplessness that come when the elder's family neglects or avoids him or her can cause emotional and psychological distress.

Psychological abuse includes any behavior that causes a loss of esteem or feeling of self-worth, that causes a feeling of fear or intimidation, or that is derogatory or belittling. It can also include verbal assaults, threats, pejorative comments, stimulus deprivation, excessive critical comments, and isolation of the elder. Psychological abuse tends to be discussed in terms of acts that are likely to produce psychological or emotional damage, rather than in terms of intent or outcome. That is, an elder does not need to demonstrate psychological pathology before the abuse is held to have occurred, and psychological abuse can occur when the caretaker has no intent to be abusive.

Psychological abuse also can occur when the elder's rights are abused. Forcing the elder to leave his or her own home, to leave a nursing home, or to enter a nursing home against his or her wishes can be psychologically damaging. In these situations, the caretakers frequently experience conflict and guilt. The caretaker may perceive the elder as being at risk, may recognize that the action is against the elder's wishes, but may believe that the action is in the best interest of the elder or at least the only reasonable solution given the resources available. The force in these cases may be gentle or harsh, but psychological damage can occur when the result of gentle persuasion is placement in an environment unacceptable to the elder.

Another form of neglect is placing the elder in an environment that might not provide the resources needed for comfortable or safe living. Failure to provide adequate food, heating, cooling, stimulation, lighting, health care, personal-care supplies and services, and attention are commonly associated with poorly operated nursing homes, but these problems also occur when the elders live with their families or live alone in their own homes.

Material abuse refers to the use of the assets of an elderly person in a manner in which the elder does not approve. This includes direct theft of money, property, and items that have little cash value but do have high sentimental value. It also includes the misappropriation of resources. Funds can be spent on unwanted or unnecessary services. Personal property may be distributed among relatives without the consultation or the consent of the elder. Noncash assets can be converted to cash to promote simpler management. Actions also may be taken to restrict the ability of the elders to manage their assets as a means of preserving their estates. In essence, material abuse occurs when the assets of the elder are managed in a manner that is not consistent with the wishes of the elder.

As is the case with the other areas of domestic violence, elder abuse is complex, and physical abuse is only one dimension in the social matrix surrounding the elderly. Domestic violence with elders as the target does occur and is a legitimate concern for society.

Elder abuse in the context of the family has been affected by changes in our social structure and recently has emerged as a social problem. This relatively new phenomenon has developed because the number and proportion of those who survive beyond their productive years have increased greatly. In the past, only the strong and healthy survived to old age. With improvements in medical care, less healthy and less strong individuals who require a higher level of care are surviving to old age. Many of those who survive severe illnesses have disabilities and chronic illnesses that require much care (Steinmetz 1983).

The survival of parents with high-care needs creates stress for middle-aged children who are attempting to cope with their own children (Silverstone & Hyman 1976). In the past, the extended nuclear family that shared living space was relatively short lived: newlyweds moved in with parents until their could establish a home of their own, or an elder moved in with adult children for a short time as death approached. Although children still live with their parents for a short time after marriage, the number of elderly and the length of time they require care have increased greatly (Steinmetz 1983).

Steinmetz (1981) has advanced the concept of generational inversion to explain one emerging pattern. In generationally inverted families, adult children assume the responsibility for one or more elders who are dependent on them for emotional, financial, physical, and/or mental support. When faced with the need to care for two or more elders, the amount of stress experienced by caretakers increases greatly, particularly as the degree of dependency increases (Steinmetz 1983). The child who is forced to make this shift in role from care receiver to care giver may feel resentment and apprehension, which may be shared by the elder also experiencing a role shift (Hooker 1976; Knopf 1975; Silverstone & Hyman 1976). This resentment can produce guilt, hatred, and disappointment (Knopf 1975; Cohen & Gans 1978). The adjustment is complicated when the elder is unwilling to relinquish authority and persists in treating adult children as young children, giving them orders and violating their privacy (Steinmetz 1983). Abuse is more likely to occur when financial resources are not adequate to meet the elder's needs (Blenkner 1965), when physical and mental deterioration increases (Lau & Kosberg 1979; Knopf 1975), when psychological and emotional dependencies are great (Lau & Kosberg 1979), when family stress is high (Blenkner 1965; Steinmetz 1978), or when the decision to admit the elder to the home is made hastily (Burston 1975) or is perceived as forced (Douglas et al. 1980).

Prevalence of Elder Abuse

Interest in elder abuse as a topic of concern to researchers is sufficiently new that studies measuring the incidence of acts against the elderly have not been conducted on a broad scale. Much of the knowledge in this area is found in unpublished manuscripts, agency reports, and reports of congressional hearings.

Elder abuse has been described as the hidden problem (Quinn & Tomita 1986), as it is less visible than child abuse and spouse abuse. Elder abuse remains hidden for many of the same reasons that other forms of domestic abuse are ignored as social issues (private family matter, concealment by victims, difficulty in providing proof of the abuse). It appears that the embarrassment experienced by elders who are abused by their children is great and that a sense of family solidarity exists among elders, causing higher levels of denial and concealment.

It is believed that abuse occurs regularly in even the best of nursing homes and occurs frequently in private homes. A number of studies have gathered estimates from service providers and agency case records, and a few studies have gathered data from the general population and family-care providers.

Higher incidence levels are reported from studies of case records and social-service agency staff than from studies that collect data from caretakers or from community groups. Studies of health-care and social-service providers have indicated that from 13 percent to 17 percent had handled an elder abuse case and from 44 percent to 88 percent had been aware of a case (Block & Sinnott 1979). In 70 percent of reported cases of elder abuse, the acts of abuse had occurred more than once; in 75 percent of the cases, the elder lived with his or her abuser; and in 80 percent of the cases, a relative was the abuser (O'Malley et al. 1979). Up to one-fourth of elders living with their families reported abuse or neglect. In a Maryland study, Baltimore police reported 149 assaults against the elderly in one year, 62.7 percent of which were committed by a relative other than the elder's spouse (Block & Sinnott 1979). When estimating the extent of elder abuse, it should be noted that about 75 percent of the elderly are physically, financially, and psychologically independent (Hudson 1986).

A study designed to measure the nature and extent of elder abuse based on a sample of citizens found that about 4 percent of the elderly are abused and that about 80 percent of the abused are abused through neglect (Crouse et al. 1981), an estimate consistent with the estimates from Pepper and Oakar's (1981) multimodality study. Steinmetz (1983) conducted a study of incidence of abuse in situations in which an elder was dependent and collected data from caretakers. The results indicated a higher level of abuse and found that violence tended to be double directed. About 10 percent of the elderly were victims of violent acts, while about 18 percent of the caretakers were victims of violent acts from their elderly dependents.

The prevalence of various types of abuse varies from study to study, with one study reporting the neglect is the most prevalent form of abuse, followed by verbal and/or psychological abuse and physical abuse (Hickey & Douglass 1981). Another study found lack of care (38 percent), lack of supervision (38 percent), and lack of food (19 percent) to be fairly prevalent (Block & Sinnott 1979). In this study, psychological abuse was found to be more prevalent than neglect and less prevalent than physical abuse. A third study found a similar pattern, with higher rates of incidence for all forms of abuse (Wolf et al. 1982).

The growing concern over elder abuse is evidenced in the passage of new laws. In the first eight months of the implementation in 1977 of Connecticut's elderly protective-services law, 87 cases of physical abuse, 314 cases of neglect, 65 cases of exploitation, and 8 cases of abandonment had been reported by various police and service agencies. By the end of the first year, 700 cases had been reported, and by April 1979, 937 cases of elder abuse had been reported (Block & Sinnott 1979). A review of the records from the Connecticut experience indicates that abuse occurred in rural, suburban, and urban settings and in all economic groups (Walker 1983). In another study that focused on abuse reports from professionals, it was found that over 75 percent of the cases involved physical abuse and over 50 percent involved psychological abuse (Lau & Kosberg 1979). It should be noted that the above studies are limited to specific geographical areas, have used differing definitions of abuse, and have tended to rely on data from secondary sources. In the absence of data drawn from a broad-based sample of elders, any estimates of the scope of elder abuse are, to some extent, speculation.

Legal Dimensions

Various state and federal agencies have established a broad range of services that are available to meet the needs of the elderly. The agencies that dispense these services range from Social Security and Medicare, which now provide benefits to virtually all of the elderly, to the Veterans Administration and local welfare agencies, which dispense specifically defined services to specifically defined client groups. Penetrating these agencies and obtaining services needed to meet the needs of the elderly can be difficult. Most elderly people lack the training to understand the law and agency procedures and thus are dependent on agency staff to determine eligibility and benefits. There is increasing litigation in this area, but provisions for legal representation of the elderly are needed (Nathanson 1983).

There are two times in life when competency is an issue—childhood and old age. In the case of childhood, there is a presumption of diminished capacity, and although children mature at different rates, a set age is selected for the point at which the child becomes an adult and is responsible for his or her own welfare. As is the case with children, the ability to manage one's affairs in old age varies greatly, with some people retaining the ability to manage their own affairs past the age of one hundred and others suffering a loss of mental acuity at a relatively young age. In addition, illnesses take their toll, and although the elder is alert and rational, he or she may lack the physical strength or energy to manage his or her own affairs.

Adults who have lost the ability to manage their own affairs must be protected from relatives and agencies that might take advantage of their diminished capacities. The process in most states is to declare the elder incompetent and to appoint a guardian or conservator. The need for this action is determined on a case-by-case basis. Before this occurs, someone must be concerned about the plight of the elder and initiate action. In many cases, protective action is never taken, and the elder's assets are misappropriated.

Pressure is developing for legislation to protect elders who are no longer able to defend themselves or their interests. The adult protective-services movement seeks legislation to provide affirmative assistance for elders. Advocates for this movement assert that elder consent is an essential principle when the elder is capable of giving consent. Involuntary provision of services would require a court finding of mental disability or inability to give consent. In such cases, a least restrictive approach would be taken to preserve as much as possible the incompetent elder's right of self-determination.

Eleven states have established protective-services legislation with revision of the guardianship laws. There is considerable variation in the specific procedures required to establish incompetence, ranging from Maryland's elaborate system of hearings and requirements for guardians to Alabama's less rigorous statute that conveys greater power to the court and less protection of the elder's right to self-determination (Regan 1983).

Connecticut is one state that has adopted legislation in this area (Walker 1983). Connecticut has legislation providing for a statewide advocacy program using ombudsmen to visit nursing homes and to pursue complaints of elders. It also has legislation establishing reporting laws for the elderly, similar to those laws that require health-care and social-service workers to report child abuse. These bills, passed in 1977, were designed to control the nursing-home industry. The ombudsman program recruits and trains volunteers who visit nursing homes weekly. The protective-services component of the law identifies four types of abuse: (1) physical and mental abuse, (2) neglect, (3) abandonment, and (4) exploitation. The protective-services component of the legislation requires the consent of the elder before services are delivered unless the elder is found to be legally incompetent (Walker 1983).

Federal legislation in the area of domestic violence has tended to emerge following widespread public interest. The 1980s is the decade of the elder, and pressure for legislative reform can be seen in the protective-service movement. In addition, federal legislation is being enacted, with regular congressional hearings to examine the nature of the problem and to consider additional legislation. Federal legislation will provide guidelines and incentives for states to pursue reform (Oaker & Miller 1983).

Victim Characteristics

With the exception of sex, age, and dependency, there are no outstanding characteristics of the abused elder. Some factors have been found to be associated with a greater likelihood of occurrence of abuse. Very old females tend to be victims of domestic elder abuse more frequently than men or relatively younger women (Lau & Kosberg 1979; Block & Sinnott 1979; Giolio & Blakemore 1983; McLaughlin et al. 1980; Boydston & McNairn 1981; Wolf et al. 1982; Pennsylvania Department of Aging 1982; Sengstock & Liang 1982). Each of these studies describes the victim as elderly (more than seventy years of age) and female. One study examined victim profiles for different types of abuse (Gioglio & Blakemore 1983). White females with annual incomes less than $7,001 per year tended to be the victim of all types of abuse except financial exploitation. In financial exploitation cases, victims tended to be white widowers with annual incomes less than $7,001. The victims of neglect tended to be somewhat older than the other groups (seventy-two to eighty-nine versus sixty-six to eighty-three years of age).

The presence of a physical or mental impairment increases the likelihood of abuse (Block & Sinnott 1979; Boydston & McNairn 1981; Pennsylvania Department of Aging 1982; Burston 1975; Lau & Kosberg 1979; Luppens & Lau 1983; Sengstock & Liang 1982; Steuer 1983). The disabilities ranged from chronic illnesses to severe disability or psychological instability.

Offender Characteristics

What is known about offenders is just as limited as what is known about victims. Within the family context, the abuser is most likely to be a relative, frequently the child of the victim and usually the daughter (Lau & Kosberg 1979; Block & Sinnott 1979; Levenberg et al. 1983; O'Malley et al. 1979; McLaughlin et al. 1980; Sengstock & Liang 1982). In some cases, elder abuse overlaps with spouse abuse (Gioglio & Blakemore 1983).

Some studies indicate that females are more likely to be the abusers than males (Block & Sinnott 1979; Lau & Kosberg 1979). It is possible that women are more likely to be offenders because they are more likely to be responsible for the care of the elder (Steinmetz 1983) or because society has higher expectations for daughters when it comes to the care of both the very young and the very old dependents; thus, acts such as failure to provide care are considered abusive if committed by a woman, but are not necessarily considered abusive if committed by a man.

However, much research tends to question the role of women in elder abuse. Several studies have found that the abuser is more likely to be a male caretaker, with estimates ranging from about 52 percent in a study that queried agency staff (Pennsylvania Department of Aging 1982) to 72 percent in a study that interviewed elders (Gioglio & Blakemore 1983). A number of other studies identify males as the most frequent abusers without specifying rates (Boydston & McNairn 1981; Chen et al. 1981; Pepper & Oakar 1981; Wolf et al. 1982).

Stress also has been identified as related to elder abuse. A number of studies identify stress or stress-producing factors as a cause of elder abuse (O'Malley et al. 1979; McLaughlin et al. 1980; Boydston & McNairn 1981; Chen et al. 1981; Pepper & Oakar 1981). One study reported that the most frequently reported cause of elder abuse was frustration caused by the changes in life-style resulting from the needs of the dependent elder (Levenberg et al. 1983).

Summary

Elder abuse is unlike other types of domestic violence. Although this chapter focuses on elder abuse in the home, much of the abuse occurs outside of a domestic context. Elders are more vulnerable than other groups to fear of crime and fraud and are more likely to be abused by institutions and social-service agencies that provide services. There also appear to be greater levels of psychological abuse and misappropriation of assets than is the case with either child abuse or spouse abuse. Although physical abuse does occur in the home, it appears to be less prevalent than physical abuse of other family members and more likely to occur in a nonfamily context, such as the nursing home. The most common form of elder abuse appears to be neglect, with varying levels of abuse reported by different studies.

Much of what is asserted about elder abuse is essentially speculation. The broad surveys of victims and abuse incidents that have been conducted for cases involving children and spouses have not been conducted for cases involving elders. Much of the data presently available are found in unpublished manuscripts, reports of the proceedings of congressional committees, and reports from state and federal agencies. It is probable that this deficit will be corrected in the near future as social-science researchers pursue an understanding of this phenomenon.

References

Antunes, G.; Cook, F.L.; Cook, T.D.; and Skogan, W.G. 1977. Patterns of crime against the elderly: Findings from a national study. *Gerontologist* 17(2): 321–27.

Blenkner, M. 1965. Social work and family relationships in later life with some thoughts on filial maturity. In *Social structure and the family,* ed. E. Shanas and G. Streib. Englewood Cliffs, N.J.: Prentice-Hall.

Block, M.R., and Sinnott, J.D. 1979. *The battered elder syndrome: An exploratory study.* Final report to the United States Administration on Aging. The University of Maryland Center on Aging.

Bourestom, N., and Pastalon, L. 1981. The effects of relocation on the elderly. *Gerontologist* 21(1): 4–7.

Boydston, L.S., and McNairn, J.A. 1981. Elder abuse by adult caretakers: An exploratory study. In *Physical and financial abuse of the elderly,* Publication no. 97–297, U.S. Congress House Select Committee on Aging.

Braungart, M.M.; Hoyer, W.J.; and Braungart, R.G. 1979. Fear of crime and the elderly. In *Police and the elderly,* ed. W. J. Hoyer, and P.S. Monti. New York: Pergamon Press.

Burston, G.R. 1975. Granny battering. *British Medical Journal* 3: 5983–92.

Chen, P.N.; Bell, S.; Dolinsky, D.; Doyle, J.; and Dunn, M. 1981. Elderly abuse in domestic settings: A pilot study. *Journal of Gerontological Social Work* 4(1): 3–17.

Cicirelli, V.G. 1986. The helping relationship and family neglect in later life. In *Elder abuse: Conflict in the family,* ed. K.A. Pillemer and R.S. Wolf. Dover, Mass.: Auburn House.

Cohen, E.S. 1974. An overview for long-term care facilities. In *A Social-work guide for long-term care facilities,* ed. E.M. Body. Rockville, Md.: National Institute of Mental Health.

Cohen, E.S., and Gans, B.M. 1978. *The other generation gap: The middle-aged and their aging parents.* Chicago: Follett.

Cook, F.L.; Skogan, W.G.; Cook, T.D.; and Antunes, G.E. 1978. Criminalization of the elderly: The physical and economic consequences. *Gerontologist* 18(2): 338–49.

Crouse, J.S.; Cobb, D.C.; Harris, B.B.; Kopecky, F.J.; and Poertner, J. 1981. Abuse and neglect of the elderly in Illinois: Incidence and characteristics, legislation and policy recommendations. Illinois Department of Aging, Springfield. Manuscript.

Douglas, R.L., and Hickey, T. 1983. Domestic neglect and abuse of the elderly: Research findings and a systems perspective for service delivery planning. In *Abuse and maltreatment of the elderly: Causes and interventions,* ed. J.I. Kosberg. Boston: John Wright, PSG.

Douglas, R.L.; Hickey, T.; and Noel, C. 1980. *A study of maltreatment of the elderly and other vulnerable adults: Final report to the United States Administration on Aging and the Michigan Department of Social Sciences.* Ann Arbor: University of Michigan.

Finley, G.E. 1983. Fear of crime in the elderly. In *Abuse and maltreatment of the elderly: Causes and interventions,* ed. J.I. Kosberg. Boston: John Wright, PSG.

Gelles, R.J. 1987. *Family violence.* Beverly Hills, Calif.: Sage Publications.

George, L.K. 1986. Caregiver burden: Conflict between norms of reciprocity and solidarity. In *Elder abuse: Conflict in the family,* ed. K.A. Pillemer and R.S. Wolf. Dover, Mass.: Auburn House.

Gioglio, G.R., and Blakemore, P. 1983. *Elder abuse in New Jersey: The knowledge and experience of abuse among older New Jerseyans.* Trenton: New Jersey Department of Human Services.

Gresham, M.L. 1976. The infantilization of the elderly: A developing concept. *Nursing Forum* 15:195–210.

Hahn, P.H. 1976. *Crimes against the elderly: A study in victimology.* Santa Cruz, Calif.: David.

Halamandaris, V.L. 1983. Consequences of institutionalization of the aged. In *Abuse and maltreatment of the elderly: Causes and interventions,* ed. J.I. Kosberg. Boston: John Wright, PSG.

Hickey, T., and Douglass, R.L. 1981. Neglect and abuse of older family members: Professionals' perspectives and case experiences. *Gerontologist* 21(1): 171–83.

Hindelang, M. 1976. *Criminalization in eight American cities: A descriptive analysis of common theft and assault.* Cambridge, Mass.: Ballinger.

Hooker, S. 1976. *Caring for elderly people: Understanding and practical help.* London: Routledge and Kegan Paul.

Hudson, M.F. 1986. Elder mistreatment: Current research. In *Elder abuse: Conflict in the family,* ed. K.A. Pillemer and R.S. Wolf. Dover, Mass.: Auburn House.

Johnson, T. 1986. Critical issues in the definition of elder abuse. In *Elder abuse: Conflict in the family,* ed. K.A. Pillemer and R.S. Wolf. Dover, Mass.: Auburn House.

Kasl, S.V. 1972. Physical and mental-health effects of involuntary relocation and institutionalization of the elderly: A review. *American Journal of Public Health* 62(2): 377–84.

Knopf, O. 1975. *Successful aging, the facts and fallacies of growing old.* New York: Viking Press.

Kosberg, J.I., ed. 1983. *Abuse and maltreatment of the elderly: Causes and interventions.* Boston: John Wright, PSG.

Lau, E., and Kosberg, J. 1979. Abuse of the elderly by informal care providers. *Aging* 5:10–15.

Levenberg, J.; Milan, J.; Dolan, M.; and Carpenter, P. 1983. Elder abuse in West Virginia: Extent and nature of the problem. In *Elder abuse in West Virginia: A policy analysis of system response,* ed. L.G. Schultz. Morgantown: West Virginia University.

Ling, J., and Sengstock, M.C. 1983. Personal crimes against the elderly. In *Abuse and maltreatment of the elderly: Causes and interventions,* ed. J.I. Kosberg. Boston: John Wright, PSG.

Luppens, J., and Lau, E.E. 1983. The mentally and physically impaired elderly relative: Consequences for family care. In *Abuse and maltreatment of the elderly: Causes and interventions,* ed. J.I. Kosberg. Boston: John Wright, PSG.

McAdoo, J.L 1979. Well-being and fear of crime among the black elderly. In *Ethnicity and aging: Theory, research, and policy,* ed. D.E. Gelfand and A.J. Kutzik. New York: Springer.

McLaughlin, J.S.; Nickell, J.P.; and Gill, L. 1989. An epidemiological investigation of elderly abuse in southern Maine and New Hampshire. In *Elder abuse,* Publication no. 68–463, U.S. Congress, House Select Committee on Aging.

Mercer, S.O. 1983. Consequences of institutionalization of the aged. In *Abuse and* maltreatment of the elderly: Causes and interventions, ed. J.I. Kosberg, Boston: John Wright, PSG.

Mercer, S.O., and Kane, R.A. 1979. Helplessness and hopelessness among the institutionalized aged: An experiment. *Health and Social Work* 4: 91–113.

Nathanson, P. 1983. An overview of legal issues, services, and resources. In *Abuse and maltreatment of the elderly: Causes and interventions,* ed. J.I. Kosberg. Boston: John Wright, PSG.

Oakar, M.R., and Miller, C.A. 1983. Federal legislation to protect the elderly. In *Abuse and maltreatment of the elderly: Causes and interventions,* ed. J.I. Kosberg. Boston: John Wright, PSG.

O'Malley, H.; Segars, H.; Perez, R.; Mitchell, V.; and Knuepfel, G.M. 1979. *Elder abuse in Massachusetts.* Boston: Legal Research and Services for the Elderly.

Pennsylvania Department of Aging. 1982. *Elder abuse in Pennsylvania.* Harrisburg: Bureau of Advocacy.

Pepper, C.D. 1983. Frauds against the elderly. In *Abuse and maltreatment of the elderly: Causes and interventions,* ed. J.I. Kosberg. Boston: John Wright, PSG.

Pepper, C.D., and Oakar, M.R. 1981. *Elder abuse: An examination of a hidden problem,* Publication no. 97-277. U.S. Congress, House Select Committee on Aging.

Quinn, M.J., and Tomita, S.K. 1986. *Elder abuse and neglect.* New York: Springer.

Randall, O.A. 1965. Some historical developments of social-welfare aspects of aging. *Gerontologist* 5(1): 40–49.

Regan, J.J. 1983. Protective services for the elderly: Benefit or threat. In *Abuse and maltreatment of the elderly: Causes and interventions,* ed. J.I. Kosberg. Boston: John Wright, PSG.

Reinharz, S. 1986. Loving and hating one's elders: Twin themes in legend and literature. In *Elder abuse: Conflict in the family,* ed. K.A. Pillemer and R.S. Wolf. Dover, Mass.: Auburn House.

Schultz, R., and Aderman, D. 1973. Effects of residential change on the temporal distance of death of terminal cancer patients. *Omega: The Journal of Death and Dying* 4: 157–62.

———. 1974. Clinical research and the stages of death and dying. *Omega: The Journal of Death and Dying* 5: 50–57.

Sengstock, M., and Liang, J. 1982. Identifying and characterizing elder abuse. Wayne State University, Institute of Gerontology, Detroit. Manuscript.

Silverstone, B., and Hyman, H.K. 1976. *You and your aging parent.* New York: Pantheon Press.

Stathopoulos, P.A. 1983. Consumer advocacy and abuse of elders in nursing homes. In *Abuse and maltreatment of the elderly: Causes and interventions,* ed. J.I. Kosberg. Boston: John Wright, PSG.

Stearns, P.J. 1986. Old age family conflict: The perspective of the past. In *Elder abuse: Conflict in the family,* ed. K.A. Pillemer and R.S. Wolf. Dover, Mass.: Auburn House.

Steinmetz, S.K. 1978. The politics of aging, battered parents. *Society* (July/August): 54–55.

———. 1981. Elder abuse. *Aging* 7: 6–10.

———. 1983. Dependency, stress, and violence between middle-aged care givers and their elderly parents. In *Abuse and maltreatment of the elderly: Causes and interventions,* ed. J.I. Kosberg. Boston: John Wright, PSG.

Steuer, J.L 1983. Abuse of the physically disabled elder. In *Abuse and maltreat-*

ment of the elderly: Causes and interventions, ed. J.I. Kosberg. Boston: John Wright, PSG.

Steuer, J.L., and Austin, E. 1980. Family abuse of the elderly. *Journal of the American Geriatrics Society* 28(2): 372–76.

Sundeen, R.A., and Mathieu, J.T. 1976. The urban elderly: Environments of fear. In *Crime and the elderly,* ed. J. Goldsmith and S.S. Goldsmith. Lexington, Mass.: Lexington Books.

Walker, J.C. 1983. Protective services for the elderly: Connecticut's experience. In *Abuse and maltreatment of the elderly: Causes and interventions,* ed. J.I. Kosberg. Boston: John Wright, PSG.

Wolf, R.S.; Strugnell, C.P.; and Godkin, M.A. 1982. *Preliminary findings from three model projects on elderly abuse.* Worcester, Mass.: University of Massachusetts Medical Center, University Center on Aging.

Wolk, R.L., and Reingold, J. 1975. The course of life for older people. *Journal of Personality and Social Psychology* 31(2): 376–79.

4
Violence in America

S pouse abuse and child abuse have been growing steadily in importance as areas of concern for scholars, social-service personnel and criminal-justice personnel. Although these social problems have many dimensions, two areas of concern stand out above the others. Sexual abuse of children and violence in the home receive considerable attention and are the focus of most treatment and intervention programs. The prohibition of sex with young children is accepted by all except some of the offenders, yet the rightness and wrongness of domestic violence is not clear. Domestic violence frequently is characterized in terms of the use of physical force among family members. The use of physical force with children often is confused with issues of discipline and the rights and responsibilities of parents to raise their children in a manner they believe is correct. The use of force between spouses at times is perceived as a private matter that does not concern the general public.

In the justice system, the issue often is further obscured by recantation on the part of the victim, a phenomenon that is confusing to police and prosecutors alike. An Alabama prosecutor recently responded to an open offer of assistance from researchers with a request for a research project that would provide information to help him understand the reasons and dynamics underlying recantation. He wanted to move affirmatively in prosecuting domestic violence cases, but he was frustrated by victims who recanted even when he was prepared to provide them with protection from the abusers. Recantation is only one aspect of the confusion surrounding domestic violence.

The definition of women's roles and the social values that define the relationships between men and women have been changing. These changes have been a result of the contemporary feminist movement, which has identified cultural and legal precedents that have reduced a woman's freedom and made her dependent upon and under the control of the males in her environment (Brownmiller 1975). This control can take the form of physical force (Dobash & Dobash 1979). In the process of creating an atmosphere for change, proponents of women's rights sought to introduce accountability into the social-service and justice systems for dealing effectively with domestic complaints (Dobash & Dobash 1979). These agencies responded by moving to adopt policies and practices that were more sympathetic to female victims of domestic violence. These responses were reactive, based on limited knowledge, and designed to satisfy those who were demanding effective societal intervention for the abused wife.

As attention shifted to the nature and extent of spouse abuse, concern developed about a collateral issue—child abuse. Pressure for the reduction of child abuse developed, creating some of the same pressures for social-service and justice-system agencies to deal with the problem in an affirmative manner.

Domestic violence is the most important dimension of domestic abuse because of its nature. Scholars can identify neglect, psychological abuse, emotional abuse, and financial abuse. However, these types of abuse are less substantial in that they do not leave physical traces and thus tend to be more difficult to perceive on a case-by-case basis. Violence does leave physical traces, and in extreme cases, the impact of this evidence is startling and dramatic. In the extreme cases, the traces of physical abuse not only provide a basis for successful criminal action, but they tend to horrify and disgust the general public. It is then that the public rises to assist those who seek reform in the law, in the performance of the justice system, and in the development of support systems for the victims of domestic abuse.

Still, the case for the control of domestic violence is not clear and incontrovertible. Domestic violence is part of the generally high level of violence that is present in American society. In this society, violence itself appears to enjoy a relatively high level of acceptance. In some contexts violence is the right response. A man who is unwilling to defend "his" woman's honor or safety with physical force frequently is not seen as manly. Self-defense, with the degree of threat present highly variable, is a time-honored rationale for the use of physical violence, and most citizens would assert a right to defend their property with such force as might be necessary. Historically, domestic violence has fallen within the boundaries of acceptable violence if the amount of force was reasonable given the degree of provocation. The labeling of the use of force in domestic settings as improper behavior is fairly recent and may not enjoy universal acceptance.

If domestic violence is to be understood, it must be placed in the cultural context in which it occurs. Information is needed about both the extent to which the public endorses the domestic abuse, and domestic violence must be placed in the context of violence itself. Isolating domestic violence only leads to confusion and misdirection among those who seek to address this social problem from an intervention or treatment perspective.

Definitions of Violence and Aggression

Violence and aggression are linked in the most well-known theoretical approaches. In spite of this, definitions of aggression and violence often are unclear (Siann 1985). *Agression* has considerable common usage, and as is the case with many terms in social science, colloquial uses vary from the technical definitions and thus introduce confusion. In addition, questions as to intent, affective orientation, motivation, and inclusion of violence introduce additional confusion. The most common usages of *aggression* involve concepts of power, dominance, defense of territory, or the imposition of the will of one person on another.

Violence is a concept which tends to be more clearly conceptualized. Violence is the use of physical force by one person against another. Confusion is introduced by the concept of justification. That is, the use of physical force is not bad or wrong in all cases. In some circumstances, the use of physical force is acceptable or even expected.

Siann's definitions are suitable for placing aggression and violence in context. She suggests that "aggression involves the intention to hurt or emerge superior to others, does not necessarily involve physical injury and may or may not be regarded as being underpinned by different kinds of motives" (Siann 1985, 12). She goes on to define violence as involving "the use of great physical force or intensity and, while it is often impelled by aggressive motivation, may occasionally be used by individuals engaged in a mutual violence interaction which is regarded by both parties as intrinsically rewarding" (Siann 1985, 12).

Violence or the use of physical force may be an instrument of aggression, but violence can occur outside of the context of aggression, and aggression can occur without violence. In much the same way, domestic violence can be an act of aggression; however, it may be nonaggressive. In particular, it is possible in some cases that domestic violence can be understood best as a mutually beneficial or ritual exchange. If such were the case, then recantation could be viewed as a natural outcome. If violence was ritual or mutually beneficial, then police would be called to set boundaries regarding the limits of the violence or to restore a balance if the violence became excessive. In such a case, the service needed is provided either when the police arrive or when the abuser is temporarily restrained, and recantation should be the expected response of the victim.

An illustration may be useful in clarifying this situation. A young man was observed beating a young woman who stood on the steps of an apartment building. Four other people shouted at the man to stop. Police sirens could be heard. As the sirens became louder, indicating that the police were approaching the scene, the man put down the stick he had used to beat the woman and began to walk away. When the police arrived, the victim stated that she could not identify her assailant, even though he was still within sight. Later that evening in a conversation with some of the residents, the parents of the woman indicated that the man was their daughter's husband. He had been shamed because he had caught his wife in bed with another man. However, the husband and wife loved each other and did not want to part. By publicly beating his wife, the man regained his honor, and the woman was able to return to their apartment.

No assertion is made that this incident is typical or even common. However, the inability to distinguish between incidents of this nature and incidents in which the wife is an unwilling victim with limited options produces a situation in which the general public and the criminal justice system are less likely to provide effective support and assistance in situations involving domestic violence or to understand the usefulness of placing limits on violence.

Historical Perspectives on Violence

A conclusion that can be drawn quickly when one evaluates violence in the history of the United States is that there has been a great deal of it (Brown 1969). It is also obvious that the most extreme forms of violence have been justified in the name of the greater good, beginning with the Revolutionary War and the Declaration of Independence. Organized violence in the form of war generally is accepted, whether the target be Hitler in World War II or the American Indians during the Indian wars. Support for these activities is and has been used to justify other organized acts of violence committed in the name of the stabilization of the western frontier and the establishment of the rights of the laborer (Brown 1969). The use of extreme physical violence by posses, vigilantes, and unions has been both praised and condemned, depending on the times. Violence is good or bad, depending on the currently prevailing beliefs of the public.

It has been argued that the immigrant nature of American society has produced a condition in which violent resolution of differences between immigrant groups, including newcomers and established groups, can be expected and has been so common that it is accepted as normal (Graham & Gurr 1969a). The United States was settled by many different ethnic, religious, and cultural groups with conflicting fundamental values. Competition for resources conserved by the established immigrants created a condition of violence among newer groups of immigrants with different backgrounds. During a three-hundred-year process of settlement, the Indians were defeated, European presences were forced to withdraw, some Mexicans were forcibly annexed, and immigrant minorities were forced into fierce competition. The results have been a legacy of nativism, vigilantism, and ethnic aggression (Graham & Gurr 1969a).

The American frontier created a condition that fostered a legitimization of violence. It was attractive to new immigrants who saw the United States as a land of opportunity and the frontier as the place where this opportunity could be realized. Thus, the conflict between immigrant groups moved west with the new settlers. The frontier extended beyond civilization and beyond the control of established law and order. Social control was essentially informal, and individuals protected their persons and their property with their own resources. The use of force was commended when the property rights had to be protected from native Americans who expressed competing rights and extended to protecting property rights from other new Americans. When concerted community action was required, vigilante committees, courts, or posses were formed and justice was dispensed (Frantz 1969).

Vigilantism is an established American tradition that existed in the early colonies as well as in the western frontier and continuously has been held in high regard (Brown 1969). The level of physical violence authorized in this context was extreme but usually was held to be good or justifiable even when poorly supported by the facts of the situation (Brown 1969). Acts of vigilantism consistently have been characterized as justifiable in popular literature (Lynn 1969). Outlaws, marshals, and posses have been immortalized in film and in print. Stories stress the courageous, independent, self-justifying nature of the American character and provide unending examples in which violence is good if the cause is good and the actor is good. During the settlement of the frontier, the feud and its near relative, the range war, also emerged. Extreme uses of physical force were justified in these cases, although both have fallen into some disrepute today (Frantz 1969).

The emergence of the labor movement in the United States has been more violent than in other parts of the world (Taft & Ross 1969). Most of the violence has been directed toward strikebreakers or striking employees, with acts against employers tending to be characterized as acts against property. Conflicts between strikers and strikebreakers have been particularly violent. In one instance, striking miners ambushed a train that was bringing strikebreakers to open a mine closed by the strikers. Almost all of the strikebreakers were killed, with only a few of those who were fleet of foot successfully escaping (Angle 1952). This ambush is still excused as an appropriate response in the communities surrounding the site, even though it occurred so long ago that none of those involved are still alive.

The use of violence to achieve labor goals began with the emergence of the labor movement in the late 1800s and continues today. Each year, there are news reports of shots fired and occasional deaths of strikebreakers in a labor dispute. This violence is accepted as legitimate by the general public and justified as necessary and appropriate by representatives of organized labor.

Efforts to separate the organizations themselves from the violence have more to do with liability than with a belief that the acts themselves are wrong.

An acceptance of violence as appropriate behavior is rooted in ample historical precedent. While much of the material presented here reports the approved use of violence by various groups, the underlying values created support individual use of violence. If violence is right if the reasons are right, and if individual initiative and independence are valued, then individuals should be able to decide to use violence if that use is justified by the circumstances. This reasoning can be seen most clearly in the self-defense argument and other collateral defenses in our legal system. The use of force is justified in a number of circumstances, with diminished capacity and the heat of passion included in the list of rationales that mediate responsibility.

The use of force is sufficiently embedded in our culture that the question often is not should force be used, but what are the circumstances under which force can be used. Every American believes that he or she has the right to use force to deal with his or her problems. The differences between those who believe that they have the right to use force to protect their lives, those who believe that they have the right to use force to protect their property, and those who believe that they have the right to use force to gain publicity for their political beliefs is simply a matter of degree. Each of these individuals would assert that their cause is right; therefore, their use of force is right.

Domestic violence falls within this arena. There are surely those who assert that their use of force in domestic settings is right and justified. There are also those who will extend to these men and women the right to make this decision. Attempts to deal with domestic violence as a social problem are hindered by cultural values deeply rooted in the history and culture of the United States, even if the roles and expectations for women and men are changing.

Explanations for Violent Acts

The explanations for violent acts are exceptionally varied and range from those based in biological makeup theories to those based in various learning theories. The biological makeup theories link tendencies to violence with a biological dysfunction. They generally are concerned only with extreme acts of violence and at times assume that aggression and lesser violence are relatively normal. According to these theories, the list of factors that can cause a person to exhibit violent behavior includes genetics (or the so-called bad seed), including the XYY chromosome factor; dysfunctions of the limbic areas of the brain; epilepsy-related disorders; head injuries; and biochemical and endocrinal imbalances (Siann 1985).

Ethnological and sociobiological approaches tend to link violence with aggression and treat violence as an extension or consequence of aggression. Lorenz (1966) advanced the original ethnological theoretical perspective, adapted by sociobiologists, that links violence and aggression to instinctual behavior. The sociobiologists posited that an instinct for aggression (the fighting instinct) is directed against other members of the same species and results from natural selection (the survival of the fittest) and protection of one's territory. A variation of this perspective was developed by Ardrey (1966), who suggested that man exhibits violence because he has an instinct to develop ever more efficient weapons that are used to defend his territory. Ardrey's work is less rigorous than Lorenz's, though both perspectives can be seen to have influenced the work of Wilson (1975) and other sociobiologists (Siann 1985). Wilson's work attempts to apply the concepts of evolution to social behavior. Aggression and the attendant violence are instinctual responses that have been selected for their survival value as man struggled for survival in his environment. These instincts are expressed in terms of emotions, which are determined by genetic predispositions (Wilson 1975).

Aggression also has been addressed by the psychoanalytic school. This perspective also holds that aggression is an instinctual drive. Freud first asserted that aggression is related to sadism, and in his later work, aggression emerged as an element in the resistance of Thanatos, or the striving for death (Siann 1985). The mechanism works by directing self-destructive forces outward; aggression is related to both sadism (turning the destructive forces outward) and masochism (turning the destructive forces inward). Freud's work in aggression was a minor part of his overall work and had little impact until it was expanded by Storr (1968) and Fromm (1977) in their work on aggression.

Storr (1968) suggested that aggression is essential for survival and is broad, encompassing many different behaviors. Aggression includes inquisitiveness, controversy, and competition. Storr is consistent with traditional psychoanalytic theory in that he holds that the manner in which the individual handles this basic instinct is determined by early development and can be distorted to form psychopathology. Aggression can be normal or can appear in distorted or extreme forms, which are mental illnesses.

Although Fromm's (1977) work is more complex and differs in detail from Storr's, he also accepts these basic psychoanalytic principles. Fromm does have several categories of benign or positive aggression that are related to defense, unintentional harm, conformist aggression, or self-assertive aggression. Fromm's perspective identifies most aggression as normal, with pathological aggression occurring less frequently.

Siann (1985) summarized the psychoanalytic perspective regarding aggression and violence. Aggression is seen as being instinctual, as involving either hurting or dominance, as being potentially nonphysical, as having both positive and negative aspects, as being potentially normal, and as being potentially psychopathological when problems occur in development. Violence involves the use of great or intense physical force. With the exception of Fromm, psychoanalysts see violence as motivated by a drive for aggression. Violence can be used in mutually rewarding exchanges, with acts occurring in the sexual context emphasized by these theorists.

From the psychoanalytic perspective, domestic violence is relatively normal unless it becomes excessive, or when it becomes sadism and/or masochism. Excessive domestic violence is determined by the environment or by the presence of pathology in the participants. Extreme violence for one couple might be normal for another couple and pathological for another.

Modeling, a drive-based social-learning theory, is an other psychological perspective that deals with aggression theory. Bandura (1973) has focused on aggression from this perspective. His research indicates that aggression is learned by observing others perform aggressive acts. The observer (child) learns or models the behavior of the actor (adult). From this perspective, a drive exists and is channeled by the environment in which all behaviors are learned responses for drive reduction and are environment specific. As his work matured, Bandura moved from a focus on drive to a focus on learning and reinforcement.

Baron (1977) combined the work of the social-learning theorists with other psychological perspectives to introduce the concept of social determinants. He argued that aggressive behavior is a drive response mediated by such factors as frustration, emotional arousal, experience of physical pain, modeling, and pressures toward conformity. Baron stressed that aggression is learned and suggested that the treatment of aggression involves controlled exposure to violence and aggression and reinforcement of nonviolent behaviors in the child-rearing process. The environment needs to be reshaped so that children are not exposed to aggression and violence and are exposed to nonaggressive and nonviolent models. The environment also must provide positive or acceptable outlets for dissipating arousal responses.

Sociologists have been less inclined to address violence and aggression directly. Instead, violence and aggression often are addressed in terms of broader theory or from a descriptive perspective. An exception has been the work of Wolfgang and Ferracuti (1967). They asserted that violence occurs in a subculture that is supportive of violence—that is, there is a subculture in which violence is more likely to occur. Values, norms, roles, and expectations establish a condition that predisposes the members of the subculture to violence. In the lower-income subculture, commitment to subculture values commits young men in particular to regard the exchange of physical force as illustrating daring and courage and the avoidance of fighting as nonmasculine behavior leading to ostracism from the group. For these young men, most violent behavior is caused by adherence to cultural values that endorse or prescribe violence as appropriate in a particular context. From this perspective, violence is normal, not pathological.

Sutherland and Cressey (1974) and Toch (1977) accept the influence of the cultural context but place violence in a broader context. Although Sutherland and Cressey focus on the acquisition of criminal behavior, they assert that all behaviors are learned based on differential exposure to expectations and behaviors in the environment. From this perspective, aggression and violence are learned behaviors that are seen as correct, appropriate, or right in a particular context.

Toch (1977) examined individuals who tend to be very violent, rather than on violence as a general behavior. Although he agreed that the social context in which the individual is immersed is an important determinant in the development of violent behavior, he focused on attitudes toward violence and the expectations held for violent behavior by violent offenders. Toch analyzed the perceptions of violent exchanges held by both criminals and police officers with histories of the use of physical force. From the analysis of his interviews, a number of types of perceptions emerged, based on (1) the dimensions of maintaining a reputation, (2) conformity, (3) enhancement of self-esteem or self-concept, (4) self-defense, (5) conflict resolution or problem solving, (6) bullying, (7) exploitation, (8) self-satisfaction or pleasure, and (9) catharsis. According to Toch, violence can be habitual or can occur without thought or planning when environmental circumstances provide the appropriate cues. The tendency toward violence varies from man to man, with some men identified as having violence-prone orientations. Toch recommended that men who are violence prone should be exposed to treatment programs designed to change their orientations toward violence.

For most mainstream criminologists with a sociological orientation, violence is one dimension of the broader field of deviance. Research and theory tend to focus on general explanations of sets of behavior that are unacceptable to society. Criminality is linked with anomie (Merton 1957), subcultural values (Cohen 1955; Cloward & Ohlin 1960), youthful alienation (Matza 1964), social expectations (Lemert 1951; Becker 1963), or culture conflict (Miller 1976). Most of these perspectives either consider violence as a peripheral issue or product of a social condition or do not consider violence at all. Crime is regarded by most of these theorists as a natural result of the social context in which it occurs. Although there may be differences of opinion about what is right and wrong, for the actor, his or her criminal behavior (violence) is an acceptable or expected behavior.

Discussions focusing on sex differences in aggression and violence consistently stress that excessive aggression and violence tend to be primarily a male phenomenon. When theorists speak of the violent man, they are using the term in the sexual sense, not in the sense of mankind. The difference in aggression between men and women has been attributed to chemical differences occurring at puberty (Moyer 1976). This link between sexual chemistry and aggression provides some support for those who argue for castration as a treatment (Mazur 1983). However, experimental evidence generally does not support such a course of action. Sex differences in animals in terms of aggression have been used to explain this difference between males and females; however, there are exceptions in the animal kingdom, particularly in primates (Siann 1985). The psychoanalysts base their defintion of men as aggressive and women as passive in psychosexual development and differing drives and drive levels in men and women (Siann 1985). Experimental evidence regarding different levels of violence in the laboratory is also inconclusive. The areas in which there is consistent support for the differences between men and women include crime statistics (and this is changing), observational field studies, and ethnographics. It is possible that any differences between men and women in terms of aggression and violence are learned, or created during the socialization process.

Explanations for violence are varied and identify causes ranging from biological agents to social pressure. The one thing that all explanations have in common is an acceptance of the normality of violence. In other words, violence in the right amounts and in the right context is either good, acceptable, or to be expected. The rightness or wrongness of violence in each case is determined by such factors as degree, nature of the intent, social setting, expectations, the need for self-protection, and the protection of property. It is in this framework that scholars and practitioners work, and it is a framework that contributes additional confusion to an already confusing area.

Domestic Violence as Violence

Spouse abuse and child abuse are sensitive matters, and emotions tend to run high when they are discussed. In particular, examples of extreme violence or exploitation are graphic and compelling and thus gain attention. The response to this phenomenon has tended to be reactive and emotional, rather than rational and analytical.

In most cases, little attention has been paid to the dynamics of the situations. Domestic violence has tended to be classified in terms of the type or degree of violence, rather than as a function of specific types of situations involving specific types of people. Some attention has been paid to the characteristics of the victims; however, most studies have tended to stress the vulnerability and dependencies of the victims. Little attention has focused on the contemporary cultural context, the definitions in use by the public for these variables, or the relationship between ordinary violence and domestic violence.

It is possible to propose a model based on the information available from various studies and from various theoretical perspectives. Although such a model is not empirically grounded, it can provide a framework for subsequent research. The model can also serve as a preliminary classification scheme for researchers and practioners, although it is not a well articulated typology.

One fundamental assumption underlying the development of the model is that domestic violence is ordinary violence. That is, there is nothing special or different about domestic violence other than that it occurs in a domestic environment. This difference can be used to explain victim selection and the restricted options for the victim in avoiding the violence, but it does not explain the violence itself.

A second collateral assumption is that violence is a characteristic of the violent actor, who may be keyed or shaped by environmental factors. This assumption discounts theories that focus on victim precipitation as a dominant factor. If a scapegoat is present, there will be no violent response unless there is a violence-prone actor in the setting. The scapegoat may provide an attractive target but does not cause the violence. "She asked for it" in this sense is a rationale, not a cause.

With these assumptions, a number of categories can be developed to classify acts against either women or children. These categories focus on cause rather than on type of victim or form of abuse. The types of causes are physical, psychological, emotional, and cultural or learned behavior. Each of these, or a combination of one or more, can cause the violent behavior.

There is ample evidence to indicate that there are cases in which violent behavior can be attributed to organic causes. Some cases involve chemical or hormonal imbalance; others involve physical injury. It appears that these cases are rare; however, it may be that these cases often are not diagnosed. Medical tests to detect these physical abnormalities are expensive. In addition, with the general level of acceptance of violence in our society, a physical abnormality is not likely to be suspected. It is much easier to assume a personality pathology or a social cause than to look for underlying physiological causes. Although it is not likely, it is possible that the number of cases of violence that have a biological cause is substantial. Domestic violence occurs because the domestic environment provides ample opportunity for the pathology to be expressed.

There is a collateral category that is probably more common. There appears to be a biological component to the expression of emotions that may create a disposition to unanticipated types of behavior. Some people are less able to control their emotions than others. In the area of aggression and violence, temper and anger reflect these emotions. People who have lower thresholds for losing their temper will be more apt to exhibit violent behavior. This lack of control may be caused by a basic endocrinal physiological reaction or by inadequately learned control mechanisms. Domestic violence occurs when the domestic situation is such that it keys the loss of temper and the subsequent violence. These causes may be associated with alcohol, as alcohol reduces the effectiveness of learned control mechanisms. An actor under the influence of alcohol would be more likely to lose his or her temper and commit violent acts.

Violence can be an expression of a psychological or emotional pathology. A number of psychological pathologies can produce violent behavior as well as sadism. The occurrence of these pathologies appears to be limited. As is the case with physiological conditions, these conditions are difficult and expensive to diagnose, and thus may be more common than expected.

Emotional pathologies are more common and are more likely to be observed by the relatively untrained layman. If a man who has not been violent in the past and who has lost his job becomes violent, a prosecutor or untrained caseworker would be likely to note the presence of frustration and conclude that the violent behavior was caused by the frustration and loss of self-worth. In this case, the actor may be aware of the nature of the problem, which aids diagnosis. It is possible that such factors function as causes of violence at a higher rate than suspected.

In some cases, the actor believes that the use of physical force is an appropriate behavior, a belief at times shared by the victim. Many of the theories reviewed state that aggression and violence are learned. The mechanism may be socialization, differential association, modeling, or subcultural values. The end result is that the actor has learned to respond to specific social situations with violence. At times, both offender and victim believe that the behavior is appropriate, and social-service agencies or justice-system agencies become aware of the incidence of this violence from secondary sources. When child victims are involved, the use of physical force is often characterized as discipline. This contributes to the limited response possible in many child-abuse cases and can explain the court's reluctance to intervene in domestic violence involving child targets unless the violence is extreme. There appears to be no set standard for the use of force allowed a parent when discipline is involved, and discipline is a parental responsibility, with parents held accountable for the behavior of an undisciplined child.

Sexual abuse of a spouse is not included as a separate category. Sexual access can be obtained through exchange, contract, the use of guilt, love, as a gift, or through force. The use of force is the operator in this case, not sexual access. The same factors that explain violence in other situations can explain the use of violence in obtaining sexual access.

Sexual abuse of children has an additional dimension. Although sexual access to one's spouse is considered normal in this society, sexual access to children generally is universally rejected (Gebhard et al. 1967). Sexual activity with children with or without force is considered wrong. In order to fit this activity into the proposed typology, the two components of the behavior must be separated. When the act involves violence, the typology suggested can explain the use of violence. The selection of the child as a sexual target requires a different orientation. However, it is possible that the same factors are operating with the addition of one factor. A strong sexual appetite or drive may be a contributing factor. The focus of investigation is on men who seek sexual access to children, primarily girls. These men may be driven by an organic abnormality, by psychological or emotional pathologies, or by a belief that their behavior is acceptable. One defense of the pedophile is that he is providing a benefit to the child by assuring that the child's first experience with sex is a positive one involving a caring, understanding adult. Although that argument generally is not acceptable to most adults in our society, it reflects a real position for the pedophile.

Here, too, the question of frequency is relevant. The rate of incidence of sexual abuse of children is not known and is difficult to measure. Those cases that come to the attention of social-service agencies and criminal justice agencies frequently are referred by secondary sources, such as teachers, neighbors, and relatives. Investigation frequently encounters denial from all involved and recantation on the part of the victim. Such denials often confuse investigators and prosecutors who can not understand why anyone would condone or tolerate such behavior. As is the case with domestic violence, before appropriate policies and programs can be developed and implemented, much more must be known about this area.

Summary

Domestic abuse has been defined as a social problem based in part on changing social values regarding the role of women and men in society and in domestic settings. Domestic violence is the dimension of domestic abuse that is visible, provable, and in extreme cases, shocking. As a result, the proponents for value change have focused on the violence dimension. As the value system has changed, the social institutions that are responsible for dealing with pathology have had to adapt, frequently while under attack for being insensitive, ineffective, and possibly guilty of malfeasance. The resulting response has been somewhat unfocused as these agencies have moved to satisfy the critics and complete their assigned tasks. Before effective responses to domestic violence can be developed, it must be understood. A first step in increasing understanding is to recognize that domestic violence is violence and to place it in a social context.

The United States appears to have a high tolerance for violence. Violence is acceptable behavior in some social situations. A review of violence in history provides virtually unlimited examples. The American frontier experience, combined with the pressures of assimilating diverse immigrant groups, led to direct citizen action in the protection of person and property and in maintaining social order and expansion. This direct action frequently involved violence on the part of individuals acting for the so-called right reasons and on the part of vigilante groups. To this day, citizens of the United States assert their right to use physical force to protect themselves and their property.

The rise of organized labor also was characterized by violence, which was judged appropriate given the circumstances. Violence as a form of social protest has a lengthy history and recently has been advocated as a means of achieving racial equality, protesting war, making a political statement, and protesting justice-system discrimination. Throughout history, the rightness or wrongness of violence has been determined by the intention of the actor and the social context in which the acts occur.

Theoretical explanations that have addressed the commission of violent acts are as broad and varied as the social sciences themselves, with violence addressed from biological, ethnological, sociobiological, psychoanalytical, psychological, sociological, and criminological perspectives. Violent behavior can be caused by organic pathology, psychological or emotional pathology, diminished capacity, or any of a variety of learning contingencies. Common to all of these approaches is the assumption that violence and aggression are normal conditions that are pathological only when they are excessive.

Domestic violence can best be understood as a form of violence caused by different factors in different cases. These factors have been identified through various theoretical perspectives, which have advanced organic pathology, psychological or emotional pathology, and belief that the behavior is acceptable. Accepting the multidimensionality of domestic violence and of sexual abuse of children is a first step in moving toward the development of effective responses to this social problem.

There is a need for additional information about domestic violence before program development can take place. More needs to be known about the social context in which the violent acts occur. What are the public definitions of domestic abuse? What is the level of the public's tolerance for this type of violence? What factors in individual settings precipitate the use of violence? What are the interactional characteristics of these situations? What are the factors that cause some people to be more violent thatn others? When such questions are answered, resources can be allocated effectively and efficiently.

References

Angle, P.M. 1952. *Bloody Williamson: A chapter in American lawlessness.* New York: Alfred A. Knopf.

Ardrey, R. 1966. *The territorial imperative.* New York: Antheneum.

Bandura, A. 1973. *Aggression: A social learning analysis.* Englewood Cliffs, N.J.: Prentice-Hall.

Baron, R.A. 1977. *Human aggression.* New York: Plenum.

Becker, H. 1963. *Outsiders: Studies in the sociology of deviance.* New York: Free Press.

Brown, R.M. 1969. Historical patterns of violence in America. In *Violence in America: A staff report to the National Commission on the Causes and Prevention of Violence,* ed. H.D. Graham and T.R. Gurr. Washington, D.C.: Government Printing Office.

Brownmiller, S. 1975. Against our will: Men, women, and rape. New York: Simon and Schuster.

Cloward, R.A., and Ohlin, L.E. 1960. *Delinquency and opportunity.* Glencoe, Ill: Free Press.

Cohen, S. 1955. *Delinquent boys: The culture of the gang.* Glencoe, Ill.: Free Press.

Dobash, R.E., and Dobash, R. 1979. *Violence against wives: A case against the patriarchy.* New York: Free Press.

Frantz, J.B. 1969. The frontier tradition: An invitation to violence. In *Violence in America: Historical and comparative perspectives,* vol. 1, ed. D. Graham and T.R. Gurr. Washington, D.C.: Government Printing Office.

Fromm, E. 1977. *The anatomy of human destructiveness.* Harmondsworth, England: Penguin.

Gebhard, P.H.; Gagnon, J.H.; Pomeroy, W.B.; and Christenson, C.V. 1967. *Sex offenders.* New York: Bantam Books.

Graham, D.G., and Gurr, T.R. 1969a. *Violence in America: Historical and comparative perspectives,* vol. 1. Washington, D.C.: Government Printing Office.

———. 1969b. *Violence in America: Historical and comparative perspectives,* vol. 2. Washington, D.C.: Government Printing Office.

Lemert, E.M. 1951. *Social pathology.* New York: McGraw-Hill.

Lorenz, K. 1971. *On aggression.* New York: Bantam Books.

Lynn, K. 1969. Violence in American literature and folklore. In *Violence in America: Historical and comparative perspectives,* vol. 1, ed. H.G. Graham and T.R. Gurr. Washington, D.C.: Government Printing Office.

Matza, D. 1964. *Delinquency and drift.* New York: John Wiley and Sons.

Mazur, A. 1983. Hormones, aggression, and dominance in humans. In *Hormones and aggressive behavior,* ed. B.B. Svare. New York: Plenum.

Merton, R.K. 1957. *Social theory and social structure.* Glencoe, Ill.: Free Press.

Miller, W. 1976. Youth gangs in the urban crisis era. In *Delinquency, crime, and society,* ed. J.F. Short. Chicago: University of Chicago Press.

Moyer, K.E. 1976. *The psychobiology of aggression.* New York: Harper and Row.

Mulvihill, D.J., and Curtis, L.A. 1969. *Crimes of violence: A staff report submitted to the National Commission on the Causes and Prevention of Violence,* vols. 11, 12, 13. Washington, D.C.: Government Printing Office.

Siann, G. 1985. *Accounting for aggression and violence.* London: Allen and Unwin.

Storr, A. 1968. *Human aggression.* Harmondsworth, England: Penguin.

Sutherland, E.H., and Cressey, D.R. 1974. *Criminology.* 9th ed. Philadelphia: Lippincott.

Taft, P., and Ross, P. 1969. American labor violence: Its causes, character, and outcome. In *Violence in America: Historical and comparative perspectives,* vol. 1, ed. H.G. Graham and T.R. Gurr. Washington, D.C.: Government Printing Office.

Toch, H. 1977. *Police, prisons, and the problem of violence.* Rockville, Md.: National Institute of Mental Health.

Wilson, E.O. 1975. *Sociobiology: The new synthesis.* Cambridge: Belknap Press of Harvard University.

Wolfgang, M., and Ferracutti, F. 1967. *The subculture of violence.* London: Travistock.

5
Research Design

D omestic abuse has gained increasing stature as an appropriate focus for social-science research. While a number of the more recent studies have made respectable inroads in expanding the knowledge base in this area, much of the existing research has been bound by a number of conceptual constraints. The most important of these have to do with the tendency to establish boundaries around specific subsets of domestic abuse.

Domestic abuse generally is identified in terms of violence. Studies designed to examine the prevalence and characteristics of domestic abuse tend to measure acts of violence and to consider additional factors as collateral to or as a cause of the violence. This narrow focus restricts the ability of researchers to consider the complete dynamics of the abusive situation; thus, potential developmental phases are not discovered and abusive situations that do not include physical force as a factor are not examined.

Much of the research has been victim oriented and has, to some extent, focused on the physically abused woman and the physically or sexually abused child. Numerous designs have been used to gather data from victims; these have included extensive use of case histories, document research based on agency records, and surveys of victims using questionnaires or interviews. Although these studies have greatly expanded our knowledge of the nature and extent of victimization, this knowledge may have come at the expense of understanding the dynamics of the abusive situation. At present, the general consensus appears to be that abuse is an interactive condition. The consistent examination of any interactive process from a single perspective is certain to lead to distorted and inaccurate explanatory models. This distortion is intensified when the perspective is further limited by data gathering only from victims whose victimization was sufficiently severe that they sought assistance from social-service agencies.

It is possible that domestic abuse is a behavior that ranges from the relatively normal, nonharmful, aggressive interaction that can occur in any dyad when participants press for individual advantage to a situation in which one participant dominates the other participant through psychologically or physically damaging techniques. The narrow focus created through the use of restrictive parameters prevents an assessment of the full range of these dynamics and of the context in which the interaction occurs.

Recent research has begun to erode the tendency to use restrictive parameters in studies of domestic abuse by measuring the incidence of observed domestic violence in nonvictim populations. It is time to move away from the advocacy mission of research in domestic abuse. Although a focus on domestic abuse occurring outside of the family may be warranted because of the overlap among family, social-service agencies, and the justice system, that focus should begin with attempts to identify the real parameters of domestic abuse, including an assessment of the context in which the interaction occurs. The series of studies presented in this chapter were designed to investigate one dimension of this context.

Reforms are under way in the justice system as a result of the activities of groups that advocate increasing the resources available to battered women and children. Pressure for legal reform creates a difficult enforcement situation when the reform specifies behaviors that are unacceptable to or opposed by the general public such as criminalization of some forms of discipline. Although it is probable that the activities of the pressure groups have created a condition in which the public supports an assertive, proactive, justice system response in cases of domestic violence, it is appropriate to measure the general public's perspective. The series of surveys that provide the basis for this and the following chapters were designed to measure the public's perspective regarding the placement of various forms of domestic abuse in the broader context of violence, the extent to which specific types of behavior that can be characterized as abuse are perceived as abuse, and the extent to which domestic abuse is perceived as requiring a criminal justice intervention.

It is suggested that the ordinary citizen sees domestic violence as violence. If this is true, and this violence is perceived as wrong, then the extent to which the public endorses criminalization should be evaluated. This line of research also seeks to identify the range of behaviors which the ordinary citizen includes in his or her definitions of abuse. This information will both increase our knowledge of domestic abuse and provide a basis for further research.

Design Characteristics

Data were collected via four self-administered questionnaires that were delivered and retrieved from randomly selected households within the city limits of Tuscaloosa, Alabama, a city with major educational and mental-health institutions and with a light industrial economic base. The four separate surveys shared a common sampling frame, common variables, and common data collection techniques.

The first survey, administered in 1986, focused on domestic violence within the broader context of social violence. The second, third, and fourth surveys, administered in 1987 and 1988, addressed the perceived dimensions of domestic abuse and the perceived need for criminalization of specific types of domestic abuse. These types, determined by victim profiles presently in use, were spouse abuse, child abuse, and elder abuse. Each survey focused on one victim type in an attempt to avoid generalization by the subjects to a common victim group.

Setting

Tuscaloosa, Alabama, is a town of approximately 80,000 people (approximately 100,000 if the contiguous bedroom communities that lie outside the city limits are included) located in Tuscaloosa County (population approximately 140,000) in west-central Alabama. Tuscaloosa has a varied economy, with educational, commercial, mental-health, and industrial presences in the community.

The educational aspect of the economy consists of one university, one college, one community college, and one technical college. The University of Alabama is one of the oldest universities in the United States. It offers a full range of academic programs to approximately 16,000 students. Stillman College, a junior college, is also an old, well-established educational institution. It is one of a number of colleges that served black students before integration. Shelton Community College presently serves local residents from two campuses; one houses the academic division and the other the technical division. Fred State Technical College offers students vocational training.

The mental-health presence in Tuscaloosa is composed of three mental-health hospitals and a Veterans Administration hospital with a psychiatric ward. The Taylor Hardin Secure Medical Facility provides treatment services to the criminally insane and to difficult-to-manage patients and provides diagnostic and evaluation services regarding mental competence and sanity to the courts of Alabama. Bryce Hospital provides treatment to the mentally insane in an institutional environment. Partlow State School provides treatment and services for the mentally retarded in an institutional setting. The Veterans Administration Hospital offers a full range of basic medical services to local veterans and maintains a substantial treatment service for veterans with psychiatric disorders. In addition, the major medical center for the area is located in the city.

Tuscaloosa is the major shopping area for residents of west-central Alabama. Commercial interests include two moderate shopping malls, more than ten shopping centers, a downtown shopping center, and a well-developed shopping area skirting the city. Tuscaloosa is the fourth largest shopping center in the state.

The light industrial component is composed of a variety of manufacturing and processing industries, including frozen-food processing, steel-pipe manufacturing, electronics manufacturing, wire manufacturing, auto-carburetor assembly, roofing-materials manufacturing, and auto-tire manufacturing. Over fifty industries that provide goods for sale outside of the Tuscaloosa area are listed by the area's chamber of commerce. They range from businesses with less than 20 employees to two with over 2,000 employees, with the largest (Jim Walter Industries) employing over 3,500 people.

Because of the educational and mental-health presence, Tuscaloosa has a greater proportion of highly educated professionals than many towns of comparable size. However, the size of the town and the presence of an industrial base create a condition in which the university and the mental-health facilities do not dominate the community. In addition, many of these highly educated professionals live in the contiguous bedroom communities, rather than within the city limits.

Variables

Although the variables remain fairly constant across the four surveys, there are some differences in the scales used to measure some of the variables. *Violence,* one variable common to all four surveys, has some variation in operationalization. For this study, *violence* is defined as the intentional aggressive use of physical force between two people. There is a great deal of variance in the definition of violence from one study to another, particularly at the operational level. For this study, physical contact must actually occur for the action to be included within the definition of violence. Striking at or throwing at or near someone is not violence unless physical contact occurs. Actual physical damage is not required. A soft or deflected blow is considered violence. Although it is legitimate in many contexts to define degree of violence based on extent of damage, the purpose here is to examine violence as an interactive pattern, rather than in terms of the amount of resulting physical damage.

Although *violence* is a key variable for this study, it is not a measured variable. All four questionnaires include measures of the perception of the rightness or wrongness of the use of physical force in a number of environmental contexts and toward a number of specific targets.

The focus of the first survey was the measurement of the public's perception of the use of physical force. There were two measures of this perception. The first asked the subjects to assign a degree of wrongness to a set of behaviors in which varying levels of force were directed toward different targets. The targets were chosen to reflect differing degrees of social distance. The second asked the subjects to indicate the likelihood that they would call police if they observed varying uses of force. The behaviors in the list were identical to the behaviors in the first list. These lists measured the interplay between four variables: (1) *perception of the wrongness of the use of physical force,* (2) *willingness to report use of physical force to police,* (3) *degree of force,* and (4) *social distance.* A fifth variable, *social context,* was also incorporated into the measures in that the use of force was defined in specific terms, such as when fighting and during the commission of a crime.

For the remaining three questionnaires, violence was one dimension of abuse. Subjects were presented with a number of acts (some of which included the use of physical force) and were asked to rate these acts in terms of the extent to which each act constituted abuse.

Prior to the collection of data, no attempt was made to establish a definition of domestic abuse other than the acceptance of the concept that abuse consists of acts that one person directs toward another person that cause harm. Intent is not a component of this concept, and no parameters were established for types of behaviors or for types of outcomes. One purpose of this line of research is the identification of parameters that contribute to the public definition of abuse. In short, the definitions in use should emerge from the data.

The measurement of the parameters of abuse was accomplished by asking the subjects to label specific behaviors in terms of the extent to which those behaviors were characteristic of the type of abuse examined by that particular survey. As much as possible, the lists of behaviors were similar. Because the types of abuse were determined by type of victim, each of the lists included behaviors specific to that particular type of victim. The behaviors were selected to be representative of the abusive behaviors discussed in the earlier chapters of this book.

Criminalization, another primary variable for this study, is defined as the identification of an act as sufficiently harmful and sufficiently uncontrolled by techniques of informal social control to require control through the use of the justice system. Criminalization includes the passage of new legislation providing criminal sanctions for the target behaviors and the subsequent enforcement of the resulting laws by the justice system. In theory, criminalization also can include the innovative application of existing statutes to control a behavior that has not been included previously as a controlled behavior.

Endorsement of criminalization was measured indirectly in the first questionnaire, which asked the subjects to indicate for which acts of physical force they would call police. *Criminalization* was measured directly in the following three questionnaires, which were designed to measure subject definitions of abuse. A set of items measured (1) *endorsement of specific penalties for abuse,* (2) *perception of the effectiveness of criminalization,* (3) *support for specific legislation,* and (4) *preferred approach to the disposition of abusers.*

In addition to the primary variables, a number of standard demographic variables were measured. These variables include *sex, race, age, education, occupation, marital status, religious activity,* and *political activity.* The last two variables were examined through scales that measured affiliation and perceived level of activity.

Survey Instruments

Four survey instruments were used to collect the data for this study. The first survey (concerning perceptions of violence) consisted of a cover letter and five pages of questions. The second through fourth questionnaires (concerning definitions and criminalization of abuse) each consisted of a cover letter and three pages of questions. The four cover letters were essentially identical, with the one sentence that identified the focus of the study changed. The cover letters were printed on University of Alabama's Department of Criminal Justice letterheads and identified the project as university sponsored. Protection of human-subject provisions was included, as were the home and office telephone numbers of the primary researcher.

The first pages of all four questionnaires were also identical, with the exception of the title, which varied to reflect the focus of the particular phase of the study. The first page measured the secondary demographic variables with a set of twelve items.

The first questionnaire was designed to measure community attitudes toward the use of physical contact. Subjects were asked to rate twenty-eight behaviors according to the extent to which they were "wrong." The subjects then were asked to rate the same items based on the extent to which the subjects were willing to call police if they saw the act occurring. The items varied by degree of force, social distance, and context. The domestic-violence items were included in this part of the study to permit comparisons between these acts and other acts that can be characterized as violence.

The second questionnaire was designed to measure community attitudes toward child abuse. Fifteen items designed to measure the parameters of the subjects' definitions of child abuse were presented following the demographic measures. The items represented the range of acts that can be characterized as child abuse. They were followed by two items designed to identify conditional parameters operating when the subjects stated that an act was sometimes abusive. The next set of items measured the subjects' willingness to criminalize what they perceived to be child abuse; the questionnaire concluded with two open-ended items that permitted the subjects to express their preferences for a method for dealing with child abuse or to volunteer any information about child abuse.

The third and fourth questionnaires were designed to measure community attitudes toward spouse abuse and toward elder abuse. The formats of these two questionnaires were the same as the format of the child-abuse question-naire. Nineteen items measured definitions of elder abuse, and fifteen items measured spouse abuse. All other items were identical to the items in the questionnaire concerning perceptions of child abuse.

Population

The population for the four surveys was the adult resident population of the city of Tuscaloosa. The geographical boundaries of the city constituted the physical boundaries for the study. Several areas within these boundaries were excluded to eliminate nonresident adults. The campuses of Stillman College and the University of Alabama and the student housing area adjacent to the university campus were excluded to eliminate nonresident students from the population. The reservations of the mental-health facilities and the Veterans Administration Hospital were excluded to eliminate nonresident patients from the population. This process may have excluded a small number of Tuscaloosa residents, thus introducing a small bias. This is outweighed by the bias that would result if the student and patient populations were included.

Sample

Four separate stratified random samples were drawn from the population. The questionnaires for the spouse abuse and child abuse phases were administered at the same time to different samples. At the beginning of each data-gathering session, a city map was obtained from the city engineer's office. The grids formed by the latitude and longitude lines on the maps constituted the first strata, and city blocks constituted the second strata. The number of city blocks in each section was counted, and a number of units were assigned to each section based on its portion of the total blocks in the city. Most sections were equivalent, producing a situation in which all of the main sections were assigned the same number of units, with four peripheral sections assigned a reduced number of units.

In all, 150 blocks were selected for each session. The blocks were selected from each grid by using a table of random numbers to select three-digit numbers and by counting blocks from the upper right-hand corner from left to right and down for each grid until the block number was reached. The block was marked in ink on the map, and the next block was selected. This process continued until 150 blocks had been identified and marked. One house was selected from each block using a list of two-digit random numbers drawn from a table of random numbers by the researcher. If an apartment building was selected, the list of random numbers was used to select an apartment. The next-birthday method was used to select one adult from each household. *Adult* was defined as a permanent Tuscaloosa resident over eighteen years of age.

Data Collection

The questionnaires were administered in three separate data-gathering sessions. The questionnaires concerning public perceptions of physical contact were administered during the first session, the questionnaires concerning perceptions of spouse abuse and child abuse were administered during the second session, and the questionnaires concerning perceptions of elder abuse were administered during the third data-gathering sessions.

The questionnaires were placed in campus mail envelopes (reusable 9-inch by 12-inch manila envelopes) for delivery. All of the campus mail envelopes had been used several times and listed the researcher as the last recipient. These envelopes were delivered and retrieved by research assistants working in teams. Each team consisted of one driver and one contact person. In the first two sessions, the contact persons were all black females. In the third session, the contact person was a white female. All contact persons dressed in clothing selected to project a neutral image.

Each data-gathering session extended over a four-month period. The team would leave the office with a map, a set of questionnaires, and a list of random numbers. They would proceed to a section of town and locate a block. Using the list of random numbers, they would select a house. In the third session, two houses were randomly chosen from each block. The first house chosen received a spouse-abuse questionnaire, and the second house chosen received a child-abuse questionnaire. When a block was completed, the team would move to the next closest block marked for inclusion in the study.

The contact person would approach the house and make contact. She would introduce herself and ask for the adult who would be the next adult to have a birthday. When that person came to the door, the contact person would describe the research and ask for participation. If the subject was not at home, the contact person would leave the questionnaire with the person who answered the door with instructions to give the questionnaire to the subject with an explanation and request for assistance.

The contact person would make arrangements to return to retrieve the questionnaire two days later. If no one was home on the return trip, the team would make up to three additional trips in an attempt to retrieve the questionnaire.

If no one answered the door at the first house selected, the next house on the block was selected. If the door was not answered at the second house, the researchers returned to the original selection at a later date. If the selected subject refused to accept the questionnaire, the next house was selected. If a block had no homes, the next block was selected.

This approach was relatively successful. There were only five refusals to accept a questionnaire, and about 80 percent of the surveys were retrieved in completed usable form from each sample. From the 150 questionnaires concerning community attitudes toward the use of physical force, 121 were returned; 120 of the 150 child-abuse questionnaires were returned; 111 of the 150 spouse-abuse questionnaires were returned; and 117 of the 150 elder-abuse questionnaires were returned. The final sample was 469 returned of 600 distributed questionnaires, for an overall return rate of about 78 percent. Two questionnaires were returned through the campus mail. One of these was a spouse-abuse questionnaire, the other a child-abuse questionnaire. Two telephone complaints were received, both regarding the spouse-abuse questionnaire. In both cases, the subjects agreed after a short discussion to complete the questionnaires.

Data Analysis

The data were recorded on optical scanning sheets for transfer to a computer file for analysis using selected routines from version 10 of the *Statistical Package for the Social Sciences* (SPSSX), 3d edition. The open-ended items on the abuse questionnaires were precoded. Each response was read and reduced to simple statements that constituted points on a scale. Similar statements were combined to form a single scale point. The relevant questionnaire items were read a second time and assigned a scale value, which was recorded on the optical scanning sheets.

Because this was a descriptive, exploratory survey, the primary statistical procedure for reporting the findings was percentages. When comparisons were made between variables, chi square, simple analysis of variance, and the *t*-test were applied to the data when appropriate. The results were sufficiently clear and straightforward that a more sophisticated statistical analysis was not warranted, as it would not have produced an increase in the level of knowledge and would have served primarily to make the findings less comprehensible to the average reader.

A comparison of totals from the 1980s census adjusted for the removal of students and for nine years of population change, with the characteristics of the combined sample found that the sample approximated the population for all variables except sex. There were more women in the sample than in the population. Although women are slightly overrepresented in the population, they are highly overrepresented in the sample.

Table 5–1
Selected Demographic Characteristics of Samples

Characteristic	Physical Contact (N = 121)	Spouse Abuse (N = 111)	Child Abuse (N = 120)	Elder Abuse (N = 117)	All Subjects (N = 469)
Mean age *	47.1	36.9	36.4	45.2	40.9
Sex					
Male (*percent*)	42.1	34.5	28.3	35.0	35.5
Female (*percent*)	57.9	65.5	70.8	65.0	64.5
Race *					
Black (*percent*)	23.5	34.2	28.3	17.9	31.2
White (*percent*)	74.8	64.9	70.8	81.2	67.7
Other (*percent*)	1.7	.9	.8	.9	1.1
Marital status					
Never married (*percent*)	15.0	33.3	31.1	13.7	23.3
No longer married (*percent*)	31.7	13.9	13.4	21.4	20.1
Married (*percent*)	52.3	52.8	55.5	65.0	56.4
Approximate mean family income (*thousands of dollars*) *	28.1	30.0	29.8	34.3	30.6

* Significance for chi square or *F* less than .001 for comparisons between groups.

The total sample approximated the population, yet there were some differences among the four samples (see table 5–1). The subjects in the physical-contact sample and the elder-abuse sample tended to be older than those in the spouse-abuse and child-abuse samples, while the child-abuse and spouse-abuse samples tended to have higher percentages of blacks than the two other samples. The elder-abuse sample appeared to be somewhat more affluent than the other three samples. In addition to the variables in table 5–1, a significant difference was found for education, which was measured on an ordinal scale with degrees as points on the scale (*p* for chi square = .0009). A greater number of subjects in the spouse-abuse and the child-abuse samples had baccalaureate degrees than subjects in the other two samples.

The subjects in the sample had a mean age of about forty-one years and a mean income of about $27,000. About 35 percent were male, and 31 percent were black. Over two-thirds of the sample had attended college, about 22 percent had earned a baccalaureate degree, and about 7 percent had advanced degrees.

The differences among the four samples were relatively small. An examination by sample for significant relationships between the demographic variables and the measures of abuse and criminalization did not produce evidence of a consistent pattern of difference. Such differences as were observed are discussed in the next chapter.

The responses for the various types of force and the various behaviors characterized as abuse were examined as individual scales and as combined scales. For the physical-contact variables, a number of subscales were constructed to permit evaluation of the impact of the secondary variables: social distance, type of force, and type of offense. For the three definition-of-abuse questionnaires, a single subscale was created by counting any endorsement of the acts as abuse responses. These variables were compared with the demographic and criminalization measures.

Summary

A study was designed and implemented to examine public perceptions of domestic violence and domestic abuse. The study had four components. The first focused on the placement of domestic violence within the context of violence in general. Both the wrongness of specific acts and the willingness to report observed acts to police were measured. The second through fourth components focused on the types of acts that subjects were willing to identify as domestic violence and the extent to which subjects were willing to endorse the criminalization of domestic abuse. Each of the three components focused on separate targets of domestic abuse (children, elders, and spouses).

The data were collected from a random stratified sample of adult residents of Tuscaloosa, Alabama. Over a three-year period, a self-administered questionnaire was distributed to a selected adult in selected homes and was retrieved later by research assistants. The 78 percent complete questionnaire return rate produced a sample of 469 usable surveys. The sample approximated the population with the exception of sex. More women than men returned completed questionnaires. There were some variations among the four components for the demographic variables, but these tended to be relatively small. No persistent pattern was found in a comparison of the demographic variables with the primary study variables. The analysis of data is fairly basic and straightforward, with percentages as the primary statistic and chi square, *t*-test, and analysis of variance used for selected comparisons.

6
Community Beliefs

The purpose of the series of studies discussed in this chapter was to examine public perspectives regarding domestic violence. The data were analyzed in terms of perceived denotative definitions of types of abuse, the identification of selected acts involving the use of physical force as wrong, the willingness of citizens to call police when they observed acts involving the use of force, and perspectives on the criminalization of domestic abuse.

Definitions of Child Abuse

As discussed in previous chapters, child abuse tends to be defined in terms of the use of excessive physical force and in terms of involving children in explicit sexual acts. Concern for children's rights has been present for more than two centuries, but firm community support for children's rights has developed only in recent years (Farson 1979). The child-saver movement first produced the juvenile and family courts before resulting in legislation giving children basic rights (Platt 1969).

More recently, the area of sexual abuse has expanded to include all cases in which children are used to satisfy adult sexual desires, including child pornography (Furness 1984). This dimension of the mistreatment of children tends to be salient because of its strong emotional content and because of the severity of the damage that can occur to child victims. The unacceptability of sexual abuse of children has been recognized in law for some time and rarely is defined as acceptable behavior. In order to avoid the anticipated dominance of the unacceptability of child sexual abuse as a factor in the measurements of criminalization, acts of sexual abuse were deleted from the range of behaviors assessed in the study.

The definition of the mistreatment of children can include passive acts, such as neglect, and other behaviors that cause no physical damage but inflict psychological or emotional damage. Neglect and psychological damage are more difficult than physical damage to understand, more difficult to prove, and more difficult to explain to well-educated laymen as well as to skilled professionals. These nonphysical, low-emotional-value forms of mistreatment are more difficult to portray as serious forms of misbehavior.

To some extent, conflicting values come into play in all forms of child abuse. Particularly in areas of neglect and the less extreme acts that reduce a child's self-respect and mental health, values or differences about the acceptability of some behaviors can be a key ingredient. In addition, values regarding discipline, including parental responsibility for their children's behavior, place barriers between the treatment of children by their parents and community intervention or even condemnation (Adams et al. 1971). In fact, it may be that parents who do not discipline their children are as likely to be the focus of community condemnation as are parents whose discipline includes a greater use of force than is used by most parents. Because of these elements in the context in which child abuse occurs, conventional wisdom suggests that only the more extreme forms of child mistreatment are sufficiently "wrong" to be classified as child abuse. Thus, the first set of scales following the demographic measures on the survey instrument attempted to evaluate the extent to which a specific range of behaviors was included by the subjects in the denotative definitions of child abuse.

The patterns of endorsement of specific acts as constituting child abuse are presented in table 6-1. One striking finding is the very low level of absolute exclusion of items from the definition of abuse. The items were selected to range from very mild acts to very severe acts. None of the acts were excluded by more than about 14 percent of the subjects.

There appear to be higher levels of support for the inclusion of neglect and psychological abuse in the definition of child abuse than conventional wisdom predicts. Relatively mild acts that could be expected to cause emotional or psychological abuse were endorsed at relatively high levels, as were relatively minor acts of negligence. In fact, mild levels of use of physical force were endorsed at lower levels than the abuse and neglect items.

The use of force was strongly endorsed as child abuse. Although there is a great deal of variation among items, the severe use of force consistently was endorsed as abuse by more than 90 percent of the subjects. The *always* endorsement is reduced as the frequency and severity of the use of force declines, but the *never* category was endorsed only by a small number of the subjects. This pattern can be better understood through evaluation of the conditional statements.

There were two measures of rationale for conditional endorsement of the selected behaviors as abuse. One measured the reasons for including the act in the abuse category; the other measured the reasons for excluding the act from the abuse category. Factors identified as influencing the decision to label the act as abusive include *duration and severity* (20.5 percent), *type of force*

Table 6–1
Endorsement of Selected Behaviors as Child Abuse
(percentage)

Behavior	Never Child Abuse	Sometimes Child Abuse	Always Child Abuse
Criticizing child in front of others	12.6	64.7	22.7
Telling child that he/she is worthless	10.0	15.0	74.2
Cursing child	11.8	25.2	63.0
Not loving child	9.4	8.5	82.1
Not allowing child out of the house	10.9	43.7	45.4
Trying to lock up child	6.7	.8	91.7
Not feeding child enough	6.8	15.3	78.0
Not giving child adequate clothing	10.1	26.1	63.9
Hitting occasionally with open hand	14.4	67.8	17.8
Hitting frequently with open hand	7.6	20.2	72.3
Hitting occasionally with fist	5.9	3.4	90.8
Hitting frequently with fist	5.9	0.0	93.3
Hitting occasionally with belt or stick	11.0	45.8	43.2
Hitting frequently with belt or stick	8.4	13.4	78.2
Putting child in extremely hot water	8.4	.8	90.8

used (14.1 percent), *frequency of the use of force* (11.5 percent), *characteristics of the situation* (9.0 percent), and *presence of anger* (7.7 percent). Reasons identified for excluding the act from classification as abuse are *identification of the act as discipline* (35.8 percent), *moderation in use* (16.4 percent), *frequency of use* (10.4 percent), and *ability of the child to understand the purpose of the act as discipline* (11.9 percent).

Discipline and severity appear to be related to the acceptability of both acts of physical force and acts that could cause psychological damage. All four of the acts with uncertainty endorsements by over 40 percent of the subjects are acts that could be characterized as common forms of discipline. The most frequent criteria provided by subjects for determining the extent to which acts are abusive tend to be related to either the disciplinary nature of the act or to the excessiveness of the behavior. In other words, as the behavior was identified as discipline and was used to "reasonable degrees," it was less likely to be labeled as abuse.

Each of the selected behaviors was compared with the demographic variables. Although there are occasional instances of significance, the levels of association are low, and no patterns have emerged. In order to facilitate the comparison of the abuse variables with other variables, one variable was constructed by researchers summing the responses to the individual items, with a value of 1 assigned to *never,* a value of 2 assigned to *sometimes,* and a value of 3 assigned to *always.* The constructed variable, *level of abuse,* was thus measured on a high-level ordinal scale. For some comparisons, this variable was treated as an interval variable to facilitate clear presentation of the results. Such comparisons were treated carefully to compensate for the distortion caused by entering high-level ordinal measures in equations that require interval-level data. When *level of abuse* was compared with the demographic variables, no significant relationships were found.

On the whole, demographic characteristics are not related to definitions of abuse. The definition of child abuse is fairly consistent across the sample. Differences among economic levels, which are suggested in some literature, do not appear. In essence, all economic, political, racial, religious, and sexual strata endorsed the items as child abuse in much the same way.

Definitions of Spouse Abuse

Spouse abuse was the first area in which domestic abuse was labeled as unacceptable behavior (Dobash & Dobash 1979). It is also one of the most controversial, with some people suggesting that behavior between two consenting adults is private and of no interest to society (Parker 1985). In studies of spouse abuse, the focus has been on wife beating; that is, spouse abuse usually is perceived by researchers and experts in the field in terms of husbands using physical force toward wife victims (Steinmetz 1977). Neglect and psychological and emotional abuse tend to be ignored or treated as collateral to the use of physical force. Sexual abuse as wife abuse is a contemporary issue that does not appear to be perceived by the public as a behavior that should be criminalized when characterized as rape (Sigler & Haygood 1988). In order to maintain consistency, sexual abuse was deleted from the spouse-abuse questionnaire as it was from the child-abuse questionnaire.

The women's-shelter movement has emerged as a dynamic force for providing services for abused wives and for providing pressure for criminalization of wife abuse (Martin 1976). The movement to criminalize wife abuse, specifically wife beating, has met with considerable success, as is reflected in the passage of family-protection legislation (Paterson 1979). The question raised in this study addresses the extent to which the general public shares the focus on the use of physical force as spouse abuse and the extent to which there is support for criminalization of spouse abuse. As was the case with child abuse, the first set of items following the demographic variables were designed to measure the rate of endorsement of selected behaviors that could be characterized as abuse.

The patterns of responses to selected items chosen to measure the denotative definition of spouse abuse are listed in table 6–2. Because spouse abuse presently is somewhat consistently defined in terms of wife abuse, the items reference women as the targets. The subjects consistently rejected the use of

Table 6–2
Endorsement of Selected Behaviors as Spouse Abuse
(percentage)

Behavior	Never Spouse Abuse	Sometimes Spouse Abuse	Always Spouse Abuse
Criticizing wife in front of others	14.3	56.2	29.5
Telling her that she is worthless	14.3	16.2	69.5
Cursing her	11.4	36.2	52.4
Never staying at home	17.9	37.7	44.3
Making all of her decisions for her	17.0	34.0	49.1
Never allowing her to have money	16.2	21.0	62.9
Not allowing her to have food	12.3	4.7	83.0
Not talking with her	17.9	38.7	43.4
Hitting occasionally with open hand	11.3	8.5	80.2
Hitting frequently with open hand	11.3	1.9	86.8
Hitting occasionally with fist	10.4	2.8	86.8
Hitting frequently with fist	10.4	2.8	86.8
Hitting occasionally with belt or stick	11.3	2.8	85.8
Hitting frequently with belt or stick	11.3	.9	87.7
Not allowing her to leave the house	8.7	8.7	82.6

physical force as appropriate. All the items that measured use of force were endorsed as always constituting spouse abuse by over eighty percent of the subjects. Although these rates of endorsement were lower than for child abuse, the results were more consistent. In other words, all types of force were rejected. The results were mixed for items measuring neglect and psychological abuse, yet there was some support for including these acts in the definitions of abuse. The *never* categories were selected by less than 18 percent in all cases, and the *always* categories for some items were endorsed by most of the subjects.

Approximately half of the subjects responded to the open-ended items designed to measure the conditions that influence uncertainty in defining an act as abusive. Those who did respond tended to focus on the item that received the highest level of *sometimes* endorsement: criticism. Factors that influenced the decision to label the act as abuse include *severity* (18.6 percent), *type of criticism* (13.6 percent), *intent to do harm* (13.6 percent), *if done frequently* (13.6 percent), *if done in anger* (10.2 percent), and *if done in front of others* (10.2 percent). Reasons for not labeling an act as abuse include the *nature of the situation* (14.5 percent), *if done in fun* (12.7 percent), and fourteen other factors endorsed by from one to five subjects.

A comparison of the demographic variables with the items selected to measure the subjects' endorsement of abuse shows no significant relationships. In order to facilitate comparison of the level of endorsement of abuse with other central variables, a new variable, *level of abuse,* was constructed using the same techniques as those used to construct the *level of abuse* variable for child abuse. A comparison of this variable with the demographic variables shows a significant relationship with age (Spearman's rho = .1754, *p* = .044). The endorsement of the use of physical force as abuse and the inclusion of neglect and psychological abuse within the parameters of spouse abuse tend to be consistent across the population and not particular to any one segment. Thus, concepts of class differences are not supported by these data.

Definitions of Elder Abuse

Elder abuse is the newest of the emerging areas of domestic abuse. As is the case with other forms of domestic abuse, the use of physical force is just one dimension of elder abuse. Although use of force tends to dominate research and policy interest, a great deal of attention has been directed toward other forms of elder abuse, particularly neglect. A number of changes, including longer life spans, improved medical care with related survival to invalid or semi-invalid status, and increased dependency ratio (care receivers to care givers in the family) have placed stress on family support structures (Steinmetz 1983). The outcome has been the expansion and increased use of nursing and retirement homes designed to function on the Social Security income of the elderly (Stathopoulos 1983).

Much of what is characterized as elder abuse is not domestic abuse. In many cases, elder abuse tends to occur outside of the family. When the elderly move to retirement and nursing homes, they become dependent upon non-family members for their care (Bourestom & Pastalon 1981). When they are abused in this situation, nondomestic elder abuse occurs.

There is a high potential for contradictory expectations in situations in which family members are responsible for elders. The elders may have high expectations for personal service, while the care givers may have expectations for lower levels of service. The difference in expectations can lead to a situation in which the elders perceive themselves as neglected (abused), while the care givers perceive themselves as providing more than adequate care. In these situations, it could be expected that there would be low levels of endorsement, by the general public, of neglect and related psychological-abuse items as constituting abuse.

Table 6–3 presents the rates of endorsement of the behaviors selected to measure the denotative definition of elder abuse. The subjects showed no tolerance for the use of physical force with elders. The endorsement of the *never* response was about 94 percent for all physical-force items. Unlike attitudes toward the use of physical force with children and wives, there was no ambivalence. Physical force was not considered appropriate under any circumstances by these subjects.

Table 6–3
Endorsement of Selected Behaviors as Elder Abuse
(percentage)

Behavior	Never Elder Abuse	Sometimes Elder Abuse	Always Elder Abuse
Criticizing elder in front of others	4.4	50.4	45.1
Telling elder that he/she is worthless	7.0	5.2	87.8
Cursing elder	7.0	10.4	82.6
Not loving elder	9.7	38.1	52.2
Forcing elder out of his/her own home	6.1	21.9	71.9
Tying or locking up elder	6.1	7.9	86.0
Not feeding elder enough	6.1	.9	93.0
Not giving elder adequate clothing	6.0	5.2	88.8
Hitting occasionally with open hand	6.0	.9	93.1
Hitting frequently with open hand	6.0	0.0	94.0
Hitting occasionally with fist	5.2	0.0	94.8
Hitting frequently with fist	6.0	0.0	94.0
Hitting occasionally with belt or stick	6.0	0.0	94.0
Hitting frequently with belt or stick	6.1	0.0	93.9
Not providing medical care	6.1	7.0	87.0
Threatening elder	7.0	13.0	80.0
Not spending time with elder	9.7	61.1	29.2
Preventing elder from spending own money	6.1	58.1	34.8
Spending elder's money without permission	6.1	20.9	73.0

There also was relatively high endorsement of the neglect and psychological abuse items as abuse, with the exception of *spending time with the elder, criticizing the elder,* and *allowing the elder to spend his or her own money.* For these items, the *sometimes* categories were the most frequently endorsed.

As with child abuse and spouse abuse, reasons for categorizing some items as uncertain and for not categorizing them as abuse were measured. The reasons for characterizing certain acts as abuse include *being overly critical of the elder* (18.6 percent), *the elder was mentally competent* (12.9 percent), *the best interests of the elder were not the basis for the action* (10.0 percent), and *the elder's financial interests were not being protected* (10.0 percent). The patterns for not categorizing the acts as abuse are similar. The factors include *acting in the best interest of the elder* (27.4 percent), *constructive criticism* (16.1 percent), *mental incompetence of the elder* (11.3 percent), and *maintaining financial affairs* (11.3 percent).

The subjects study were willing to define a broad range of acts as abuse. They recognized that the mental competence of the elder was an issue and would tolerate some behaviors if they were in the best interests of the elder. They had no tolerance at all for the use of physical force with elders.

A comparison of the demographic variables with the acts selected to measure endorsement of abuse shows that there are no consistent patterns among the variables. The limited significant relationships demonstrate relatively low levels of association. In order to permit a comparison of overall level of endorsement of abuse with other variables, a new variable, *level of abuse,* was constructed with the same procedures used for spouse-abuse and child-abuse data sets.

A comparison of level of abuse with the demographic variables shows no significant relationships. As is the case with child abuse and spouse abuse, there are no differences among the various components of the sample, nor is there a high level of consistency in beliefs about elder abuse.

Identification of Acts as Wrong

We have seen that violence is just one component of the definitions of domestic abuse in use by the subjects of this study. The denotative definitions include behaviors that do not involve the use of force. The next task of the research was to examine the subjects' perceptions concerning the placement of acts of domestic physical force in context among other acts of physical force.

As discussed in earlier chapters, violence (the use of physical force) has been present throughout written history and has been praised as frequently as it has been decried. Throughout history, grievances have been settled through violence, with some public acceptance (Wolfgang & Ferracuti 1967). As the rule of law emerged, the legally accepted use of violence to address grievances passed from the individual to the state (Wolin 1970).

This movement to the state of the use of physical force in social control has not prevented the legitimization of violence as an appropriate individual response. The acceptability of physical force as a tool to redress grievances has continued to the present. The use of physical force has been defined as an appropriate response when the cause is right or when circumstances justify the use of force. As a result of this orientation toward violence, many scholars suggest that violence is a relatively normal and healthy aspect of social life and that there is no consistent, accepted method for assessing the rightness or wrongness of any act involving force (Stange 1975). To some extent, the rightness or wrongness of the use of force is determined by the beliefs in use at a particular time and place.

The data to investigate perceptions of domestic violence were collected with a relatively short survey that sought to measure subjects' perceptions of the wrongness of specific acts of violence and the extent to which they would call police if they observed the acts. The primary variables for this phase of the study are *violence, perception of wrongness, willingness to call police, social distance,* and *type of assault. Violence* is defined as the use of physical force by one person against another. *Perception of wrongness* is defined as the endorsement of an act as wrong. *Willingness to call police* is defined as the endorsement of an act that the subjects would report to police. *Social distance* is defined as the extent to which the position held by one actor is removed from the position of another actor in terms of social relationship. The categories used here focus on family, friend, and stranger relationships. *Type of assault* is defined as the circumstances of a physical attack and includes type of weapon and context. *Perception of wrongness* was measured with twenty-eight items, and twenty-eight items measured *willingness to call police*. These fifty-six scale items used three-point responses: *always, depending on the circumstances,* and *never.*

In order to examine the social distance, type of force, and context variables, researchers constructed fourteen scales by summing the subjects' scores on specific sets of items. Four of these scales summed the extent to which the subjects saw the use of force as wrong for each of four types of assault: hitting someone, fighting, using a weapon, and any type of assault occurring during the commission of a crime involving theft. Four of the scales summed the extent to which the subjects were willing to call police for each of the four types of assault. Three of the scales summed the subjects' perceptions of the use of force as wrong for each of three types of social relationship: friend, neighbor, and stranger. Family items were evaluated separately. Three scales summed the subjects' willingness to call police when abusive acts using physical force were observed for the three types of social relationship. The scales and the family items were compared with the demographic measures. All interval variables approximated normal distributions (kurtosis and skewness < ±1).

The extent to which the subjects perceived the acts of violence as wrong is greater than expected (see table 6–4). Over 80 percent of the subjects stated that sixteen of the acts were always wrong, and over 90 percent of the subjects stated that ten of the acts were always wrong. The lowest levels of endorsement were for the items that specified fighting or hitting. The lowest levels of endorsement for acts as always being wrong were for *an adult hitting his or her own child* (24 percent) and for *a man fighting to protect his woman's honor* (11 percent).

Although the general patterns of response are similar to when the subjects indicated their willingness to call police (see table 6–4), the levels of endorsement are lower, with the exception of *violence in the commission of a crime* and *the use of a knife or a gun.* Over 90 percent of the subjects stated that they would always call police for all items specifying violence during a property crime or involving the use of a knife or a gun. All other items received less than 45 percent endorsement of the *always* response. It is noted that the most frequently chosen response for these items was the *depends on the circumstances* response.

Table 6–4
Endorsement of Wrongness of Specific Acts and Willingness to Report Observed Use of Force to Police
(percentage)

Act	Never	Sometimes	Always
		Act is Wrong	
Adult hitting own child	3.4	72.3	24.4
Adult hitting other's child	.9	29.1	70.1
Hitting spouse	2.6	11.3	86.1
Hitting friend during argument	2.6	19.7	77.8
Hitting neighbor during argument	3.4	17.1	79.5
Hitting stranger during argument	2.6	25.0	72.4
Two boys fighting	3.4	59.5	37.1
Two men fighting	4.4	31.9	63.7
Two girls fighting	2.6	40.9	56.5
Two friends fighting	2.6	31.6	65.8
Two neighbors fighting	3.5	29.2	67.3
Two strangers fighting	2.6	40.9	56.5
Man fighting to protect woman's honor	29.9	59.0	11.1
Hitting friend with stick during argument	0	16.1	81.8
Hitting neighbor with stick during argument	0	16.1	81.8
Hitting stranger with stick during argument	.8	30.0	69.2
Stabbing friend with knife during argument	0	5.8	94.2
Stabbing neighbor with knife during argument	0	5.8	94.2
Stabbing stranger with knife during argument	0	11.9	88.1
Shooting friend with gun during argument	.8	5.0	94.1
Shooting neighbor with gun during argument	0	5.9	94.1
Shooting stranger with gun during argument	1.7	12.7	85.7
Shoplifter hitting someone while shoplifting	1.7	2.5	95.8
Burglar hitting someone during burglary	.8	4.2	95.0
Robber hitting someone during robbery	.8	4.2	95.0
Shoplifter using weapon to avoid arrest	.8	2.5	96.7
Burglar using weapon during burglary	.8	4.2	95.0
Robber using weapon during robbery	1.7	3.3	95.0

Table 6–4 (Continued)

Act	Report Act to Police		
	Never	Sometimes	Always
Adult hitting own child	2.5	90.8	6.7
Adult hitting other's child	25.0	70.8	4.2
Hitting spouse	25.2	68.1	6.7
Hitting friend during argument	16.9	70.3	12.7
Hitting neighbor during argument	26.1	64.7	9.2
Hitting stranger during argument	26.7	64.2	9.2
Two boys fighting	14.3	72.3	13.4
Two men fighting	32.8	61.3	5.9
Two girls fighting	14.7	75.0	10.3
Two friends fighting	29.7	64.4	5.9
Two neighbors fighting	28.8	66.1	5.1
Two strangers fighting	36.2	58.6	5.2
Man fighting to protect woman's honor	21.2	72.0	6.8
Hitting friend with stick during argument	39.3	55.6	5.1
Hitting neighbor with stick during argument	43.2	52.5	4.2
Hitting stranger with stick during argument	44.9	53.4	1.7
Stabbing friend with knife during argument	93.3	6.7	0
Stabbing neighbor with knife during argument	95.0	5.0	0
Stabbing stranger with knife during argument	95.8	4.2	0
Shooting friend with gun during argument	96.7	3.3	0
Shooting neighbor with gun during argument	97.5	2.5	0
Shooting stranger with gun during argument	96.7	3.3	0
Shoplifter hitting someone while shoplifting	90.8	7.5	1.7
Burglar hitting someone during burglary	97.5	1.7	.8
Robber hitting someone during robbery	98.3	.8	.8
Shoplifter using weapon to avoid arrest	95.0	3.3	1.7
Burglar using weapon during burglary	97.5	1.7	.8
Robber using weapon during robbery	98.3	.8	.8

The lowest levels of endorsement of the *always* response continue to be assigned to *an adult hitting his or her own child* (*always,* 2 percent; *depends,* 90 percent) and *a man fighting to defend his woman's honor* (*always,* 21 percent; *depends,* 72 percent). More subjects were willing to call police (79 percent) in the latter case than subjects who perceived the act as wrong (70 percent). It is possible that the subjects would stop the fighting in such a case, even though the fighting was not perceived as wrong, or that police would be called to save a man who is doing right from those who are doing wrong.

For domestic violence, the results are mixed. As indicated earlier, few of the subjects perceived hitting a child as always wrong or as a reason to call the police. Over 82 percent of the subjects stated that hitting one's husband or wife was always wrong; however, only 25 percent would always call the police.

Fourteen scales were constructed to permit evaluation of changing patterns of endorsement for *type of force* (figure 6–1) and *social distance* (figure 6–2). In the case of *type of force,* hitting and fighting less often were seen as wrong and were less likely to be reported to police than the use of a weapon or the use of force in the commission of a crime (paired t, all comparisons, $p < .05$). However, differences between hitting and fighting and between weapon and crime are very small.

Social distance does not appear to be a factor in assessments of the wrongness of the use of force or in the willingness of subjects to call police. The higher levels of endorsement for the wrongness of the act than for endorsement for calling police, found when the *always* response was considered, continue when all responses are considered (paired t, all comparisons, $p < .05$).

Examination of the relationships between the various scales and the demographic variables failed to identify any patterns of association with two exceptions, *religious activity* and *political activity*. The more religiously active the subjects were, the more likely they were to perceive the use of force as wrong (for rho, all categories, $p < .05$). The more politically active the subjects were, the more likely they were to call police (for rho, all categories except for crime, $p > .05$).

In summary, the data indicate that the subjects had a relatively low tolerance for violence. The use of physical force in almost all situations was defined as *always wrong* by substantial numbers of the subjects. Although there was some tolerance for fighting, this behavior was usually seen as wrong unless a man was defending "his" woman. The support for intervention by the justice system was weaker but still substantial, particularly when a crime was involved. Most subjects saw the acts as wrong, yet there was some hesitancy to call police when these wrong acts were observed. Calling the police is an affirmative act, which people will avoid for many reasons. People often don't want to get involved when they are not participants in or affected by a situation, and some people prefer to avoid contact with the police. The need for

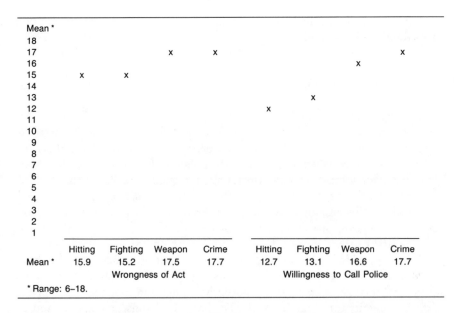

Figure 6–1. Perception of Wrongness of Use of Force and Willingness to Call Police by Type of Force

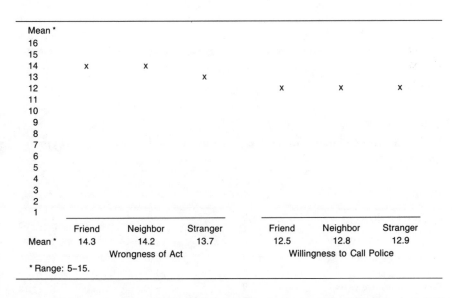

Figure 6–2. Perception of Wrongness of Use of Force and Willingness to Call Police by Social Distance

a behavior to be controlled by the justice system is just one factor that influences the decision to call the police.

Criminalization of Domestic Abuse

The willingness to criminalize abuse was measured with several scales. The subjects who responded to each of the three definition-of-abuse questionnaires were asked to choose a preferred penalty from a list of penalties. In addition, they were asked if they would be in favor of a law making the target abuse behavior a misdemeanor; then a similar question asked if they would favor making the behavior a felony offense. Another set of items measured perceived effectiveness of such a law in preventing the abuse and in shaping people's perception of the wrongness of the act.

The first of these items asked the subjects to choose a preferred penalty from a list provided. Table 6–5 presents the responses concerning the three components that focus on the definitions of abuse. The small percentage of subjects who chose no penalty supports the contention that there is support in the community for criminalization. For both child abuse and spouse abuse, substantial numbers of subjects supported relatively severe penalties. For elder abuse, milder penalties were endorsed by most subjects. There appears to be some ambiguity among subjects regarding the status of elder abuse.

The differences among groups disappear when endorsement of specific legislation is requested (see table 6–6). Support for both felony and misdemeanor legislation was endorsed by high percentages of the subjects for all categories of abuse. Although about three-fourths of the subjects believed that abuse would be perceived as wrong if it were illegal, smaller percentages believed that the law would be enforced or that it would be effective in preventing abuse.

Table 6–5
Endorsement of Penalty for Domestic-Abuse Offenders by Target Type
(percentage)

Penalty	Child Abuser (N = 104)	Spouse Abuser (N = 100)	Elder Abuser (N = 85)
No legal penalty	1.0	2.0	3.5
Grounds for divorce	11.5	2.0	8.2
Fine	4.8	29.0	10.6
Misdemeanor	14.4	6.0	29.4
One year in jail	8.7	10.0	28.2
Felony: up to five years	27.9	14.0	7.1
Felony: six to ten years	8.7	21.0	12.9
Felony: eleven to twenty years	23.1	16.0	0.0

Table 6–6
Affirmative Responses to Statements Regarding Criminalization of Abuse by Abuse Type
(percentage)

Statement	Child Abuse	Spouse Abuse	Elder Abuse
Abuse perceived as wrong if illegal	73.3	79.4	76.1
Abuse enforced if against the law	65.0	55.9	47.9
Law would be effective in preventing abuse	51.7	51.4	45.3
Would favor law making offense a misdemeanor	60.0	63.1	71.8
Would favor law making offense a felony	85.0	73.0	75.2

Although most subjects appeared to be in favor of the use of the justice system to control domestic abuse, they did not necessarily see criminalization as the best method for dealing with abuse. The subjects were asked to express their opinions regarding the best method for dealing with abuse. The responses from the open-ended question were coded and recorded. There were up to nineteen different responses for each category. Following preliminary analysis, these responses were reduced to a three-point ordinal scale with *treatment, other,* and *use of the justice system* as the points.

For spouse abuse and child abuse, the majority of subjects were equally divided into the *treatment* and *use of the justice system* categories (see table 6–7). Some of those subjects who were willing to endorse the use of criminal sanctions to control domestic abuse apparently believed that abuse would be best handled with treatment. The measure was not sufficiently precise to permit a distinction between treatment for the offender and treatment for the victim; however, a review of the raw data indicates that when the treatment target could be identified, the target was the offender.

Table 6–7
Endorsement of Selected Best Methods for Dealing with Abuse
(percentage)

Best Method	Child Abuse (N = 58)	Spouse Abuse (N = 80)	Elder Abuse (N = 77)
Treatment	39.2	33.3	0.0
Other	13.9	28.2	93.5
Criminal sanctions	46.8	38.5	6.5

The results of this process for elder abuse are unusual (see table 6–7). Over 90 percent of subjects who responded to this item were placed in the *other* category. That is, the subjects did not perceive treatment or arrest as the best method for dealing with elder abuse. It appears that there was some degree of uncertainty among the subjects about the nature of elder abuse. Over 24 percent of the subjects stated that additional research was the best method for dealing with elder abuse, while research was not mentioned by a single subject in the spouse-abuse or child-abuse samples. A small percentage identified the elderly as responsible for the abuse (6.5 percent), while the largest percentage listed various forms of improved treatment of elders as the best method for handling elder abuse. Over 65 percent of subjects believed that elder abuse occurs primarily in the home, and 29 percent believed that elder abuse occurs primarily in nursing homes.

The criminalization variables were compared with the demographic variables, with each other, and with *level of endorsement of abuse* in the denotative definitions. For the most part, the variables appear to be relatively independent. The best method for dealing with spouse abuse was related to *marital status* (Spearman's rho = .2389, p = .017), age (Spearman's rho = .4911, p < .0001), and *the potential for people to see spouse abuse as wrong if it were illegal* (p for chi square = .0243). *Marital status* and *best method for dealing with spouse abuse* were recoded into three-point ordinal variables. *Marital status* measures degree of involvement in a marital relationship, and *preferred method for dealing with spouse abuse* measures the extent to which the subjects preferred the use of the justice system or the use of treatment with domestic-abuse victims and offenders. As age and marital involvement increase, the degree of endorsement of involvement with the justice system increases. In the comparison of *best method for dealing with spouse abuse* and *the potential for people to see abuse as wrong if it were illegal,* those who favored the use of the justice system were more likely to see a law as effective in preventing abuse.

For child abuse, the only significant relationships observed occur between *preferred punishment, preferred method of dealing with child abuse,* and *willingness to endorse misdemeanor and felony penalties. Preferred method of dealing with child abuse* was recoded into a three-point scale measuring the extent to which the subjects endorsed the use of the criminal justice system, as was the case with spouse abuse. *Preferred punishment* was related to *preferred method of dealing with child abuse* (Spearman's rho = .2827, p = .007), subjects' *willingness to endorse a misdemeanor penalty* (Spearman's rho = .2165, p = .016), and subjects' *willingness to endorse the use of a felony* (Spearman's rho = −.2411, p = .007). As the severity of the penalty endorsed increases, the willingness to endorse the use of a misdemeanor penalty increases while the willingness to endorse a felony penalty decreases. An examination of the patterns in tabular form reveals that many of the subjects who would accept the use of a felony penalty preferred a lesser penalty. As the severity of the preferred penalty increases, the selection of the justice system as the best method for dealing with the problem increases.

Comparisons were limited for elder abuse. Because the responses to *best method for dealing with elder abuse* did not "fit" the treatment/use of the justice model and were too diverse for recoding into a coherent ordinal scale, a five-point nonordinal scale was constructed. The categories were: *better treatment for the elder* (33.9 percent), *more research* (27.4 percent), *the elder is wrong* (6.5 percent), *use of the justice system* (6.5 percent), and *other* (25.8 percent). In this form, *best method for dealing with elder abuse* is not significantly related to any of the other variables. As is the case with child abuse, *preferred penalty* is related to *endorsement of a misdemeanor* (Spearman's rho = .4308, p < .001) and *endorsement of a felony law* (Spearman's rho = −.4152, p < .001). For this sample the *level of abuse* was significantly related to *preferred level of punishment* (Spearman's rho = .2952, p = .007) and *race* (p for t = .002). As the level of severity of preferred punishment increases, the level of endorsement of behaviors identified as abuse increases. For *race,* the level of endorsement of behaviors as abuse is higher for blacks (mean = 54.6667) than for whites (mean = 51.4659).

The significant relationships between the central variables are sparse, indicating that to a great extent, the variables are independent. Even relationships that might be anticipated do not occur. It would seem that there should be at least some degree of interrelationship between the criminalization measures for all of the studies, but only limited patterns emerge for two of the samples, and no significant relationships are observed in the third. This suggests that the concept of domestic abuse is more complex than anticipated or that domestic abuse was not a single phenomenon in the perceptions of the subjects.

Summary

The denotative definitions of the selected categories of domestic abuse clearly include the use of physical force. The items concerning use of physical force were highly endorsed as violence by the subjects, with lower levels of endorsement for items that can be characterized as discipline for children. In addition, for all three target groups, there was consistent endorsement of items designed to measure types of behavior that can be characterized as neglect or as psychological abuse. The data from this study support the contention that the general public holds a broad definition of domestic abuse.

The data also indicate that the subjects had relatively low tolerance for the use of physical force. A high percentage of the subjects always thought that the use of force was wrong, with greater tolerance for fighting than for other activities. This was less true when willingness to call police was assessed. Unless a crime was involved, the subjects were less likely to state that they would call police if they observed a violent act. The most frequent category checked for all of these items was the conditional response.

It has been suggested that domestic violence is tolerated because it is part of general social violence that is present in American society. These data do not support such a contention. In addition to a general willingness to identify the use of force as wrong, the subjects' willingness to identify the use of force between husband and wife as wrong is higher than for all categories other than those involving the use of a weapon or the commission of a crime. The same is not true for items that ask for an opinion about the use of force with children. It is possible that the issue of discipline, which appears to have generally been rejected in the case of adult women, is still valid for children.

The results for the subjects' willingness to criminalize domestic abuse are mixed. When given an opportunity to select a penalty from a list, the subjects who selected noncriminal options (including fines) ranged from 16.5 percent for child abuse to 33 percent for spouse abuse, while over 75 percent were willing to support the passage of legislation creating a felony penalty for all three forms of domestic abuse. It should be remembered that substantial numbers of the subjects endorsed nonviolent acts as being classified as abuse. At the same time, over one-third of the subjects thought that the best method for dealing with spouse abuse and child abuse was treatment.

References

Adams, P.; Berg, L.; Berger, N.; Duane, M.; Neil, A.S.; and Ollendorff, R. 1971. *Children's rights: Toward the liberation of the child.* New York: Praeger.

Bourestom, N., and Pastalon, L. 1981. The effects of relocation on the elderly. *Gerontologist* 24: 4–7.

Dobash, R.E., and Dobash, R. 1979. *Violence against wives: A case against the patriarchy.* New York: Free Press.

Farson, R. 1979. The children's rights movement. In *The future of children and juvenile justice,* ed. L.T. Empry. Charlottesville: University of Virginia Press.

Furness, T. 1984. Organizing a therapeutic approach to intrafamilial child sexual abuse. *Journal of Adolescence* 7: 309–17.

Martin, D. 1976, *Battered wives.* San Francisco: Glide.

Parker, S. 1985. The legal background. In *Private violence and public policy: The needs of battered women and the response of public services,* ed. J. Pahl. Boston: Routledge and Keagan Paul.

Paterson, E.J. 1979. How the legal system responds to battered women. In *Battered women,* ed. D.M. Moore. Beverly Hills, Calif.: Sage Publications.

Platt, A. 1969. *The child savers.* Chicago: Chicago University Press.

Sigler, R., and Haygood, D. 1988. The criminalization of forced marital intercourse. *Marriage and Family Review* 16(2): 121–30.

Stange, S.M. 1975. *Reason and violence.* Totowa, N.J.: Rowman and Littlefield.

Stathopoulos, P.A. 1983. Consumer advocacy and abuse of elders in nursing homes. In *Abuse and maltreatment of the elderly: Causes and interventions,* ed. J.I. Kosberg. Boston, John Wright, PSG.

Steinmetz, S.K. 1977. Wife beating, husband beating: A comparison of the use of physical violence between spouses to resolve marital fights, in *Battered women,* ed. M. Roy. New York: Van Nostrand Reinhold.

———. 1983. Dependency, stress, and violence between middle-aged care givers and their elderly parents. In *Abuse and maltreatment of the elderly: Causes and interventions,* ed. J.I. Kosberg. Boston: John Wright, PSG.

Wolfgang, M., and Ferracuti, F. 1967. *The subculture of violence.* London: Tavistock.

Wolin, S.S. 1970. Violence and the western political tradition. In *Violence: Causes and solutions,* ed. R. Hartogs and E.D. Artzt. New York: Dell Press.

7
Looking to the Future

A s is the case with many studies, more questions have been raised than answered by the research project reported in this book. The project was designed to examine public perceptions of domestic abuse from three perspectives: (1) the extent to which domestic violence is perceived as violence, (2) the extent to which nonviolent dimensions of domestic abuse are included in the denotative definitions in use by the public, and (3) the extent to which the criminalization of domestic abuse is endorsed. This exploratory project was intended to be the first step in the long-term task of gaining sufficient knowledge to understand the phenomenon of domestic abuse.

Study Findings

To some extent, these study findings deviate from the patterns that would have been expected if hypotheses had been derived from the contemporary literature. As noted in previous chapters, there has been little empirical investigation of many of the assumptions that constitute conventional wisdom in the area of domestic abuse and violence and that much of what is known is relatively ignored by both researchers and practitioners.

The data indicate that the definition of domestic abuse in use by the general public is broader than the definition implied by the bulk of the research in this area. The general public, or at least the subjects in this study, perceives neglect and psychologically offensive behavior as domestic abuse when the behavior occurs in a domestic context. The set of items designed to measure domestic abuse were too limited to measure the scope of domestic abuse in the areas of child abuse, spouse abuse, and elder abuse. In addition, more of the items focused on the use of physical force than were needed to accurately map this aspect of domestic abuse. The threshold for the use of force as abuse is considerably lower than anticipated. The range of the items designed to measure neglect and psychological abuse need to be expanded to provide a more accurate measure of the parameters of these types of abuse.

In addition, other dimensions of domestic abuse need to be measured. In particular, the sexual abuse aspect of spouse abuse and child abuse should be evaluated, as well as the potential conflict due to differences in expectations for elder abuse. Although this line of research focused on public perceptions, the same dimensions might be examined for relevance in studies that focus on the nature of domestic abuse itself.

The scales used to examine the placement of domestic violence in the general context of violence were more elaborate on the upper end of the scale than on the lower end. The study subjects generally rejected the use of physical force across the board once a relatively low threshold was crossed. Additional refinement of the lower end of the scale would permit the identification of additional parameters involved in the acceptance of the use of physical force. There is support for the contention that domestic violence fits within the context of general violence. However, the contention that Americans generally endorse the use of physical force is subject to question.

The data can be taken to indicate some general willingness to criminalize domestic abuse. The results are not consistent, indicating that there is a need for clarification. In this study, *treatment* was not sufficiently differentiated from *use of the justice system* to define accurately the subjects' placement of the best/preferred/acceptable disposition for the forms of abuse and did not permit discrimination between treatment for the offender and treatment for the victim. With the identification of treatment as the best method for dealing with abuse by many of the subjects, a finer measure of this dimension also is warranted.

It is possible that confusion is created by treating domestic abuse as a single, unified phenomenon. The boundaries around the set of behaviors constituting domestic abuse are conceptual, rather than natural. It has been demonstrated that domestic violence can be placed within the context of general violence. If this and other dimensions of domestic abuse are identified more closely with the general classes of behavior into which they fall, then different dispositions of response might be selected for different types of abusive situations.

It also is possible that treatment and the use of the justice system are not perceived as independent, exclusive alternatives. Treatment might be combined with the power to intervene inherent in law enforcement, with emphases on different aspects of the process.

Elder abuse may not have been sufficiently defined in the subjects' perceptions to permit the selection of a best method for handling it. Elder abuse is a new field that is still in the process of definition. Coverage of elder abuse by the news media has been less complete than coverage of spouse abuse or child abuse and has not been as graphic in the presentation of cases of extreme abuse. It is also possible that confusion is created by the involvement of non-family agents in elder abuse. Elder abuse may be perceived as more a matter of nondomestic abuse than as a matter of domestic abuse.

If domestic abuse is to develop fully as a legitimate area of research, then a firm knowledge base must be developed. Some of the basic areas for further research are indicated by the results reported in this book, while others are suggested by the existing knowledge base.

Community Perceptions

The study is just a beginning in the process of collecting basic information about the operation of abuse in American society. As a first step, it suggests some of the parameters of the public's perception of a set of specific, selected behaviors as constituting abuse. Although the data do support the contention that neglect and nonphysical behaviors defined as causing psychological or emotional damage are perceived as abuse, these perceptions need to be measured more precisely. In addition, linkages between the dimensions of abuse and the general set of behaviors associated with each need to be measured. For example, dimensions such as child neglect and spouse neglect should be identified by their placement in the general set of behaviors that constitute neglect.

More precise measures are needed to determine the extent to which domestic abuse is: (1) perceived as an integrated phenomenon; (2) perceived as integrated by specific target, with differing patterns or parameters depending on the nature of the specific target; (3) perceived as a set of interlinked areas, with the nature of the linkage varying by type of target, context, or some other factor; (4) perceived as a figment of the imagination; or (5) perceived as a product of the structure imposed by research in this area. Of course, it is likely that an imposed structure will become real as the pattern is promoted and becomes part of the perceptions of the general public.

Preferred Remedies

Until the public's perception of the various facets of domestic abuse can be identified accurately, it will be difficult to assess the public's preference for the appropriate method for dealing with abuse. Further study is needed to determine the linkages among the various types of domestic abuse and use of the justice system, treatment, and degree of wrongness of abusive acts. It is possible that some acts seen as abuse will be perceived as criminal, while other acts seen as abuse will be perceived as wrong but not criminal. It also is probable that some acts will be seen as abusive or as not abusive based on a range of contextual variables, such as intent, intensity, frequency, strength of the victim/target, mutuality of the behavior, cultural values, and the presence of stressors.

The role of treatment deserves some attention in its own right. The treatment preference in this study emerged from an item designed to measure criminalization. That is, the survey instruments focused attention on penalties, law, and criminal sanctions. The emergence of treatment as an option under these conditions is an indication that it is present as an important variable in the preferred-remedy area and must be considered when assessing community perspectives. Included in this line of research should be the separation of preference for treatment for the victim from preference for treatment for the offender, as well as an examination of the circumstances under which treatment is appropriate and of the forms/types of abuse amenable to treatment.

Knowledge of Abuse

It has been suggested that research influences reality. When a line of research is pursued diligently, particularly when it is interesting or serves the interests of activist groups, the results tend to become a part of the general cultural base. That is clearly a possibility with research in the area of domestic abuse. The potential for cultural assimilation is particularly high for physical abuse and for sexual abuse, as these forms of abuse can be presented in dramatic format and appeal to the public interest because of the sensitive nature of the behavior. Extreme cases attract public attention and public support for action. Any research focusing on these issues is highly likely to have public exposure simply because it is interesting. When the efforts of reform activists to promote their causes are added, the potential for research results to become a part of the cultural knowledge base fairly rapidly becomes high.

For these reasons, research in the area of domestic violence carries an additional ethical burden. When the results of a research project or line of research are likely to have an effect on the way in which people live, the extent to which people are labeled deviant, or the manner in which the justice system is called into action, extra care must be taken to protect the quality and validity of the results. It is not enough to produce valid results if those results reflect only a partial understanding, especially if the partial truth is shaped by activist perspectives.

In the area of domestic abuse, this high standard has not been met. Much of the research in this area appears to have been narrowly focused on the victims and their trauma. At times, the research seems oriented toward establishing an argument for those who seek to emphasize the scope and magnitude of the problem. Although researchers clearly may specify their measures, the fact that a measure includes all acts of force, even if directed away from the target, or that a single act in a lifetime of marriage constitutes domestic violence is often neglected. Thus, when the results are presented, the perceived scope and frequency of occurrence of domestic abuse may be inflated. Some very well conceptualized and operationalized studies contribute to this state of affairs by consistently focusing on one aspect of domestic abuse.

If the assumption that results from this line of research are highly likely to become a part of the public belief system is correct, then researchers have a strong ethical obligation to conduct comprehensive investigations. The range of studies must be broad, examining every aspect of domestic abuse. This may be difficult at times, given the commitment of activists to finding support for their position. Domestic abuse also must be investigated from several perspectives. Regardless of intent, most research to date has focused on a relatively narrow aspect of domestic abuse, the damage done to the victims of physical abuse. There is a need to broaden the focus of research to provide a more comprehensive view. A number of recent studies have begun to undertake this task, and the area of domestic abuse will benefit if that trend continues.

Emphasis has been placed on the use of physical force and on sexual abuse directed against women and children by men, while other forms of abuse inflicted by one person on another in the domestic environment have been neglected. Relatively little is known about the incidence and impact of neglect or psychological abuse. It is possible that neglect is relatively passive or is a simple failure to provide. It may also be an active, aggressive act of denial of access to resources, or it could be a combination of both. As neglect has generally been studied only when other forms of abuse are present, it has not been examined in its own right. The same is true of psychological abuse. Behaviors that cause emotional or psychological damage may be thoughtless or careless acts not intended to damage, or they may be carefully calculated, consistent patterns of behavior designed to hurt the target. It also is possible that some behaviors causing harm in the family have not been discovered. In short, a line of research designed to map the scope, and subsequently the boundaries, of abuse will add to our knowledge base.

Attention also needs to be directed toward the volume of domestic violence. Studies designed to measure the incidence of physical abuse present a wide range of estimates. This variance probably can be explained primarily in terms of differences in the measurement of violence. The instruments range from measures that focus on damaging force or persistent force to studies that focus on any act that might cause physical harm. To some extent, this variance in definitions and measurement is normal in an emerging field, but it seems prudent to establish categories of violence for studies with broad definitions of violence. A sound study is needed to set thresholds based on degree of harm, on intent to do physical harm, or both. Failure to set realistic thresholds distorts the assessment of the seriousness of the behavior. Treating a single act of thoughtless violence in the same manner as a consistent pattern of the use of force prevents a clear assessment.

Other dimensions of abuse also have not been effectively measured. Some attention has been directed toward some forms of sexual abuse, but most studies measure abuse toward a target, such as an elder or a child, without specifying the behaviors involved. Thus, forms of abuse are not clearly identified. This is particularly likely to occur when archival data is used. However, it is difficult to measure a variable that has not been clearly defined, so exploratory research designed to establish parameters for the full range of behaviors one family member directs toward another will need to precede studies designed to measure volume or impact.

Studies that focus on targets may be confusing the nature of the abusive situation. It is possible that there are factors or combinations of factors, indicative of an abusive situation, that are independent of the particular target. While attention needs to be directed toward the nature of the relationship between the abuser and the target, limiting this focus to categories defined by the type of target may obscure an understanding of abuse as a behavior in and of itself. The target may be determined simply by convenience or may be selected because of a specific set of factors in the family environment. Some behaviors and patterns may be found to be normal, or occasional and not typical. It also is possible that the severe patterns with which activists are concerned occur persistently in a small number of families and are not representative of the majority of the population. The measures of the subjects' perceptions in the study reported here suggest that the prevalence of abuse might be a fruitful line of research, as the subjects identified behaviors as wrong, as abusive, and as subject to control by the justice system.

Threshold Identification

The normality or wrongness of the behaviors classified as abuse is not likely to be a matter of absolute inclusion or exclusion. It is likely that most of the behaviors will be defined as abuse or as not abuse depending on several factors, such as frequency, severity, intent, degree of damage caused, and mutuality of the behavior. In order to permit effective coordinated research, thresholds must be defined that will permit the effective classification of behaviors. When these thresholds are established, accurate measures can be made of the incidence of abuse, and research focused on examination of the dynamics of the abusive situation can be properly targeted and compared.

Thresholds can be sufficiently flexible to include situational factors, with initial thresholds including both a point beyond which the behavior is usually considered abuse regardless of the circumstances (hitting a child with a baseball bat) and a point below which the behavior is rarely considered abuse (spanking a child), with an unclear group falling between these two points (slapping a child in the face). While these thresholds should be established through sound empirical investigation with the actual damage caused by the abuse as an important dimension, such a project would be theoretical, or at least conceptual, in nature. As a result, this line of endeavor would need to be pursued with great care to improve the likelihood that the position will be accepted by those with an interest in this area.

Abusers

Although much has been written about abusers, relatively little is based on sound empirical study. A limited number of studies using a case-history approach have attempted to characterize offenders. Frequently, the data from these studies have come from the victims. Many of these studies appear to suggest that there is an abusive type or personality, or that there is a group of people (men) whose psychological, emotional, and cognitive character predisposes them to abuse others in their environment.

Some support for the contention that an abusive type exists can be found in child-abuse studies that conclude that child abuse can be multigenerational, with children who are abused becoming parents who abuse their children. Support also can be found in studies that identify offenders who abuse multiple members of their families consistently over a long period of time.

It is probable that the present body of knowledge about abusers is distorted by the fact that the data come from case studies involving severe cases. In such cases, the behavior is extreme, suggesting that these abusers would be extreme and possibly unusual. A focus on the total abusive situation would help clarify the character of the abuser, but research focused on the abuser also could produce useful information.

Gathering data about abusers will be difficult. If the behaviors of interest are defined as wrong, the validity of responses from subjects may be low. This is a design issue that can be solved in a number of ways, but this type of data will continue to be difficult to gather.

Adaptation Skills

An area in which little reseach has been conducted is in the techniques of adaptation used by victims of abuse. Clinical evidence from severe cases provides, at best, pessimistic assessments of relatively unsuccessful adaptations. Treatment efforts focus on these severe cases and are designed to assist badly damaged victims and severe abusers.

If abuse exists on a continuum from mild, nondamaging, unpleasant behavior to severe, damaging, aggressive acts, then the milder aspects of this behavior could be accommodated with relatively minor coping skills. It also is possible that there are victims who are adequately coping with varying levels of abuse with a range of adaptation skills that is not presently anticipated. The identification of these skills would both enhance the present level of knowledge about domestic abuse and provide valuable information for those who seek to assist victims of abusive situations.

Present research indicates that the majority of victims remain in their situations as victims or return to the situations after they flee. If this is true and continues to be true, then information about coping skills is particularly relevant to the assistance process.

Elder Abuse

Although elder abuse should be included in any study of general abuse, there is a need for additional information about the ways in which elders are harmed. It may be that abuse in institutions is similar to abuse in the home when elders are involved, or there may be important differences.

The operation of differential expectations is an important and interesting focus for research in all aspects of domestic abuse, but it is particularly salient in the area of elder abuse. Although no accurate estimate has been made of the amount, form, and distribution of elder abuse, it appears likely that there is a substantial amount of behavior that can be characterized as neglect. Neglect is passive rather than active and occurs when a service is not provided. It is possible that much of what the elderly classify as neglect reflects a disagreement about the level of services due, rather than an intent to abuse. If an elderly man expects his son to visit for two to three hours a day and the son expects to visit one or two hours once or twice a week, the elder may perceive himself as neglected if the son conforms to his own expectations. In this case, the son would not perceive himself as neglecting his parent.

This is a simple example of a set of interactions that probably are fairly complex and that occur in both domestic and nondomestic situations. Once the nature of the interaction is understood, research efforts can focus on the consequences of patterns of perceived neglect and on the patterns of interaction, including active forms of abuse, such as psychological and emotional abuse. Given the increasing level of activity in the field of gerontology, it is likely that elder abuse will be the focus of comprehensive evaluation in the near future.

Community Response

The study reported in this book focused on community perceptions of domestic abuse from a denotative-definition perspective and from a context perspective. Additional areas of public response would benefit from further investigation.

Information needs to be gathered about responses of community members who observe various acts of abuse. Factors such as kinship, social setting, degree of relationship between the various parties, form of abuse, severity of abuse, response of the victim, and power differentials among the parties could influence the form and intensity of the response.

Relatively few data sets have been gathered about the response of social-service agencies to domestic abuse. While considerable attention has been directed toward the response of the justice system, this attention takes the form of case examples, review of policies, and analysis of projected consequences of types of response. The same statements can be made for the response of the shelter movement. There have been studies of shelter populations and descriptive statements about how shelters for battered women should be operated, but few studies have collected data about shelter operations and impact, other than those studies that evaluate client process outcomes.

If the development of domestic abuse and the options available to victims are to be understood, then more must be known about the manner in which social-service agencies respond to abuse cases. It appears from the literature that these agencies presently are pursuing aggressively domestic-abuse cases with affirmative programs for case management. Data collected might measure actual responses, policies, resource commitment, and priority of domestic-abuse cases. Efforts to respond effectively will continue to be difficult until better information about the nature of domestic abuse is available for agencies to use in planning and program implementation.

Violence

Perhaps the more noteworthy results from this study are not related to domestic abuse. The subjects in this study consistently demonstrated low levels of tolerance for the use of physical force in a wide range of circumstances. This finding is contrary to what would be expected given the review of literature in this area. It frequently is asserted that Americans are by nature and historical perspective more violent and more tolerant of violence than their European and Far Eastern colleagues. It also is stated that Americans as a group own more weapons, use more physical force in settling disputes, and approve of the use of force by others whenever the cause is seen as just.

The data in this study tend to suggest that this perspective may be a myth reflected only in fiction. At the same time, it is difficult to deny that violence occurs with some frequency in the United States. A simple review of crime statistics demonstrates the prevalence of murder, rape, and assault. It is possible, however, that prevalence, common occurrence, and approval of acts of violence are not interrelated.

Violence is present but may be atypical and generally unacceptable behavior to the general public. There may be a small segment of the population that uses violence and that endorses the use of violence. Because this minority is not openly opposed, it is assumed that the general public approves, or at least accepts, this behavior. In both domestic abuse and in the use of physical force, it may be that the behavior and perspectives of a small minority are taken to reflect the values and beliefs of the majority.

It appears that additional research in this area would be productive. It is possible that the data from this study, collected from one geographical area, are not representative of other areas or that a more precise measure would produce other results. It also may be that the accepted view of the violent nature of the American public is inaccurate.

Concluding Thoughts

This research was designed to be a preliminary, exploratory examination of the public's perception of domestic abuse, with a focus on the denotative definitions in use and the placement of domestic violence in the context of violence. The data tend to support the contention that the public endorses a broad definition of domestic abuse regardless of the target of the abuse and that domestic violence fits within the context of general violence. On the whole, the general public finds the use of physical force unacceptable in almost any context but is less willing to call police than to label the behavior as wrong. The public also is willing to endorse the use of the justice system in domestic-abuse cases but believes that treatment is an acceptable method of dealing with domestic abuse.

Several areas of potential for further research have been identified. An ethical issue is prominent for this line of research. Research in the area of domestic violence is highly likely to become a part of the general knowledge base used by the public to make decisions. Policy decisions, legislation, and criminalization can emerge from this area of research. As a result, care must be taken to not only develop designs that produce accurate, valid data, but also to produce data of high quality for all aspects of domestic abuse. Research to date generally has not met this test, as there is a consistent bias introduced by the persistent focus on the victim and on the more extreme forms of physical abuse and sexual abuse.

The study of domestic abuse is still an emerging field. As it continues to develop, the breadth and depth of the data developed by research efforts are certain to increase. In this process, researchers may find themselves subject to criticism from their more activist colleagues, but dedication to the advancement of knowledge is likely to prevail.

Bibliography

Abbott, G. 1938. *The child and the state*, vol. 2. Chicago: University of Chicago Press.

Abramson, L.; Garber, J.; and Seligman, M. 1980. Learned helplessness in humans: An attributional analysis. In *Learned helplessness: Theory and application*, ed. J. Garber and M. Seligman. New York: Academic Press.

Ackley, D. 1977. A brief overview of child abuse. *Social Casework* 58(1): 21–24.

Adams, C. 1986. *Wife beating as a crime and its relation to taxation*. Philadelphia: Philadelphia Social Science Association.

Adams, M.S., and Neel, J.V. 1967. Children of incest. *Pediatrics* 40(1): 55.

Adams, P.L. 1981. Language patterns of opponents to a child protection program. *Child Psychiatry and Human Development* 11 (Spring): 135–57.

Adams, P.; Berg, L.; Berger, N.; Duane, M.; Neill, A.S.; and Ollendorff, R. 1971. *Children's rights: Toward the liberation of the child*. New York: Praeger.

Adams, W. 1982. The dilemma of anonymous reporting in child protective services. *Child Welfare* 61(1): 3–15.

Adams-Tucker, C. 1985. Defense mechanisms used by sexually abused children. *Children Today* 14(1): 9–12, 14.

Adrian, M. 1978. *Montana: A study of spouse battering*. Helena: Montana Board of Crime Control.

Advocate's guide to elder abuse, neglect, and exploitation. 1983. Seattle: Evergreen Legal Services.

Allen, C., and Straus, M.A. 1980. Resources, power, and husband-wife violence. In *The social causes of husband-wife violence*, ed. M.A. Straus and G. Hotaling. Minneapolis: University of Minnesota Press.

Alliance/Elder Abuse Project. 1983. *An analysis of states' mandatory reporting laws on elder abuse*. Syracuse, N.Y.

Alter, C. 1985. Decision-making factors in cases of child neglect. *Child Welfare* 64(1): 99–111.

American Humane Association. Children's Division. 1967. *Child protective services— A national survey*. Denver.

———. 1974. *Child abuse legislation in the 1970s*. Denver.

———. 1978. *National analysis of official child neglect and abuse reporting*. Washington, D.C.: Government Printing Office.

An appraisal of New York's statutory response to the problem of child abuse. 1971. *Columbia Journal of Law and Social Problems* 7(1): 51.

Anastasio, C.J. 1981. Elder abuse: Identification and acute-care intervention. Paper presented at the National Conference on Abuse of Older Persons, March, Boston.

Andersen, I. 1977. Wife battering in the Netherlands: Needs and incidence. Paper presented at the International Sociological Association Seminar on Sex Roles, Deviance, and Agents of Social Control, Dublin, Ireland.

Anderson, D., and Ten-Bensel, R.W. 1979. Counseling the family in which incest has occurred. *Medical Aspects of Human Sexuality* 13(1): 143–44.

Anderson, G.A., and Lythcott, S. 1978. *Information on domestic violence in Wisconsin, extent and services available.* Rockville, Md.: NCJRS Microfiche Program.

Anderson, G.M. 1977. Wives, mothers, and victims. *America* 137 (30 July): 46–50.

Anderson, M.L., and Shafer, G. 1979. The character-disordered family: A community treatment model for family sexual abuse. *American Journal of Orthopsychiatry* 49(3): 436–45.

Anderson, S. 1981. *Management of child abuse and neglect, overview and protocol.* Seattle: Harborview Medical Center.

Andrews, D.R., and Linden, R. 1984. Preventing rural child abuse: Progress in spite of cutbacks. *Child Welfare* 63(5): 443–52.

Antler, S. 1981. The rediscovery of child abuse. In *The social context of child abuse,* ed. L.H. Pelton. New York: Human Sciences Press.

———. 1983. *Child abuse and child protection: Policy and practice.* Silver Springs, Md: National Association of Social Workers.

Antunes, G.; Cook, F.L.; Cook, T.D.; and Skogan, W.G. 1977. Patterns of crime against the elderly: Findings from a national study. *Gerontologist* 17(2): 321–7.

Appleton, W. 1980. Battered women syndrome. *Annals of Emergency Medicine* 9 (February): 84–91.

Araji, S., and Finkelhor, D. 1985. Explanations of pedophilia: A review of empirical research. *Bulletin of the American Academy of Psychiatry and Law* 13(1): 17–37.

Aries, P. 1962. *Centuries of childhood.* Trans. R. Baldick. New York: Alfred A. Knopf.

Armstrong, L. 1978. *Kiss Daddy goodnight: A speak-out on incest.* New York: Hawthorn Press.

Aronson, M.K. 1984. Update on Alzheimer's: Introduction. *Generations, Quarterly Journal of the Western Gerontological Society* 9(2): 5–6.

Atchley, R.C. 1980. *The social forces in later years.* 3d ed. Belmont, Calif.: Wadsworth.

Auerbach, J.S. 1978. Perceptions of police and psychiatric mandates in family disputes. *Dissertation Abstracts International* 39(3): 1465-B.

Aumer, S.M. 1979. *Battered women: An effective response.* St. Paul: Minnesota Department of Corrections, Programs and Services for Battered Women.

Author, D. 1973. Protecting neglected and abused children—a community responsibility. In *Proceedings of the second national symposium on child abuse.* Denver: American Humane Association, Children's Division.

Awana, R. 1973. An interdisciplinary child protective services unit. In *Proceedings of* the second national symposium on child abuse in Denver; American Humane Association, Children's Division.

Axelberd, M., and Valle, J. 1978. Development of the behavioral scale for measuring police effectiveness in domestic disputes. *Crisis Intervention* 9: 69–80.

Bacon, G.M. 1977. Parents anonymous. *Victimology* 2(2): 331–37.

Bagley, C. 1969. Incest behavior and incest taboo. *Social Problems* 16(3): 505–19.

Bailey, B. 1977. Child abuse: Causes, effect, and prevention. *Victimology* 2(3): 337–42.

Bailey, C.F. 1979. Incest—practical investigative guide. *Police Chief* 46: 36–38.

Bakalar, H.R. 1981. Psychological dynamics of pediatric burn abuse. *Health and Social Work* 6: 27–32.

Bakan, D. 1971. *Slaughter of the innocents: A study of the battered child phenomenon.* Boston: Beacon Press.

Ball, M. 1977. Issues of violence in family casework. *Social Casework* 58(1): 3–12.

Ball, P.G., and Wyman, E. 1978. Battered wives and powerlessness: What can counselors do? *Victimology* 2(3/4): 545–52.

Ballew, J.R. 1985. Role of natural helpers in preventing child abuse and neglect. *Social Work* 30(1): 37–41.

Ban, T.A. 1978. The treatment of depressed geriatric patients. *American Journal of Psychotherapy* 32: 93–104.

Bancroft, S. 1978. *Programs providing services to battered women.* Rockville, Md.: NCJRS Michrofiche Programs.

Bard, M. 1969. Extending psychology's impact through existing community institutions. *American Psychologist* 24: 610–12.

———. 1974. The study and modification of intrafamilial violence. In *Violence in the family,* ed. S. Steinmetz and M. Straus. New York: Harper and Row.

Bard, M., and Zacker, J. 1971. The prevention of family violence: Dilemmas of community intervention. *Journal of Marriage and Family* 33(4): 677–82.

———. 1974. Assaultiveness and alcohol use in family disputes. *Criminology* 12(3): 282–92.

Bard, P., and Johnson, M. 1973. *At the risk of being a wife.* Grand Rapids, Mich.: Zondervan.

Barden, C., and Barden, J. 1976. The battered wife syndrome. *Viva Magazine,* May, 79–81, 108–10.

Barden, J.C. 1974. Wife beaters: Few of them ever appear before a court of law. *New York Times,* 21 October, sect. 2, 38.

Barry, K. 1981. *Female sexual slavery.* New York: Avon Books.

Barry, S. 1980. Spousal rape—the uncommon law. *American Bar Association Journal* 66(4): 1088–91.

Bart, P.B. 1985. Reaction to abused and nonabused women: MMPI profile differences. *Journal of Counseling and Development* 63: 326.

Barth, R.P. 1983. The contribution of stress to child abuse. *Social Services Review* 57(3): 477–89.

———. 1983. Self-control training with maltreating parents. *Child Welfare* 62(2): 33–24.

———. 1985. Collecting competent evidence in behalf of children. *Social Work* 30(1): 130–6.

Bass, D., and Rice, J. 1979. Agency responses to the abused wife. *Social Casework* 60(2): 338–42.

Bassett, S. 1980. *Battered rich*. Port Washington, N.Y.: Ashley Books.

Baxter, A. 1985. *Techniques for dealing with child abuse*. Springfield, Ill.: Charles C. Thomas.

Beck, M.J. 1979. Pathological narcissism and the psychology of the married victim. *Family Therapy* 6: 155–9.

Beck, R.A.; Loseke, D.R.; Beck, S.F.; and Rauma, D. 1980. Bringing the cops back in: A study of efforts to make the criminal-justice system more responsive to incidents of family violence. *Social Science Research* 9: 193–215.

Becker, J. 1978. Evaluating the social skills of sexual aggressives. *Criminal Justice and Behavior* 5(2): 357–67.

———. 1978. Men and the victimization of women. In *Victimization of women*, ed. J.R. Chapman and M. Gates. Beverly Hills, Calif.: Sage Publications.

Becker, T. 1968. *Child protective services and the law*. Denver: American Humane Association, Children's Division.

———. 1972. Due process in child protective proceedings. In *Proceedings from a national symposium on child abuse*. Denver: American Humane Association, Children's Division.

———. 1973. Protecting the legal rights through judicial process. In *Proceedings of the second national symposium on child abuse*. Denver: American Humane Association, Children's Division.

Bedrosian, R.C., and Kagel, S.A. 1979. A woman under the influence: An example of multiple victimization within a family. *American Journal of Family Therapy* 7(1): 51–58.

Bell, M. 1977. Issues of violence in family casework. *Social Casework* 58(1): 3–12.

Bender, L., and Abram, B. 1937. The reaction of children to sexual relations with adults. *Journal of American Orthopsychiatry* 7(10): 500–18.

Benedek, E.P. 1978. Incidents of battered wives said underreported. *Psychiatric News* 13(10): 25–29, 31.

Bentil, J.K. 1978. Spouse bashing—wife not a compellable witness against her husband. *Justice Peace* 142: 704–6.

Benward, J., and Densen-Gerber, J. 1975. Incest as a causative factor in antisocial behavior: An exploratory study. *Contemporary Drug Problems* 4 (Fall): 323–40.

Berger, A. 1980. The child abusing family . . . parent-related characteristics. *American Journal of Family Therapy* 8(1): 53–66.

Berger, L., and Berger, M. 1973. A holistic group approach to psychogeriatric out-patients. *International Journal of Group Psychotherapy* 23(4): 432–45.

Berk, R.A. 1985. Does arrest really deter wife battery? *American Sociological Review* 50(2): 253–62.

Berliner, L. 1977. Child sexual abuse: What happens next? *Victimology* 2(2):327–31.

———. 1984. The testimony of the child victim of sexual assault. *Journal of Social Issues* 40(1): 125–47.

Berliner, L., and Stevens, D. 1976. *Special techniques for interviewing child witnesses*. Seattle: Harborview Medical Center.

Bernard, J. 1974. Age, sex, and feminism. *Annals of the American Academy of Political and Social Science* 415: 120–37.

Bernard, J.L., and Bernard, M.L. 1984. The abusive male seeking treatment: Jekyll and Hyde. *Family Relations* 33(4): 543–7.

Besharov, J.D. 1975. Building a community response to child abuse and maltreatment. *Children Today* 4: 2.

————. 1985. Right versus rights, the dilemma of child protection. *Public Welfare* 43(1): 19–27, 46.

Biaggi, G.R. 1979. *Battered women—a legal handbook for New Jersey women.* Trenton: New Jersey State Law Enforcement Planning Agency.

Biggs, J.M. 1962. *The concept of matrimonial cruelty.* Atlantic Highlands, N.J.: Athlone Press Humanities.

Birnbaum, R. 1979. The battered wife—the legal system attempts to help. *University of Cincinnati Law Review* 48: 419–34.

Bischof, N. 1972. The biological foundation of the incest taboo. *Social Science Information* 11 (December): 7–36.

Blackstone, J. 1965. *Justification for no obligation.* New York: Random House.

Blake, R. 1984. What disables the American elderly. *Generations, Quarterly Journal of the Western Gerontological Society* 8(4): 6–9.

Blake-White, J. 1985. Treating the dissociative process in adult victims of childhood incest. *Social Casework* 66(3):394–402.

Blau, P. 1964. *Exchange and power in social life.* New York: John Wiley and Sons.

Blay, S., and Coster, D.L. 1980. Marital rape in California: For better or worse. *San Fernando Valley Law Review* 8: 239–61.

Blenkner, M. 1965. Social work and family relationships in later life with some thoughts on filial maturity. In *Social structure and the family,* ed. E. Shanas and G. Streib. Englewood Cliffs, N.J.: Prentice-Hall.

————. 1969. The normal dependencies of aging. In *The dependencies of old people,* ed. R. Kalish. Ann Arbor: University of Michigan Institute of Gerontology.

Blenkner, M.; Bloom, M.; and Nielson, M. 1971. A research and demonstration project of protective services. *Social Casework* 52(8): 483–97.

Blink, L., and Porter, L. 1982. Group therapy with female adolescent sexual abuse victims. In *Handbook of clinical intervention in child sexual abuse,* ed. S. Sgroi. Lexington, Mass.: Lexington Books.

Block, M.R. 1983. Special problems and vulnerability of elderly women. In *Abuse and maltreatment of the elderly: Causes and interventions,* ed. J.I. Kosberg. Boston: John Wright, PSG.

Block, M.R., and Sinnott, J.D. eds. 1979. *The battered elder syndrome: An exploratory study.* Final report to the United States Administration on Aging. University of Maryland, Center on Aging.

Bloom, M. 1978. Conciliation court—crisis intervention in domestic violence. *Crime Prevention Review* 6 (October): 19–27.

Bloom, M., and Nielson, M. 1971. The older person in need of protective services. *Social Casework* 52(8): 500–509.

Bluglass, R. 1979. Incest. *British Journal of Hospital Medicine* 22: 152, 154–57.

Blumberg, M. 1964. When parents hit out. *Twentieth Century* 4: 39–44.

————. 1974. Psychopathology of the abusing parent. *American Journal of Psychotherapy* 28(1): 21–29.

Blumenthal, M. 1972. *Justifying violence: The attitudes of American men.* Ann Arbor: University of Michigan, Institute for Social Research.

Boehn, B. 1964. The community and the social agency define neglect. *Child Welfare* 43(9): 453–64.

Boekelheide, P.D. 1978. Incest and the family physician. *Journal of Family Practice* 6: 87–90.

————. 1978. Sexual adjustment in college women who experience incestual relationships. *Journal of the American College Health Association* 26(2): 327–30.

Bogard, M. 1984. Family systems approaches to wife battering: A feminist critique. *American Journal of Orthopsychiatry* 54(8): 558–68.

Boisvert, M.J. 1972. The battered-child syndrome. *Social Casework* 53(8): 475–80.

Bolin, D.C. 1980. The Pima County victim/witness program: Analyzing its success. *Evaluation and Change,* special issue: 120–26.

Bolton, F.G. 1980. Domestic violence continuum—a pressing need for legal intervention. *Women Lawyers' Journal* 66 (Winter): 11–17.

————. 1985. Prevention screening of adolescent mothers and infants: Assessing risk for child maltreatment. *Journal of Primary Prevention* 5: 169–87.

Borup, J.H. Transfer trauma and the law. 1984. *Generations, Quarterly Journal of the Western Gerontological Society* 8(3): 17–20.

Boszormeny-Nagy, I., and Spark, G.M. 1973. *Invisible loyalties: Reciprocity in intergenerational family therapy.* Hagerstown, Md.: Harper & Row.

Boudouris, J. 1971. Homicide and the family. *Journal of Marriage and the Family* 33(11): 667–76.

Boulding, E. 1977. A "children's rights." *Society* 15: 39–43.

Bourestom, N., and Pastalon, L. 1981. The effects of relocation on the elderly. *Gerontologist* 21: 4–7.

Bourne, R. 1985. Family violence: Legal and ethical issues. In *Unhappy families,* ed. E.H. Newberger and R. Bourne. Littleton, Mass.: PSG.

Bourne, R., and Newberger, E.H., eds. 1979. *Critical perspectives on child abuse.* Lexington, Mass.: Lexington Books.

Bowen, N.H. 1982. Guidelines for career counseling with abused women. *Vocational Guidance Quarterly* 31: 123–27.

Bowker, L. 1983. *Beating wife beating.* Lexington, Mass.: Lexington Books.

Bowling, D. 1977. An attitudinal study of child abuse in Tuscaloosa, Alabama. Master's thesis, University of Alabama.

Boyd, R.V., and Woodman, J.A. 1978. The Jekyll-and-Hyde syndrome: An example of disturbed relations affecting the elderly. *Lancet* 2: 671–2.

Boylan, A.M.; Schulman, J.; Williams, A.; and Woods, L. 1982. *Legal advocacy for battered women.* New York: National Center for Women and Family Law.

Brain, J.L. 1977. Sex, incest, and death: Initiation rites reconsidered. *Current Anthropology* 18 (June): 191–208.

Braungart, M.M.; Hoyer, W.J.; and Braungart, R.G. 1979. Fear of crime and the elderly. In *Police and the elderly,* ed. A.P. Goldstein, W.J. Hoyer, and P.S. Monti. New York: Pergamon Press.

Bremner, R.H. 1970. *Children and youth in America: A documentary history.* Cambridge: Harvard University Press.

Brenton, M. 1977. What can be done about child abuse. *Today's Education* 66: 51–53.

Breton, M. 1977. Nurturing abused and abusive mothers: The hairdressing group. *Social Work with Groups* 2(1): 161–74.

Brieland, D. 1966. Protective services and child abuse: Implications for public child welfare. *Social Service Review* 40(4): 369–77.

Briffault, R., and Malinowsky, B. 1971. *Marriage—past and present.* Boston: P. Sargent.

Brisson, N. 1982. Helping men who batter women. *Public Welfare* 40(1): 28–34.

Britain: Battered wives. 1973. *Newsweek,* 9 July, 39.

Brody, E.M. 1966. The aging family. *Gerontology* 6(2): 201–6.

———. 1970. The etiquette of filial behavior. *Aging and Human Development* 1: 70–84.

———. 1979. Aged parents and aging children. In *Aging parents,* ed. P. Ragan. Los Angeles: University of Southern California Press.

———. 1981. "Women in the middle" and family help to older people. *Gerontologist* 21(5): 471–79.

———. 1985. Parent care as a normative family stress. *Gerontologist* 25(1): 19–29.

Brody, E., and Spark, G.M. 1966. Institutionalization of the elderly: A family crisis. *Family Process* 5(1): 76–90.

Brody, S.; Poulschock, W.; and Maschiocchi, C. 1978. The family caring unit: A major consideration in the long-term support system. *Gerontologist* 18(6): 556–61.

Brotman, H. 1982. *Every ninth American.* Prepared for House Select Committee on Aging. 97th Cong. Committee Publication no. 97-332.

Brown, B.W. 1980. Wife employment, marital equality, and husband-wife violence. In *The social causes of husband-wife violence,* ed. M.A. Straus and G. Hotaling. Minneapolis: University of Minnesota Press.

Brown, J.A., and Daniels, R. 1968. Some observations on abusive parents. *Child Welfare* 47(2): 89–94.

Browne, A. 1987. *When battered women kill.* New York: Free Press.

Browning, D.H., and Boatman, B. 1977. Incest: Children at risk. *American Journal of Psychiatry* 134(1): 69–72.

Brownmiller, S. 1975. *Against our will: Men, women, and rape.* New York: Simon and Schuster.

Broy, E.M. 1979. Women's changing roles, the aging family, and long-term care of older people. *National Journal* 11: 1828–33.

Bryant, H.D. 1963. Physical abuse of children: An agency study. *Child Welfare* 42(1): 125–30.

Buehler, C.J. 1981. Counseling the romantic. *Family Relations* 30(3): 452–8.

Bullough, V.L. 1974. *The subordinate sex: A history of attitudes toward women.* Baltimore: Penguin.

Bulter, S. 1978. *Conspiracy of silence: The trauma of incest.* San Francisco: New Guide Publications.

Burgess, A.W.; Groth, N.; Holmstrom, L.L.; and Sgroi, S.M., eds. 1978. *Sexual assault of children and adolescents.* Lexington, Mass.: Lexington Books.

Burgess, A.W., and Holmstrom, L.L. 1977. Child sexual assault by a family member: Decisions following disclosure. *Victimology:* 2(3): 236–50.

———. 1978. The child and family during the court process. In *Sexual Assault of children and adolescents,* ed. A.W. Burgess, A.N. Goth, L.L. Holmstrom, and S.M. Sgroi. Lexington, Mass.: Lexington Books.

Burgess, A.W.; Holmstrom, L.L.; and McCausland, M.P. 1977. Child sexual assault by a family member: Decisions after disclosure. *Victimology* 2(2): 236–50.

———. 1978. Divided loyalty in incest cases. In *Sexual assault of children and adolescents,* ed. A.W. Burgess, A.N. Goth, L.L. Holmstrom, and S.M. Sgroi. Lexington, Mass.: Lexington Books.

Burke, R.J., and Weir, T. 1976. Relationship of wives' employment status to husband, wife, and pair satisfaction performance. *Journal of Marriage and the Family* 29(3): 325–36.

Burnside, I.M. 1971. Long-term group work with the hospitalized aged. *Gerontologist* 11(3): 231–18.

Burr, J.J. 1982. *Protective services for adults.* Publication no. 82–20505. Washington, D.C.

Burston, G.R. 1975. Granny battering. *British Medical Journal* 3: 5983–92.

———. 1978. Do your elderly parents live in fear of being battered. *Modern Geriatrics* 11.

Burt, M.R., and Balyeat, R. 1973. A new system for improving the care of neglected and abused children. *Child Welfare* 53(3): 167–79.

Burt, M.R., and Blair, L.H. 1971. *Options for improving the care of neglected and dependent children.* Washington, D.C.: Urban Institute.

Burton, R.V. 1973. Folk theory and the incest taboo. *Ethos* 1: 504–16.

Busch, R.D., and Gundlach, J. 1977. Excess access and incest: A new look at the demographic explanation of the incest taboo. *American Anthropologist* 79 (December): 912–14.

Butler, R.N. 1963. The life review: An interpretation of reminiscence in the aged. *Psychiatry* 26: 65–76.

———. 1975. *Why survive: Being old in America.* New York: Harper and Row.

Butler, R., and Lewis, M. 1973. *Aging and mental health: Positive psychosocial approaches.* St. Louis: C.V. Mosby.

———. 1977. *Aging and mental health.* 2d ed. St. Louis: C.V. Mosby.

Butz, R.A. 1985. Reporting child abuse and confidentiality in counseling. *Social Casework* 66(1): 83–90.

Bybee, R. 1979. Violence toward youth. *Journal of Social Issues* 35(1): 1–14.

Caballin, H. 1966. Incestuous fathers: A clinical report. *American Journal of Psychiatry* 122(10): 1132–38.

Caldwell, S. 1963. There is a child. *Child Welfare* 42(3): 111.

Calhoun, L.G.; Selby, J.W.; and Warring, L.J. 1976. Social perception of the victim's causal role in rape: An exploratory examination of four factors. *Human Relations* 29(6): 517–26.

California Department of Justice. 1979. *Handbook on domestic violence.* Los Angeles: California Office of the Attorney General Crime Prevention Unit.

Calvert, R. 1974. Criminal and civil liability in husband-wife assaults. In *Violence in the family,* ed. S. Steinmetz and M.A. Straus. New York: Dodd, Mead.

Cameron, J.M., and Rae, L.J. 1975. *Atlas of the battered child syndrome.* London: Churchill Livingston.

Campbell, R.V. 1983. In-home parent training . . . An ecobehavioral approach to prevent child abuse. *Journal of Behavioral and Experimental Psychiatry* 14: 147–54.

Cannavale, F. 1976. *Witness cooperation.* New York: Lexington Press.

Cantoni, L. 1981. Clinical issues in domestic violence. *Social Casework* 62(1): 3–12.

Cantwell, H.B. 1978. *Standard of child neglect.* Denver: Department of Social Services.

———. 1981. Sexual abuse of children in Denver, 1979: Reviewed with implications for pediatric intervention and possible prevention. *Child Abuse and Neglect* 8: 75–85.

Caplan, P. 1984. The myth of women's masochism. *American Psychologist* 39: 130–9.

Caplan, G., and Killiea, M. 1976. *Support systems and mutual help.* New York: Grune and Stratton.

Carleson, C.L. 1984. Peer assessment of the social behavior of accepted, rejected, and neglected children. *Journal of Abnormal Child Psychology* 12: 189–98.

Carlson, B.E. 1977. Battered women and their assailants. *Social Work* 22(4): 455–60.

———. 1984. Causes and maintenance of domestic violence: An ecological analysis. *Social Service Review* 58(4): 569–87.

Carroll, J.C. 1977. The intergenerational transmission of family violence: The long-term effects of aggressive behavior. *Aggressive Behavior* 3: 289–99.

Carrozza, P., and Heirsteiner, C.L. 1983. Young female incest victims in treatment: Stages of growth seen with a group art therapy model. *Clinical Social Work Journal* 10(1): 165–75.

Carruthers, E.A. 1973. The net of incest. *Yale Review* 63: 211–27.

Cavan, R. 1956. Family tensions between the old and the middle-aged. *Marriage and Family Living* 18(2): 323–7.

Cazenave, N.A. 1983. Elder abuse and black Americans: Incidence, correlates, treatment, and prevention. In *Abuse and maltreatment of the elderly: Causes and interventions,* ed. J.I. Kosberg. Boston: John Wright, PSG.

Cazenave, N.A., and Strauss, M.A. 1979. Race, class, network embeddedness, and family violence: A search for potent support systems. *Journal of Comparative Family Studies* 10(2): 281–300.

Chapman, J.R. 1978. Economics of women's victimization. In *Victimization of women,* ed. J.R. Chapman and M. Gates. Beverly Hills, Calif.: Sage Publications.

Chapman, J.R., and Gates, M. 1977. *Women into wives: The legal and economic impact of marriage.* Beverly Hills, Calif.: Sage Publications.

———. eds. 1978. *The victimization of women.* Beverly Hills, Calif.: Sage Publications.

Chen, P.N.; Bell, S.; Dolinsky, D.; Doyle, J.; and Dunn, M. 1981. Elderly abuse in domestic settings: A pilot study. *Journal of Gerontological Social Work* 4: 3–17.

Chesser, E. 1952. *Cruelty to children.* New York: Philosophical Library.

Chimbos, P.D. 1978. *Marital violence: A study of interspouse homicide.* Palo Alto, Calif.: R and E Research.

Christy, D.W. 1972. Child abuse—a protective service responsibility. In *Proceedings of a national symposium on child abuse.* Denver: American Humane Association, Children's Division.

———. 1975. Marshaling community resources for prevention of child neglect and abuse. In *Proceedings of the fourth national symposium on child abuse.* Denver: American Humane Association, Children's Division.

Cicirelli, V.G. 1986. The helping relationship and family neglect in later life. In *Elder abuse: Conflict in the family,* ed. K.A. Pillemer and R.S. Wolf. Dover, Mass.: Auburn House.

Clark, H.H. 1963. *The law of domestic relations in the United States.* Saint Paul: West.

Clark, M. 1969. Cultural values and dependency in later life. In *The dependencies of old people, occasional papers in gerontology no. 6,* ed. R.A. Kalish. Ann Arbor: University of Michigan, Institute on Gerontology.

Clark, N.M., and Rakowski, W. 1983. Family caregivers of older adults: Improving helping skills. *Gerontologist* 23(6): 637–42.

Clark, S.M., and Lewis, D.J. 1977. *Rape: The price of coercive sexuality.* Toronto: Women's Education Press.

Coates, C.J., and Leong, D.J. 1980. *Conflict and communication for women and men in battering relationships.* Washington, D.C.: U.S. Department of Justice, Law Enforcement Assistance Administration.

Cohen, E.S. 1974. An overview for long-term care facilities. In *A social work guide for long-term care facilities,* ed. E.M. Body. Rockville, Md.: National Institute of Mental Health.

Cohen, E.S., and Gans, B.M. 1978. *The other generation gap: The middle aged and their aging parents.* Chicago: Follett.

Cohen, S.J., and Sussman, A. 1975. The incidence of child abuse in the United States. *Child Welfare* 54(6): 432–43.

Cohn, A.H. 1979. Effective treatment of child abuse and neglect. *Social Work* 24(4): 513–9.

Cohn, A.H.; Ridge, S.; and Collingnon, F. 1975. Evaluating innovative treatment programs. *Children Today* 4(3).

Coleman, K.H. 1980. Factors affecting conjugal violence. *Journal of Psychology* 105: 197–202.

Collins, A., and Pancoast, D.L. 1976. *Natural helping networks: A strategy for prevention.* Washington, D.C.: National Association of Social Workers.

Collins, M., and La France, A.B. 1982. *Improving the protective services of older Americans: Social worker role.* Portland, Maine: University of Southern Maine, Human Services Development Institute, Center for Research and Advanced Study.

Comfort, R. 1985. Sex, strangers, and safety. *Child Welfare* 64(4): 541–45.

Conrad, M., and Thomas, J. 1985. The family stress team approach and curbing domestic violence. *Police Chief* 52: 66–67.

Consortium for Elder Abuse Prevention. 1983. *Protocols.* San Francisco: Mount Zion Hospital and Medical Center.

Conte, J. 1984. Progress in treating the sexual abuse of children. *Social Work* 29(2): 258–63.

Conte, J., and Berliner, L. 1981. Sexual abuse of children: Implications for practice. *Social Casework* 62(5): 601–6.

Cook, F.L.; Skogan, W.G.; Cook, T.D.; and Antunes, G.E. 1978. Criminalization of the elderly: The physical and economic consequences. *Gerontologist* 18(2): 338–49.

Cook, M.J. 1976. Battered wives and the law. *Law Society Gazette* 73: 123.

Corfman, E. 1979. Family violence and child abuse. Rockville, Md.: NCJRS Microfiche Program.

Cormier, B.M. 1962. Psychodynamics of homicide committed in a marital relationship. *Corrective Psychiatry and Journal of Society Therapy* 8: 187–94.

Cormier, B.; Kennedy, M.; and Sancowicz, J. 1973. Psychodynamics of father-daughter incest. In *Deviance and the family,* ed. C.D. Bryant and J. Gipson. Philadelphia: F.A. Davis.

Costin, L. 1972. *Child welfare: Policies and practice.* New York: McGraw-Hill.

Coughlin, B.J. 1979. *The rights of children.* In *Children's rights: Contemporary perspectives,* ed. P.A. Vardin and I.N. Brody. New York: Teachers College Press.

Coulborn, K. 1981. The role of social workers in multidisciplinary collaboration. In *Social work with abused and neglected children,* ed. K.C. Faller. New York: Free Press.

Coult, A.D. 1963. Causality and cross-sex prohibition. *American Anthropologist* 65: 266–67.

Court, J. 1969. Battering parents. *Social Work* 26(1): 20–24.

Courtois, C.A. 1979. The incest experience and its aftermath. *Victimology* 4(2): 337–47.

———. 1979. Victims of rape and incest. *Counseling Psychologist* 8: 38–40.

CPSIS users guide. 1979. Richmond: Virginia Department of Welfare.

Crittenden, P.M. 1985. Maltreated infants: Vulnerability and resilience. *Journal of Child Psychology* 26: 85–86.

Cromwell, J.C., and Perkins, E.A. 1969. The battered child—dilemmas in management. *Medical Social Work* 22(5): 160–68.

Crossman, L.; London, C.; and Barry, C. 1981. Older women caring for disabled spouses: A model for supportive services. *Gerontologist* 21(5): 464–70.

Crouse, J.S.; Cobb, D.C.; Harris, B.B.; Kopecky, F.J.; and Poertner, J. 1981. Abuse and neglect of the elderly in Illinois: Incidence and characteristics, legislation, and policy recommendations. Springfield: Illinois Department of Aging. Manuscript.

Crowley, C.J.; Jordan, J.; Iperen, L.; and Vennard, P. 1978. Physically abused women and their families—the need for community services: Program development guide. Trenton: New Jersey Department of Human Services.

Crystall, S. 1986. Social policy and elder abuse. In *Elder abuse: Conflict in the family,* ed. K.A. Pillemer and R.S. Wolf. Dover, Mass.: Auburn House.

Cutler, L. 1985. Counseling caregivers. *Generations, Quarterly Journal of the American Society on Aging* 10(1): 53–57.

D'Agostino, P.A. 1972. Dysfunctioning families and child abuse: The need for an interagency effort. *Public Welfare* 30(4): 14–17.

Dahl, T.S. 1975. Violence of privacy. *Acta Sociologica* 18: 269–73.

Dale, P.; Davies, M.; Morrison, T.; and Waters, J. 1986. *Dangerous families: Assessment and treatment of child abuse.* New York: Tavistock.

Daly, M. 1978. *Gynecology: The metaethics of radical feminism.* Boston: Beacon Press.

Daniels, R. 1977. Battered women—the role of women's aid refuges. *Social Work Today* 9(12): 10–13.

Daugherty, M.K. 1979. The crime of incest against the minor child and the states' statutory responses. *Journal of Family Law* 17: 93–115.

Davidson, T. 1978. *Conjugal crime: Understanding and changing the wife-beating pattern.* New York: Hawthorn Books.

Davies, J. 1965. When the agency must intervene. *Public Welfare* 23(2): 102–5.

Davoren, E. 1975. Foster placement of abused children. *Children Today,* 4(3).

———. 1975. Working with abusive parents—a social worker's view. *Children Today* 4(3).

Day, L.E. 1978. Technical assistance project—domestic violence. Chicago: Illinois Law Enforcement Commission.

DeCrow, K. 1974. *Sexist justice.* New York: Random House.

DeFrancis, V. n.d. *The court and protective services.* Denver: American Humane Association, Children's Division.

———. 1955. *The fundamentals of child protection.* Denver: American Humane Association, Children's Division.

———. 1957. Accent on prevention. Denver: American Humane Association: Children's Division.

———. 1957. *Child protective services.* Denver: American Humane Association: Children's Division.

———. 1958. *Special skills in child protective services.* Denver: American Humane Association: Children's Division.

———. 1960. *Children who were helped.* Denver: American Humane Association: Children's Division.

———. 1961. *Protective services and community expectations.* Denver: American Humane Association: Children's Division.

———. 1963. *Child abuse—preview of a nationwide survey.* Denver: American Humane Association: Children's Division.

———. 1965. *Protecting the child victim of sex crimes committed by adults.* Denver: American Humane Association: Children's Division.

———. 1967. Child abuse—the legislative response. *Denver Law Journal* 44(1): 3–41.

———. 1971. *The status of child protective services—a national assessment.* Denver: American Humane Association: Children's Division.

———. 1972. Protecting the abused child—a coordinated approach. Paper presented at a national symposium on child abuse. Denver: American Humane Association: Children's Division.

———. 1975. Child protection—a comprehensive coordinated process. In *Proceedings of the fourth national symposium on child abuse.* Denver: American Humane Association: Children's Division.

DeFrancis, V., and Lucht, J.D. 1974. *Child abuse legislation in the 1970s.* Denver: American Humane Association: Children's Division.

Deighton, J. 1985. Group treatment: Adult victims of childhood sexual abuse. *Social Casework* 66(3): 403–10.

Delaney, J. 1972. Problems in court processing of abuse. In *Proceedings of a national symposium on child abuse.* Denver: American Humane Association: Children's Division.

——. 1975. The legal process—a positive force in the interests of children. In *Proceedings of the fourth national symposium on child abuse.* Denver: American Humane Association: Children's Division.

Delson, N. 1981. Group therapy with sexually molested children. *Child Welfare* 60(1): 175–82.

Delsordo, J.D. 1963. Protective casework for abused children. *Children* 10 (November–December): 213–8.

Demott, B. 1980. The pro-incest lobby. *Psychology Today* 13: 11–12, 15–16.

Denzin, N.K. 1984. Toward a phenomenology of domestic family violence. *American Journal of Sociology* 90(3): 483–513.

DePanfilis, D. 1982. Clients who refer themselves to child protective services. *Children Today* 11(1):21–25.

Dervin, D. 1982. Father-daughter incest. *Journal of Psychohistory* 10: 85–90.

Deschner, J.P. 1984. *The hitting habit: Anger control for battering couples.* New York: Free Press.

DeSilva, W. 1981. Some cultural and economic factors leading to neglect, abuse, and violence in respect to children within the family in Sri Lanka. *Child Abuse and Neglect* 5(3): 391–405.

DeYoung, M. 1982. Innocent seducer or innocently seduced? The role of the child incest victim. *Journal of Clinical Child Psychology* 11: 56–60.

——. 1984. Counterphobic behavior in multiple molested children. *Child Welfare* 63(3): 333–39.

Ditson, J., and Shay, S. 1984. Use of a home-based computer to analyze community data from reported cases of child abuse and neglect. *Child Abuse and Neglect* 8: 503–9.

Dobash, R.E. 1979. *Violence against wives: A case against the patriarch.* Riverside, N.J.: Free Press.

Dobash, R.E., and Dobash R.P. 1977. Love, honour, and obey: Institutional ideologies and the struggle for battered women. *Contemporary Crises* 1(4): 403–15.

——. 1977. Wife beating—still a common form of violence. *Social Work Today* 9(12): 14–17.

——. 1977–78. Wives: The appropriate victims of marital violence. *Victimology* 2(3/4): 426–42.

——. 1979. *Violence against wives: A case against the patriarchy.* New York: Free Press.

——. 1981. Community response to violence against wives: Chivalry, abstract justice, and patriarchy. *Social Problems* 28(4): 563–74.

Dolor, R.; Hendricks, J.; Meagher, M.S. 1986. Police practices and attitudes toward domestic violence. *Journal of Police Science and Administration* 14: 187–92.

Douglas, R.L., and Hickey, T. 1983. Domestic neglect and abuse of the elderly: Research findings and a systems perspective for service delivery planning. In *Abuse and maltreatment of the elderly: Causes and interventions,* ed. J.I. Kosberg, Boston: John Wright, PSG.

Douglas, R.L.; Hickey, T.; and Noel, C. 1980. *A study of maltreatment of the elderly and other vulnerable adults.* Final report to the U.S. Administration on

Aging and the Michigan Department of Social Services. University of Michigan, Institute of Gerontology.

Douglass, R.L., and Ruby-Douglass, P.A. 1988. Emergency medical response to domestic abuse and neglect of the elderly. In *Management of the physically and emotionally abused,* ed. G.R. Braen. San Diego: Appleton-Century-Crofts.

Dowd, J.J., and Bengston, L.L. 1978. Aging in minority populations: An examination of the double jeopardy hypothesis. *Journal of Gerontology* 33: 427–36.

Drabble, J.J. 1980. *The middle ground.* Toronto: Bantam Books.

Dreas, G.A. 1980. The male battered: A model treatment program for the courts. *Federal Probation* 46(1): 50–55.

Dubanoski, R.A. 1981. Child maltreatment in European and Hawaiian Americans. *Child Abuse and Neglect* 5: 457–65.

Dubanoski, R.A., and McIntosh, S.R. 1984. Child abuse and neglect in military and civilian families. *Child Abuse and Neglect* 8: 55–67.

Dubanoski, R.A., and Snyder, K. 1980. Patterns of child abuse and neglect in Japanese and Samoan Americans. *Child Abuse and Neglect* 4: 217–25.

Duberman, L. 1975. *Gender and sex in society.* New York: Praeger.

Dupont, R.L., Jr., and Gruenbaum, H. 1968. Willing victim: The husbands of paranoid women. *American Journal of Psychiatry* 125(1): 152–59.

Dutton, D. 1981. Traumatic bonding: The development of emotional attachments in battered women and other relationships of intermittent abuse. *Victimology* 6(1–4): 139–55.

———. 1987. *The domestic assault of women.* Boston: Allyn and Bacon.

Dworkin, R.J. 1979. Ideology formation: A linear structural model of the influences on feminist ideology. *Sociological Quarterly* 20(3): 345–58.

Dyer, E.D. 1963. Parenthood as crisis: A re-study. *Marriage and Family Living* 25(1): 196–201.

Eaddy, V.B. 1981. Play with a purpose: Interviewing abused and neglected children. *Public Welfare* 39(1): 43–47.

Easton, B. 1983. Feminism and the contemporary family. In *Everyday family life,* ed. B.J. Vander Mey, R.L. Neff, and D.H. Demo. Minneapolis: Burgess.

Ebeling, N., and Hill, D. 1975. *Child abuse: Intervention and treatment.* Boston: Publishing Sciences Group.

Ebersole, P., and Hess, P.A. 1981. *Toward healthy aging: Human needs and nursing response.* St. Louis: C.V. Mosby.

Eisenberg, A.D., and Seymour, E.J. 1978. The self-defense plea and battered women. *Trial* 14(7): 34–42.

Eisenberg, L. 1981. Cross cultural and historical perspectives on child abuse and neglect. *Child Abuse and Neglect* 5: 299–308.

Eisenberg, S.E., and Michlow, P.L. 1974. The assaulted wife: Catch 22 revisited. *Women's Rights Law Reporter* 3(1): 138–61.

Eist, H.I., and Mandel, A. 1968. Family treatment of ongoing incest behavior. *Family Process* 7: 216–32.

Elbow, M. 1977. Theoretical considerations of violent marriages. *Social Casework* 58: 515–26.

———. 1980. *Patterns in family violence.* New York: Family Service Association of America.

Eldeson, J.L. 1985. Men who batter women. *Journal of Family Issues* 6(2): 229–47.

Eldridge, A. 1985. Applications of self-psychology to the problem of child abuse. *Clinical Social Work Journal* 13: 50–61.

Elliott, F. 1977. The neurology of explosive rage: The dyscontrol syndrome. In *Battered women,* ed. M. Roy. New York: Van Nostrand Reinhold.

Elmer, E. 1966. Hazards in determining child abuse. *Child Welfare* 45(1): 28–33.

———. 1967. *Children in jeopardy: A study of abused minors and their families.* Pittsburg: University of Pittsburg Annual Reviews.

———. 1967. Developmental characteristics of abused children. *Pediatrics* 40(4): 596–609.

———. 1975. A social worker's assessment of medical-social stress in child abuse cases. In *Proceedings of the fourth national symposium on child abuse.* Denver: American Humane Association, Children's Division.

Emslie, G.J. 1983. Incest reported by children and adolescents hospitalized for severe psychiatric problems. *American Journal of Psychiatry* 140(8): 708–11.

Englehard, P.A. 1976. Trends in counselor attitude about women's roles. *Journal of Counseling Psychology* 23(4): 365–72.

English, R.W. 1980. *Elder abuse.* Philadelphia: Franklin Research Center.

Epstein, N.B., and Bishop, D.S. Problem-centered system therapy of the family. *Journal of Marital Family Therapy* 7: 23–31.

Erchak, G.M. 1981. The escalation and maintenance of child abuse: A cybernetic model. *Child Abuse and Neglect* 5: 153–57.

Fagan, J.A.; Stewart, D.K.; and Hansen, K.V. 1983. Violent men or violent husbands? In *The dark side of families,* ed. D. Finkelhor, R. Gelles, G. Hotaling, and M. Straus. Beverly Hills, Calif.: Sage Publications.

Fairorth, J.W. 1982. *Child abuse and the school.* Palo Alto, Calif.: R and E Research Association.

Faller, K.C. 1981. *Social work with abused and neglected children.* New York: Free Press.

———. 1984. Is the child victim of sexual abuse telling the truth? *Child Abuse and Neglect* 8: 473–81.

Farrar, M. 1955. Mother-daughter conflicts extended into later life. *Social Casework* 36(2): 202–7.

Farrington, D.P. 1980. *Stress and family violence.* In *The social causes of husband-wife violence,* ed. M.A. Straus and G. Hotaling. Minneapolis: University of Minnesota Press.

Farrow, R.G. 1972. Our abuse of children. In *Proceedings of the national symposium on child abuse.* Denver: American Humane Association, Children's Division.

Farson, R. 1979. The children's rights movement. In *The future of children and juvenile justice,* ed. L.T. Empry. Charlottesville: University of Virginia Press.

Fattah, E.A. 1984. Victim's response to confrontational victimization. *Crime and Delinquency* 30(1): 75–89.

Faulk, M. 1976. Sexual factors in marital violence. *Medical Aspects of Human Sexuality* 11(10): 30–43.

Feldman-Summers, S., and Edgar, M. 1979. Childhood molestation: Variables related to differential impacts on psychosexual functioning in adult women. *Journal of Abnormal Psychology* 88: 407–17.

Ferraro, K.J., and Johnson, J.M. 1983. How women experience battering: The process of victimization. *Social Problems* 30(2): 325–39.

Fields, M. 1978. Does this vow include wife beating? *Human Rights* 7(2): 40–45.

———. 1977–78. Wife-beating: Facts and figures. *Victimology* 2(3–4): 643–47.

Fields, M., and Fields, H. 1973. Marital violence and the criminal process: Neither justice nor peace. *Social Service Review* 47(2): 221–40.

Finkelhor, D. 1978. Psychological, cultural, and family factors in incest and family sexual abuse. *Journal of Marriage and Family Counseling* 4: 41–49.

———. 1978. Social forces in the formulation of the problems of sexual abuse. Family Violence Research Program Paper V55. Durham: University of New Hampshire.

———. 1979. *Sexually victimized children.* New York: Free Press.

———. 1979. What's wrong with sex between adults and children? *American Journal of Orthopsychiatry* 49(6): 692–97.

———. 1980. Risk factors in the sexual victimization of children. *Child Abuse and Neglect* 4: 265–73.

———. 1980. Sexual socialization in America: High risk for sexual abuse. In *Childhood and sexuality,* ed. J. Sampon. Montreal: Éditions Études Vivantes.

———. 1983. Common gestures of family abuse. In *The dark side of families,* ed. D. Finkelhor, R. Gelles, G. Hotaling, and M. Straus. Beverly Hills, Calif.: Sage Publications.

———. 1984. *Child sexual abuse: New research and theory.* New York: Free Press.

———. 1984. How widespread is child sexual abuse? *Children Today* 13(1): 18–20.

———. 1985. Sexual abuse and physical abuse: Some critical differences. In *Unhappy families,* ed. E.H. Newberger and R.B. Bourne. Littleton, Mass.: PSG.

———. 1985. The traumatic impact of child sexual abuse. *American Journal of Orthopsychiatry* 55(5): 530–41.

Finkelhor, D.; Gelles, R.J.; Hotaling, G.T.; and Murray, A.S., eds. 1983. *The dark side of families: Current family violence research.* Beverly Hills, Calif.: Sage Publications.

Finkelhor, D., and Hotaling, G.T. 1984. Sexual abuse in the national incidence study of child abuse and neglect. *Child Abuse and Neglect* 8:23–33.

Finkelhor, D., and Yllo, K. 1983. Rape in marriage: A sociological view. In *The dark side of families,* ed. D. Finkelhor, R.J. Gelles, G.T. Hotaling, and M.A. Straus. Beverly Hills, Calif.: Sage Publications.

Finley, B. 1984. The use of a battered women's shelter as a clinical agency for student learning. *Journal of Nursing Education* 23: 310–13.

Finely, G.E. 1983. Fear of crime in the elderly. In *Abuse and maltreatment of the elderly: Causes and interventions,* ed. J.I. Kosberg. Boston: John Wright, PSG.

Finn, J. 1985. Men's domestic-violence treatment groups. *Social Work with Groups* 8(3): 81–94.

———. 1985. The stresses and coping behavior of battered women. *Social Casework* 34(1): 1–9.

Fisher, R.A. 1963. *Statistical methods for research workers.* Edinburgh: Oliver and Boyd.

Flammang, C.J. 1970. *The police and the underprotected child.* Springfield, Ill.: Charles C. Thomas.

Fleming, J.B. 1979. *Stopping wife abuse.* Garden City, N.Y.: Anchor Press.

Flexner, B., and Baldwin, R.N. 1914. *Juvenile courts and probation.* New York: Century Press.

Flynn, J.P. 1977. Recent findings related to wife abuse. *Social Casework* 58(1): 13–20.

Fojtik, K.M. 1978. The NOW domestic violence project. *Victimology* 2(4): 653–57.

Fontana, V.J. 1966. An insidious and disturbing medical entity. *Public Welfare* 24(3): 235–9.

———. 1984. When systems fail: Protecting the victim of child sexual abuse. *Children Today* 13(1): 14–18.

Fontana, V.J., and Besharov, D.J. 1977. *The maltreated child.* Springfield, Ill.: Charles C. Thomas.

Ford, D.A. 1983. Wife battery and criminal justice—victim decision making. *Family Relations* 32(4): 463–76.

Forer, L.G. 1979. Rights of children: The legal vacuum. In *Children's right: Contemporary perspectives,* ed. P.A. Vardin and I.N. Brody. New York: Teachers College Press.

Forst, B.; Lucianovic, J.; and Cox, S. 1977. *What happens after arrest?* Washington, D.C.: Institute of Law and Social Research.

Fortune, M.M. 1983. *Sexual violence: The unmentionable sin.* Boston: Pilgrim Press.

Forward, S., and Buck, C. 1978. *Betrayal of innocence: Incest and its destruction.* New York: Penguin.

Foster, H.H. 1974. *"Bill of rights" for children.* Springfield, Ill.: Charles C. Thomas.

Fox, J.R. 1962. Sibling incest. *British Journal of Sociology* 13: 128–50.

Fox, R. 1980. *The red lamp of incest.* New York: E.P. Dutton.

Frances, V., and Frances, A. 1976. The incest taboo and family structure. *Family Process* 15(2): 235–44.

Frazer, G., and Kilbride, P.L. 1980. Child abuse and neglect—rare, but perhaps increasing, phenomena among the Samia of Kenya. *Child Abuse and Neglect* 4: 227–32.

Frederick, R.E. 1979. *Domestic violence: A guide for police response.* Harrisburg: Pennsylvania Coalition against Domestic Violence.

Freeman, M.D. 1979. Rape by a husband? *New Law Journal* 129(2): 332–33.

———. 1979. *Violence in the home.* Hants, England: Saxon House.

Friedman, S. 1972. *A psychiatrist's view of child abuse.* In *Proceedings of a national symposium on child abuse.* Denver: American Humane Association: Children's Division.

Friedrich, W.N. 1982. The abusing parent revisited, a decade of psychological research. *Journal of Nervous and Mental Disease* 170(4): 577–87.

Friedrich, W.N., and J.A. Boriskin. 1976. The role of the child in abuse. *American Journal of Orthopsychiatry* 46(6): 580–90.

Friedrich, W.N. and A.J. Einbender. 1983. The abused child: A psychological review. *Journal of Clinical Child Psychology* 12: 244–55.

Frieze, I. 1979. Perceptions of battered wives. In *New approaches to social problems,* ed. I. Frieze, D. Bar-Tal, and J.S. Carroll. San Francisco: Jossey-Bass.

Fritz, G.S. 1981. A comparison of males and females who were sexually molested as children. *Journal of Sex and Marital Therapy* 7: 54–59.

Froland, C.; Pancoast, D.; and Chapman, N. 1981. *Helping networks and human services.* Beverly Hills, Calif.: Sage Publications.

Frude, N., ed. 1981. *Psychological approaches to child abuse.* Totowa, N.J.: Rowman and Littlefield.

Furness, T. 1984. Organizing a therapeutic approach to intrafamilial child sexual abuse. *Journal of Adolescence* 7: 309–17.

Gage, M.J. 1889. *History of woman suffrage.* 2d ed. Rochester, N.J.: Sourcebook Press.

Gagnon, J.H. 1965. Female victims of sex offenses. *Social Problems* 12(2): 176–92.

Galbraith, M.W., and Zdorkowski, T. 1984. Teaching the investigation of elder abuse. *Journal of Gerontological Nursing* 10(12): 21–25.

Gallagher, U. 1973. Changing focus on services to teenagers. *Children Today* 2(5).

Gaquin, D.A. 1977–78. Spouse abuse: Data from the national crime survey. *Victimology* 2(3–4): 632–43.

Garbarino, J. 1976. A preliminary study of some ecological correlates of child abuse: The impact of socioeconomic stress on mothers. *Child Development* 47: 178–85.

———. 1977. The human ecology of child maltreatment: A conceptual model for research. *Journal of Marriage and the Family* 39(6): 721–35.

———. 1980. *Understanding abusive families.* Lexington, Mass.: Lexington Books.

Garbarino, J., and Crouter, A. 1978. Defining community context for parent-child relationships. *Child Development* 49: 604–16.

Garbarino, J., and Ebata, A. 1983. The significance of ethnic and cultural differences in child maltreatment. *Journal of Marriage and the Family* 45(6): 773–83.

Garbarino, J. and Gilliam, G. 1980. *Understanding abusive families.* Lexington, Mass.: Lexington Books.

Garbarino, J.; Guttmann, E.; and Seeley, J.W. 1986. *The psychologically battered child.* San Francisco: Jossey-Bass.

Garbarino, J., and Sherman, D. 1980. High-risk neighborhoods and high-risk families: The human ecology of child maltreatment. *Child Development* 51: 188–98.

Garbarino, J., and Stocking, S.H. 1980. *Protecting children from abuse and neglect.* San Francisco: Jossey-Bass.

Garber, J., and Seligman, M. 1980. *Learned helplessness: Theory and applications.* New York: Academic Press.

Garrett, T.B., and Wright, R. 1975. Wives of rapists and incest offenders. *Journal of Sex Research* 2: 149–57.

Garrison, J., and Howe, J. 1976. Community intervention with the elderly: A Social network approach. *Journal of the American Geriatric Society* 24(1).

Gayford, J. 1975. Battered wives. *Medicine and Science Law* 15(2): 237–45.

———. 1975. Wife battering: A preliminary survey of one-hundred cases. *British Medical Journal* 1: 194–97.

Geis, G. 1978. Rape-in-marriage: Law and law reform in England, the United States, and Sweden. *Adelaide Law Review* 6(6): 284–303.

Gelfand, D.E.; Olsen, J.K.; and Block, M.R. 1978. Two generations of elderly in the changing American family: Implications for family services. *Family Coordinator* 27(3): 395–411.

Gelinas, D.J. 1983. The persisting negative effects of incest. *Psychiatry* 46(3): 312–32.

Gellen, M.I. 1984. Abused and nonabused women: MMPI profile differences. *Personnel and Guidance Journal* 62: 601–4.

Geller, J. 1978. Reaching the battering husband. *Social Work with Groups* 1(1).

———. 1978. A treatment model for the abused spouse. *Victimology* 2(3/4): 627–32.

Gelles, R.J. 1972. *The violent home: A study of physical aggression between husbands and wives.* Beverly Hills, Calif.: Sage Publications.

———. 1974. Child abuse as psychopathology: A sociological critique and reformation. In *Violence in the family,* ed. S. Steinmetz. New York: Harper and Row.

———. 1976. Abused wives: Why do they stay? *Journal of Marriage and the Family* 38(5): 569–78.

———. 1977. No place to go: The social dynamics of marital violence. In *Battered women,* ed. M. Roy. New York: Van Nostrand Reinhold.

———. 1977. Power, sex, and violence: The case of marital rape. *Family Coordinator* 26(4): 9–14.

———. 1977. Violence and pregnancy. *Family Coordinator* 24(1): 81–86.

———. 1978. Violence toward children in the United States. *American Journal of Orthopsychiatry* 48(5): 580–92.

———. 1980. Violence in the family: A review of research in the seventies. *Journal of Marriage and the Family* 42(6): 873–85.

———. 1982. Applying research on family violence to clinical practice. *Journal of Marriage and the Family* 44(1): 9–20.

———. 1982. An exchange/social-control theory of interfamily violence. In *The dark side of families,* ed. D. Finkelhor, R. Gelles, G. Hotaling, and M. Straus. Beverly Hills, Calif.: Sage Publications.

———. 1985. Family violence: What we know and can do. In *Unhappy families,* ed. E.H. Newberger and R.B. Bourne. Littleton, Mass.: PSG.

———. 1987. *Family violence.* Beverly Hills, Calif.: Sage Publications.

Gelles, R.J., and Cornell, C. 1985. *Intimate violence in families.* Beverly Hills, Calif.: Sage Publications.

Gelles, R.J., and Straus, M.A. 1979. Determinants of violence in the family: Toward a theoretical integration. In *Contemporary theories about the family,* ed. W.R. Burr, R. Hill, F.I. Nye, and I.L. Reiss. New York: Free Press.

———. 1979. Violence in the American family. *Journal of Social Issues* 35(1): 15–39.

Gemmill, F.B. 1982. A family approach to the battered woman. *Journal of Psychosocial Nursing and Mental Health Services* 20(9): 22–39.

Gentemann, K.M. 1984. Wife beating: Attitudes of a nonclinical population. *Victimology* 9(1): 109–19.

Gentry, C.E. 1978. Incestuous abuse of children: The need for an objective view. *Child Welfare* 62(2): 355–64.

George, L.K. 1986. Care-giver burden: Conflict between norms of reciprocity and solidarity. In *Elder abuse: Conflict in the family,* ed. K.A. Pillemer and R.S. Wolf. Dover, Mass.: Auburn House.

Gesino, J.P.; Smith H.H.; and Keckich, W.A. 1982. The battered woman grows old. *Clinical Gerontologist* 1(1): 59–67.

Giarretto, H. 1976. Humanistic treatment of father-daughter incest. In *The family and the community,* ed. R. Helfer and H. Kempe. Cambridge, Mass.: Ballinger.

Giarretto, H.; Giarretto, A.; and Sgroi, S.M. 1978. Coordinated community treatment of incest. In *Sexual assault of children and adolescents,* ed. A.W. Burgess, A.N. Goth, L.L. Holmstrom, and S.M. Sgori. Lexington, Mass.: Lexington Books.

Gil, D.G. 1970. *Violence against children: Physical abuse in the United States.* Cambridge: Harvard University Press.

———. 1971. A sociocultural perspective on physical child abuse. *Child Welfare* 50(7): 389–95.

———. 1971. Violence against children. *Journal of Marriage and the Family* 33(4): 637–48.

———. 1977. Levels of manifestation, causal dimensions, and primary prevention. *Victimology* 2(3): 186–95.

———. 1979. Violence against children. In *Child abuse and violence,* ed. D.G. Gil. New York: AMS Press.

———. 1981. The United States versus child abuse. In *The social context of child abuse,* ed. L.H. Pelton. New York: Human Sciences Press.

———. 1984. Institutional abuse: Dynamics and prevention. *Catalyst* 4: 23–42.

———. 1985. The political and economic context of child abuse. In *Unhappy families,* ed. E.H. Newberger and R. Bourne. Littleton, Mass.: PSG.

Gil, D., and Noble, J. 1969. Public knowledge, attitudes, and opinion about physical child abuse in the United States. *Child Welfare* 48(7): 395–401.

Giles, R.J. 1982. Applying research on family violence to clinical practice. *Journal of Marriage and the Family* 44(1): 9–20.

Giles-Sims, J. 1983. *Wife battering, a systems-theory approach.* New York: Guilford.

———. 1985. A longitudinal study of the battered children of battered wives. *Family Relations* 34(2): 205–10.

Giles-Sims, J., and Finkelhor, D. 1984. Child abuse in step-families. *Family Relations* 33: 407–13.

Gilgum, J.F. 1985. Sex education and the prevention of child sexual abuse. *Journal of Sex Education and Theory* 11: 46–52.

Gillespie, D.L. 1971. Who has the power?: The marital struggle. *Journal of Marriage and the Family* 33(3): 445–58.

Gillum, I.S. 1980. Objective relations approach to the phenomenon and treatment of battered women. *Psychiatry* 43(2): 346–58.

Giordano, G.R., and Blakemore, P. 1984. *Elder abuse in New Jersey: The knowledge and experience of abuse among older New Jerseyans.* Trenton: New Jersey Department of Human Services.

Giovannoni, J. 1971. Parental mistreatment: Perpetrators and victims. *Journal of Marriage and the Family* 33(4): 649–57.

Giovannoni, J., and Billingsley, A. 1970. Child neglect among the poor: A study of parental adequacy in three ethnic groups. *Child Welfare* 49(4): 196–204.

Glasgow, J.M. 1980. The marital rape exemption: Legal sanction of spouse abuse. *Journal of Family Law* 18: 565–86.

Glasser, P., and Glasser, L. 1962. Role reversal and conflict between aged parents and their children. *Marriage and Family Living* 24: 46–51.

Glazer-Mablin, N. 1975. Old family, new family. *International Social Science Journal* 14: 507–26.

Golde, M. 1980. Federal programs provided housing assistance for battered women. *Journal of Housing* 37: 443–7.

Goldfarb, A. 1965. Psychodynamics and the three-generation family. In *Social structure and the family: Generational relations,* ed. E. Shanas and G.F. Streib. Englewood Cliffs, N.J.: Prentice-Hall.

Gondolf, E.W. 1985. *Men who batter: An integrated approach for stopping wife abuse.* Holmes Beach, Fla.: Learning Publications.

Goode, W. 1971. Force and violence in the family. *Journal of Marriage and the Family* 33(4): 624–36.

Gresham, M.L. 1976. The infantilization of the elderly: A developing concept. *Nursing Forum* 15: 195–210.

Guttmacher, M. 1960. *The mind of the murder.* New York: Farrar, Straus, and Giroux.

Hahn, P.H. 1976. *Crimes against the elderly: A study in victimology.* Santa Cruz, Calif.: David.

Halamandaris, V.L. 1983. Consequences of institutionalization of the aged. In *Abuse and maltreatment of the elderly: Causes and interventions,* ed. J.I. Kosberg. John Wright, PSG.

Hally, C.; Polansky, N.F.; and Polansky, N.A. 1980. *Child neglect: Mobilizing services.* Washington, D.C.: Government Printing Office.

Hammell, C.L. 1969. Preserving family life for children. *Child Welfare* 48(1): 591–4.

Hanks, S.E., and Rosenbaum, C.P. 1977. Battered women: A study of women who live with violent, alcohol-abusing men. *American Journal of Orthopsychiatry* 47(2): 291–306.

Harbert, A.S., and Ginsburg, L.H. 1979. *Human services for older adults: Concepts and skills.* Belmont, Calif.: Wadsworth.

Harrell, J.A. 1983. Federal dissemination of child-abuse and neglect information. *Children and Youth Services Review* 5: 65–74.

Havenmeyer, H. 1982. *Legal and social-work values in adult protection.* Lakewood, Calif.: Jefferson County Department of Social Services.

Hayes, C.L. 1984. Elder abuse and the utilization of support groups for the relatives of functionally disabled older adults. Catholic University of America, Center on Aging. Manuscript.

Heider, C.G. 1969. Anthropological models of incest laws in the United States. *American Anthropologist* 71: 693–701.

Helfer, R. n.d. *The diagnostic process and treatment programs.* Washington, D.C.: U.S. Department of Health, Education and Welfare.

———. 1975. Why most physician's don't get involved in child-abuse cases. *Children Today* 4(3): 64–78.

Helfer, R., and Kempe, C.H. 1968. *The battered child.* Chicago: University of Chicago Press.

Henderson, D.J. 1980. Incest: A synthesis of data. In *Traumatic abuse and neglect of children at home,* ed. G.J. Williams and J. Money. Baltimore: Johns Hopkins University Press.

Henderson, J. 1981. Using experts and victims in the sentencing process. *Criminal Law Bulletin* 17(3): 226–33.

Hendricks-Matthews, M. 1982. The battered woman: Is she ready for help? *Social Casework* 63(1): 131–7.

Heppner, M.J. 1978. Counseling the battered wife: Myths, facts, and decisions. *Personnel and Guidance Journal* 56: 522–5.

Hepworth, P. 1975. Looking at baby battering: Its detection and treatment. *Canadian Welfare* 4(3): 33–46.

Herman, D.M. 1985. A statutory proposal to prohibit the infliction of violence upon children. *Family Law Quarterly* 19: 1–54.

Herman, J. 1981. *Father-daughter incest.* Cambridge: Harvard University Press.

———. 1983. Recognition and treatment of incestuous families. *International Journal of Family Therapy* 5: 81.

Herman, J., and Lirschman, L. 1977. Father-daughter incest. *Signs: An International Journal of Women in Culture and Society* 2: 735–56.

Herr, J.H., and Weakland, J.H. 1978. The family as a group. In *Working with the elderly groups: Processes and techniques,* ed. I.M. Burnside. North Scituate, Mass.: Duxbury.

Herre, E.A. 1965. A community mobilizes to protect its children. *Public Welfare* 23(2): 93–98.

Herrenkohl, R.C. 1983. Circumstances surrounding the occurrence of child maltreatment. *Journal of Consulting and Clinical Psychology* 51: 424–31.

Hershorn, M., and Rosenbaum, A. 1985. Children of marital violence: A closer look at the unintended victims. *American Journal of Orthopsychiatry* 55(2): 260–66.

Hickey, T., and Douglass, R.L. 1981. Mistreatment of the elderly in the domestic setting. *American Journal of Public Health* 71(4): 500–7.

———. 1981. Neglect and abuse of older family members: Professionals' perspectives and case experience. *Gerontologist* 21(4): 171–6.

Higgins, J.G. 1978. Social services for abused wives. *Social Casework* 59(2): 266–71.

Hilberman, E.C. 1980. The wife-beater's wife reconsidered. *American Journal of Psychiatry* 137(11): 1336–47.

Hilberman, E., and Munson, K. 1977–78. Sixty battered women. *Victimology* 2(3/4): 460–70.

Hill, E. 1985. *The family secret: A personal account of incest.* Santa Barbara, Calif.: Capra Press.

Hindelang, M. 1976. *Criminalization in eight American cities: A descriptive analysis of common theft and assault.* Cambridge, Mass.: Ballinger.

Hindman, M.H. 1979. Family violence: An overview. *Alcohol Health and Research* 4(1): 1–11.

Hirsch, M. 1981. *Women and violence.* New York: Van Nostrand Reinhold.

Hobbes, T. 1977. The citizen. In *Man and citizens,* ed. T.S.K. Scott-Craig and B. Gert. Gloucester, Mass.: Peter Smith.

Hoel, H. 1973. Child protective services—a public responsibility. In *Proceedings of the second national symposium on child abuse.* Denver: American Humane Association, Children's Division.

Hoffman, E. 1979. Policy and politics: The child abuse prevention and treatment act. In *Critical perspectives on child abuse,* ed. R. Bourne. Lexington, Mass.: Lexington Books.

Holmes, S.A. 1981. A holistic approach to the treatment of violent families. *Social Casework* 62(10): 594–600.

Holter, J.C. 1968. Principals of management in child-abuse cases. *American Journal of Orthopsychiatry* 38(1): 127–36.

———. 1972. A medical social worker's view of child abuse. In *Proceedings of the national symposium on child abuse.* Denver: American Humane Association, Children's Division.

Holter, J.C., and Friedman, S.B. 1968. Child abuse: Early case findings in the emergency department. *Pediatrics* 42(1): 128–38.

Hooker, S. 1976. *Caring for elderly people: Understanding and practical help.* London: Routledge and Kegan Paul.

Hoorwitz, A.N. 1983. Guidelines for treating father-daughter incest. *Social Casework* 64(4): 515–24.

Hornung, C.A.; McCullough, B.C.; and Sugimoto, T. 1981. Status relationships in marriage: Risk factors in spouse abuse. *Journal of Marriage and the Family* 43(4): 657–96.

Hoshino, G., and Yoder, G.H. 1973. Administrative discretion in the implementation of child-abuse legislation. *Child Welfare* 52(7): 414–24.

Howze, D.C., and Kotch, J.B. 1984. Disentangling life-events stress and social support: Implications for the primary prevention of child abuse and neglect. *Child Abuse and Neglect* 8: 401–9.

Hudson, M.F. 1986. Elder mistreatment: Current research. In *Elder abuse: Conflict in the family,* ed. K.A. Pillemer and R.S. Wolf. Dover, Mass.: Auburn House.

Hudson, W.W. 1981. Assessment of spouse abuse: Two quantifiable dimensions. *Journal of Marriage and the Family* 43(5): 873–85.

Hughes, H.M. 1982. Brief interventions with children in a battered women's shelter. *Family Relations* 31(4): 495–502.

Hughes, H.M., and Barad, S.J. 1983. Psychological function of children in a battered women's shelter: A preliminary investigation. *American Journal of Orthopsychiatry* 53(5): 525–31.

Hurt, M., Jr. n.d. *Child abuse and neglect: A report on the status of the research.* Washington, D.C.: U.S. Department of Health, Education, and Welfare.

Hutchin, T. 1980. Battered women. In *Alternative social services for women,* ed. N. Gottlieb. New York: Columbia University Press.

Ireland, W. 1966. In a state-administered child welfare program. In *Community services on behalf of the abused child.* Denver: American Humane Association, Children's Division.

Jackson, J.J. 1977. Older black women. In *Looking ahead: A women's guide to the problems and joys of growing older,* ed. L.E. Trull, J. Israel, and K. Israel. Englewood Cliffs, N.J.: Prentice-Hall.

Jacobs, M. 1984. More than a million older Americans abused physically and mentally each year. *Perspectives on Aging* 13(6): 19–20, 30.

Jacobson, R. 1977. Battered women: The fight to end wife beating. *Civil Digest* 9: 2–11.

Jaffe, A.C.; Papovich, D.; and Biers, D. 1975. Sexual abuse of children. *American Journal of Disabled Children* 129(6): 689–92.

James, J. 1971. *Born to win.* Boston: Addison-Wesley.

James, J., and Meyerding, J. 1977. Early sexual experience as a factor in prostitution. *Archives of Sexual Behavior* 7: 31–42.

James, K.L. 1977. Incest: The teenager's perspective. *Psychotherapy: Theory, Research and Practice* 14: 146–55.

Jamsen, M.A., and Meyers-Abell, J. 1981. Assertive training for battered women: A pilot program. *Social Work* 26(1): 164–65.

Janeway, E. 1981. Incest: A rational look at the oldest taboo. *Ms.,* November, 61–64, 81, 109.

Jansen, R.H. 1977. Battered women and the law. *Victimology* 2(3/4): 585–90.

Jeffery, C.R. 1977. *Crime prevention through environmental design.* Beverly Hills, Calif.: Sage Publications.

Jeffords, C.R. 1981. *Demographic variations in attitudes toward marital rape immunity.* Huntsville, Tex.: Sam Houston State University.

———. 1982. Public attitudes toward criminal sanctions against forced marital intercourse. Paper presented at Academy of Criminal Justice Sciences Conference, March 1982 Louisville, Ky.

Johnson, B., and Morse, H.A. 1968. Injured children and their parents. *Children* 15(4): 147–52.

Johnson, C.L., and Catalano, D.J. 1983. A longitudinal study of family supports to impaired elderly. *Gerontologist* 23(6): 612–18.

Johnson, D. 1981. Abuse of the elderly. *Nurse Practitioner* (6): 29–34.

Johnson, E.S., and Bursk, B.J. 1977. Relationships between elderly and their adult children. *Gerontologist* 17(1): 90–96.

Johnson, J.M., ed. 1981. New research in family violence. *Journal of Family Issues* 2(4): 387–90.

Johnson, T. 1986. Critical issues in the definition of elder abuse. In *Elder abuse: Conflict in the family,* ed. K.A. Pillemer and R.S. Wolf. Dover, Mass.: Auburn House.

Johnson, W. 1984. Predicting the recurrence of child abuse. *Social Work Research and Abstracts* 20(1): 21–26.

Jones, A. 1981. *Women who kill.* New York: Fawcett Columbine.

Jones, B.; Jenstrom, L.L.; and MacFarlane, K., eds. 1980. *Sexual abuse of children: Selected readings.* Publication no. 78-30161. Washington, D.C.: U.S. Department of Health and Human Services; Administration for Children, Youth and Families. Children's Bureau National Center on Child Abuse and Neglect. November.

Jones, J.M. 1981. Reaching children at risk: A model for training child-welfare specialists. *Child Welfare* 60(1): 148–60.

Jones, M.A. 1981. Effective practice with families in protective and preventive services: What works? *Child Welfare* 60(1): 67–80.

Jouriles, E.N., and O'Leary, K.D. 1985. Interpersonal reliability of reports of marital violence. *Consulting Clinical Psychology* 53(1): 149–221.

Julian, V.; Mohr, C.; and Lapp, J. 1980. Father-daughter incest: A descriptive analysis. In *Sexual abuse of children: Implications for treatment,* ed. W.M. Holder. Denver: American Humane Association, Child Protective Division.

Junewice, W.J. 1983. A protective posture toward emotional neglect and abuse. *Child Welfare* 62(2): 243–52.

Justice, B., and Justice, R. 1976. *The abusing family.* New York: Human Sciences Press.

———. 1979. *The broken taboo: Sex in the family.* New York: Human Sciences Press.

Kadushim, A. 1978. Neglect—is it neglected too often? In *Child abuse and neglect: Issues on innovation and implementation,* vol. 1, ed. M.L. Lauderdale. Washington, D.C.: Government Printing Office.

Kahana, E., and Felton, B. 1977. Social context and personal need: A study of Polish and Jewish aged. *Journal of Social Issues* 33(4): 56–64.

Kalish, R. 1967. Children and grandfathers: A speculative essay on dependency. *Gerontologist* 7(1): 65–69, 79.

Kalmuss, D. 1979. The attribution of responsibility in a wife-abuse context. *Victimology* 4(2): 284–91.

———. 1984. The intergenerational transmission of marital aggression. *Marriage and Family* 46: 11–19.

Kalmuss, D.S., and Straus, M.A. 1982. Wife's marital dependency and wife abuse. *Journal of Marriage and the Family* 44(2): 277–86.

Kamerman, S.B. 1975. Crossnational perspectives on child abuse and neglect. *Children Today* 4(3).

Kanowitz, S. 1973. *Sex roles in law and society.* Albuquerque: University of New Mexico Press.

Kaplan, H.B. 1975. *Self-attitudes and deviant behavior.* Pacific Palisades, Calif.: Goodyear.

Kaplan, S.G. 1983. Survival skills for working with potentially violent clients. *Social Casework* 64(6): 339–52.

Kasl, S.V. 1972. Physical and mental-health effects of involuntary relocation and institutionalization of the elderly: A review. *American Journal of Public Health* 62(2): 377–84.

Kassel, V. 1983. A geriatrician's view of the health care of the elderly. In *Abuse and maltreatment of the elderly: Causes and interventions,* ed. J.I. Kosberg. Boston: John Wright, PSG.

Kastenbaum, R.S., and Candy, S. 1973. The 4 percent fallacy: A methodological and empirical critique of extended-care facility statistics. *Aging and Human Development* 4: 15–21.

Katz, K. 1979. Elder abuse. *Journal of Family Law* 18: 695–722.

Katz, S.N. 1975. Child neglect laws in America. *Family Law Quarterly* 9: 1–37.

Kaufman, I. 1954. The family constellation and overt incestuous relations between father and daughter. *American Journal of Orthopsychiatry* 24(2): 606–19.

———. 1962. Psychiatric implications of physical abuse of children. In *Protecting the battered child.* Denver: American Humane Association, Children's Division.

Kaufman, I.; Peck, A.L.; and Tagiuri, C.K. 1954. The family constellation and overt incestuous relations between fathers and daughters. *American Journal of Orthopsychiatry* 54(2):266–79.

Keefe, M. 1978. Police investigation in child sexual assault. In *Sexual assault of children and adolescents,* ed. A.W. Burgess, A.N. Groth, and L.L. Holmstrom. Lexington, Mass.: Lexington Books.

Kelley, J.A. 1983. *Treating child-abuse families.* New York: Plenum.

Kempe, C.H. 1973. A practical approach to the protection of the abused child and rehabilitating of the abusing patient. *Pediatrics* 51(41): 408–412.

Kempe, C.H., and Helfer, R. 1972. *Helping the battered child and his family.* Philadelphia: J.B. Lippincott.

Kempe, C.H.; Silverman, F.N.; Brandt, F.; Droegemueller, W.; and Silver, H.K. 1962. The battered-child syndrome. *Journal of the American Medical Association* 181(1):17–24.

Kennedy, D.B. 1983. Attitudes of abused women toward male and female police officers. *Criminal Justice and Behavior* 10(4): 391–405.

————. 1984. Battered women's evaluation of the police response. *Victimology* 9(1): 174–79.

Kercher, G.A.; Jeffords, C.R.; and Dull, R.T. 1981. *Legislative proposals about crime and criminal justice: Texas crime poll, 1980.* Huntsville, Tex.: Sam Houston State University.

Kercher, G.A.; and McShane, M. 1984. The prevalence of child sexual victimization in an adult sample of Texas residents. *Child Abuse and Neglect* 8: 495–501.

Khan, A.N. 1978. Battered wives in magistrates' courts—part 1, University of Western Australia. *Justice Peace* 142(14): 207–8.

Kidd, T. 1982. Social security and the family. In *Sex differences in Britain,* ed. I. Reid and E. Wormald. London: Grant McIntyre.

Kinard, E.M. 1982. Aggression in abused children. *Journal of Personality Assessment* 46: 139–41.

————. 1982. Experiencing child abuse: Effects on emotional adjustment. *American Journal of Orthopsychiatry* 52(1): 82–91.

Kirschner, C. 1979. The aging family in crisis: A problem in living. *Social Casework* 60(1): 209–16.

Kjonstad, A. 1981. Child abuse and neglect: Viewed in relation to twelve fundamental principles in a Western social and legal system. *Child Abuse and Neglect* 5: 421–29.

Klatt, M.R. 1980. Rape in marriage: The Law in Texas and the need for reform. *Baylor Law Review* 32:109–21.

Kleine, D. 1979. Can this marriage be saved? Battery and sheltering. *Crime and Social Justice* 12: 19–33.

Klemmack, S.H., and Klemmack, D.L. 1976. The social definition of rape. In *Sexual assault,* ed. J. Walker and S. Brodsky, Lexington, Mass.: Lexington Books.

Knapp, V.S. 1975. *The role of the juvenile police in the protection of neglected and abused children.* Saratoga, Fla.: R and E Research Association.

Knopf, O. 1975. *Successful aging, the facts and fallacies of growing old.* New York: Viking Press.

Koch, M. 1980. Sexual abuse in children. *Adolescence* 15(4): 643–48.

Komarouski, M. 1967. *Blue-collar marriage.* New York: Vintage Books.

Korbin, J.E. 1980. The cultural context of child abuse and neglect. *Child Abuse and Neglect* 4: 3–13.

Korlath, M.T. 1979. Alcoholism in battered women: A report of advocacy services to clients in a detoxification facility. *Victimology* 4(2): 292–99.

Kosberg, J.I., ed. 1983. *Abuse and maltreatment of the elderly: Causes and interventions.* Boston: John Wright, PSG.

Kovacs, M., and Celine, B. 1982. Building on battered women's strengths. *Aegis* 36: 27.

Kradita, A.S. 1965. *The ideas of the woman suffrage movement 1890–1930.* New York: Columbia University Press.

Kratcoski, P.C. 1984. Perspectives on intrafamily violence. *Human Relations* 37(6): 443–54.

Krenk, C.J. 1984. Training residence staff for child-abuse treatment. *Child Welfare* 58(2): 167–73.

Kristal, H.F., and Tucker, F. 1975. Managing child abuse cases. *Social Work* 20(3): 392–95.

Kroth, J.A. 1979. *Child sexual abuse: Analysis of a family-therapy approach.* Springfield, Ill.: Charles C. Thomas.

Kruger, L.; Moor, D.; Schmidt, P.; and Weins, R. 1979. Group work with abusive parents. *Social Work* 24(2): 337–38.

Kuhl, A.F. 1984. Personality traits of abused women: Masochism myth refuted. *Victimology* 9(3/4): 450–63.

LaBarbera, J.D.; Martin, J.E.; and Dozier, J.E. 1980. Child psychiatrists' view of father-daughter incest. *Child Abuse and Neglect* 4: 147–51.

LaBell, L.S. 1979. Wife abuse: A sociological study of battered women and their mates. *Victimology* 7(2): 258–67.

Landis, J.T. 1963. Social correlates of divorce or nondivorce among the unhappily married. *Marriage and Family Living* 25: 178–80.

Langan, P.A., and Innes, C.A. 1986. Preventing domestic violence against women. In *Bureau of Justice Statistics: Special Report.* Washington, D.C.: U.S. Department of Justice.

Langley, R., and Levy, R. 1978. Wife abuse and the response. *FBI Law Enforcement Bulletin* 47: 5–9.

———. 1978. *Wife beating: The silent crisis.* New York: Pocket Books.

Larrance, D.T. 1983. Maternal attribution and child abuse. *Journal of Abnormal Psychology* 92: 449–57.

Larson, J.F. 1973. The role of the juvenile court in protecting the rights of children. In *Proceedings of the second national symposium on child abuse.* Denver: American Humane Association, Children's Division.

Lau, E., and Kosberg, J. 1979. Abuse of the elderly by informal care providers. *Aging* September–October, 10–15.

Lefkowitz, M.M. 1977. *Growing up to be violent: A longitudinal study of development of aggression.* New York: Pergamon Press.

Legal Research and Services for the Elderly. 1979. *Elder abuse in Massachusetts: A survey of professionals and paraprofessionals.* Boston.

Lerman, L.G. 1983. Legal help for battered women. In *Abuse of women: Legislation, reporting, and prevention,* ed. J. Costa. Lexington, Mass.: Lexington Books.

Lerman, L.G.; Landis, L.; and Goldzweig, S. 1983. State legislation on domestic violence. In *Abuse of women: Legislation, reporting, and prevention,* ed. J. Costa. Lexington, Mass.: Lexington Books.

Lesse, S. 1979. The status of violence against women: Past, present, and future factors. *American Journal of Psychotherapy* 33(2): 190–200.

Lester, D. 1972. Incest. *Journal of Sex Research* 8: 268–85.

Levenberg, J.; Milan, J.; Dolan, M.; and Carpenter, P. 1983. Elder abuse in West Virginia: Extent and nature of the problem. In *Elder abuse in West Virginia: A policy analysis of system response,* ed. L.G. Schultz. Morgantown: West Virginia University.

Levinger, G. 1966. Sources of marital dissatisfaction among applicants for divorce. *American Journal of Orthopsychiatry* 26(6): 803–7.

———. 1974. Physical abuse among applicants for divorce. In *Violence in the family,* ed. S. Steinmetz and M. Straus. New York: Harper and Row.

Lewis, B.Y. 1985. The wife abuse inventory: A screening device for the identification of abused women. *Social Work* 30(1): 32–35.

Lewis, M., and Sarrel, P.M. 1969. Some psychological aspects of seduction, incest, and rape in childhood. *American Academy of Child Psychiatry Journal* 8: 606–19.

Lewis-Beck, M.S. 1980. *Applied regression: An introduction.* Beverly Hills, Calif.: Sage Publications.

Lieb, J. 1973. *The crisis team: A handbook for the mental-health professional.* Hagerstown, Md.: Harper and Row.

Lieberknecht, K. 1978. Helping the battered wife. *American Journal of Nursing* 78: 654–56.

Lifton, R.J. 1961. *Thought reform and the psychology of totalism.* New York: W.W. Norton.

Lindenthal, J. 1975. The public knowledge of child abuse. *Child Welfare* 54(7): 47–56.

Lindzey, G. 1967. Some remarks concerning incest, the incest taboo, and psychoanalytic theory. *American Psychologist* 22: 1051–59.

Ling, J., and Sengstock, M.C. 1983. Personal crimes against the elderly. In *Abuse and maltreatment of the elderly: Causes and interventions,* ed. J.I. Kosberg. Boston: John Wright, PSG.

Lion, J.R. 1977. Clinical aspects of wife beating. In *Battered women,* ed. M. Roy. New York: Van Nostrand Reinhold.

Liston, R.A. 1977. *Terrorism.* Nashville: Nelson.

Lloyd, S.A. 1983. Family violence and service providers: Implications for training. *Social Casework* 64(7): 431–35.

Lockhard, L.L. 1988. Methodological issues in comparative racial analysis: The case of wife abuse. *Social Work Research and Abstracts* 21(2): 35–41.

London, J. 1978. Images of violence againt women. *Victimology* 2(4): 510–24.

Loseke, D.R., and Cahill, S.E. 1984. The social construction of deviance: Experts on battered women. *Social Problems* 31(2): 296–310.

Lovelace, L. 1981. *Ordeal.* New York: Berkley Books.

Lowenberg, D.A. 1977. Conjugal assaults: The incarcerated or liberated women. *Federal Probation* 41(2): 10–13.

Lucht, C. 1975. Providing a legislative base for reporting child abuse. In *Proceedings of the fourth national symposium on child abuse.* Denver: American Humane Association, Children's Division.

Lukianowicz, N. 1972. Incest 1.: Paternal incest. *British Journal of Sociology* 120: 301–13.

Luppens, J., and Lau, E.E. 1983. The mentally and physically impaired elderly relative: Consequences for family care. In *Abuse and maltreatment of the elderly: Causes and interventions,* ed. J.I. Kosberg. Boston: John Wright, PSG.

Lustig, N. 1966. Incest: A family group survival pattern. *Archives of General Psychiatry* 14: 31–40.

Lynch, M.A. 1985. Child abuse before Kempe: A historical literature review. *Child Abuse and Neglect* 9: 7–15.

Lystad, M. 1975. Violence at home: A review of the literature. *American Journal of Orthopsychiatry* 45: 328–45.

———. 1986. *Violence in the home: Interdisciplinary perspectives.* New York: Brunner/Mazel.

McAdoo, J.L. 1979. Well-being and fear of crime among the black elderly. In *Ethnicity and aging: Theory, research, and policy,* ed. D.E. Gelfand and A.J. Kutzik. New York: Springer.

McCarty, L. 1981. Investigation of incest: Opportunity to motivate families to seek help. *Child Welfare* 60(4): 679–89.

McCrea, R.C. 1910. Societies for the prevention of cruelty to children. In *Preventive treatment of neglected children,* ed. H.H. Hart. New York: Russell Sage.

McEvoy, A. 1983. Responses to battered women: Problems and strategies. *Social Casework* 64(1): 92–96.

McFerran, J. 1958. Parent's groups in protective services. *Children* 5(6): 223–28.

McGovern, J.I. 1977. Delicate inquiry: The investigator's role in child abuse. *Victimology* 2(3): 277–84.

Machotka, P.; Pittman, F.S.; and Flomenshaft, K. 1967. Incest as a family affair. *Family Process* 6(March): 98–116.

McIntyre, K. 1981. Role of mothers in father-daughter incest: A feminist analysis. *Social Work* 26: 462–66.

McKerrow, W. 1972. Reactor's comments. In *Proceedings of a national symposium on child abuse.* Denver: American Humane Association, Children's Division.

———. 1977. Protecting the sexually abused child. In *Proceedings of the second national symposium on child abuse.* Denver: American Humane Association, Children's Division.

McLaughlin, J.S.; Nickell, J.P.; and Gill, L. 1983. An epidemiological investigation of elderly abuse in southern Maine and New Hampshire. In *Elder abuse,* House Select Committee on Aging. Committee Publication no. 68-463.

McLeod, M. 1983. Victim noncooperation in the prosecution of domestic assault: A research note. *Criminology* 21(3): 395–416.

McMurtry, S.L. 1985. Secondary prevention of child maltreatment: A review. *Social Work* 30(1): 42–48.

McShane, C. 1979. Community services for battered women. *Social Work* 24(1): 34–39.

Maddox, G. 1975. Families as context and resource in chronic illness. In *Issues in long-term care,* ed. S. Sherwood. New York: Holstead.

Magura, S. 1982. Clients view outcome of child protective services. *Social Casework* 63(4): 522–31.

Maisch, H. 1972. *Incest.* New York: Stein and Day.

Mallard, R. 1975. Due process—guidelines for fair play and protection of rights. In *Proceedings of the fourth national symposium on child abuse.* Denver: American Humane Association, Children's Division.

Marcovitch, A. 1979. Refuges for battered women. *Social Work Today* 7(2): 34–35.

Margolin, G. 1979. Conjoint marital therapy to enhance anger management and reduce spouse abuse. *American Journal of Family Therapy* 7(2): 13–23.

Marion, M. 1982. Primary prevention of child abuse: The role of the family-life educator. *Family Relations* 31(3): 575–82.

Marsden, D., and Owens, D. 1975. The Jekyll and Hyde marriages. *New Society* 32(657): 333–35.

Martin, D. 1976. *Battered wives.* New York: Glide Publications.

———. 1982. Wife beating: A product of sociosexual development. In *Women's sexual experience: Explorations of the dark content,* ed. M. Kirkpatrick. New York: Plenum.

Martin, J.P. 1978. *Violence and the family.* New York: John Wiley and Sons.

Martin, P. 1976. *A marital therapy manual.* New York: Brunner/Mazel.

Marvick, E.W. 1974. Nature versus nurturance. Patterns and trends in seventeenth-century French child rearing. In *The history of childhood,* ed. L. de Mause. New York: Psychohistory Press.

Marx, E. 1976. *The social context of violent behavior: A social anthropological study of an Israeli immigrant town.* London: Routledge and Kegan Paul.

Massachusetts Coalition of Battered Women Service Groups. 1981. *For shelter and beyond: An educational manual for working with women who are battered.* Boston.

Masters, W., and Johnson, V.E. 1976. Incest: The ultimate sexual taboo. *Redbook* 146(4): 54–58.

Masumura, W.T. 1979. Wife abuse and other forms of aggression. *Victimology* 4(1): 46–59.

Mause, L. de. 1974. *The history of childhood.* New York: Psychohistory Press.

Mayhill, P.D., and Norgard, K.E., 1983. *Child abuse and neglect: Sharing responsibility.* New York: John Wiley and Sons.

Meddin, B.J. 1984. Criteria for placement decisions in protective services. *Child Welfare* 63(2): 367–73.

Mehta, M.N.; Praphy, S.V.; and Mistry, H.N. 1985. Child abuse in Bombay. *Child Abuse and Neglect* 9: 107–11.

Meiselman, K. 1978. *Incest.* San Francisco: Jossey-Bass.

Melton, G.B. 1985. Sexually abused children and the legal system. *American Journal of Family Therapy* 13(1): 61–67.

Melville, J. 1976. Wife batterers. *New Society* 37(3): 400–401.

———. 1977. In search of a refuge. *New Society* 41(3): 389–90.

Mercer, S.O. 1983. Consequences of institutionalization of the aged. In *Abuse and maltreatment of the elderly: Causes and interventions,* ed. J.I. Kosberg. Boston: John Wright, PSG.

Mercer, S.O., and Kane, R.A. 1979. Helplessness and hopelessness among the institutionalized aged: An experiment. *Health and Social Work* 4: 91–113.

Merrill, E.J. 1962. Physical abuse of children—an agency study. In *Protecting the battered child.* Denver: American Humane Association, Children's Division.

Meyer, L. 1985. Battered wives, dead husbands. *Student Lawyer* 6(7): 46–51.

Micarthy, G. 1982. *Getting free: A handbook for women in abusive relationships.* Tucson: National Family Advocacy Project.

Michigan Women's Commission. 1977. *Wife assault in Michigan.* Lansing.

Mill, J.S. 1870. *The subjection of women.* New York: D. Appleton.

Miller, A. 1983. *For your own good: Hidden cruelty in child rearing and the roots in violence.* New York: Farrar, Straus, and Giroux.

Miller, C. 1985. A parent aid program. *Child Welfare* 64(3): 407–19.

Miller, D. 1982. Innovative program development for battered women and their families. *Victimology* 7(2/4): 335–41.

———. 1983. Domestic violence. *School Guidance Worker* 39(1): 20–26.

Miller, D.T., and Porter, C.A. 1983. Self-blame in victim's violence. *Journal of Social Issues* 39(1): 39–52.

Miller, F. 1969. *Prosecution: The decision to charge a suspect with crime.* Boston: Little, Brown.

Miller, J.K. 1973. An interdisciplinary approach to child protective services in the military community. In *Proceedings of the second national symposium on child abuse.* Denver: American Humane Association, Children's Division.

Miller, N. 1975. *Battered spouses, Social Service Department, Borough of Kensington and Chelsey, London.* London: G. Bell and Sons.

Miltra, C.L. 1979. . . . For she has no right or power to refuse her consent. *Criminal Law Review* 9(4): 558–65.

Minnigrode, F.A. 1976. Attitudes toward women, sex-role stereotyping, and locus of control. *Psychological Reports* 38(3): 1301–2.

Mondale, W. 1974. Child abuse: Issues and answers. *Public Welfare* 32(2): 9–11.

Moore, D.M. 1979. *Battered women.* Beverly Hills, Calif.: Sage Publications.

Moore, J.B. 1983. The experience of sponsoring a Parents Anonymous group. *Social Casework* 64(4): 585–92.

Morgan, S.M. 1982. *Conjugal terrorism: A psychological and community treatment model of wife abuse.* Palo Alto, Calif.: R and E Research.

Moroney, R.M. 1980. *Families, social services, and social policy: The issue of shared responsibility.* Rockville, Md.: National Institute of Mental Health.

Morris, D. 1969. *The human zoo.* New York: Dell.

Mouzakitis, C.M. 1985. A multidisciplinary approach to treating child neglect. *Social Casework* 66(2): 218–24.

Mowat, R.R. 1966. *Morbid jealousy and murder.* London: Tavistock.

Mowrer, E.R., and Mowrer, H.R. 1928. *Domestic discord.* Chicago: University of Chicago.

Mrazek, P. 1981. The child psychiatric examination of the sexually abused child. In *Sexually abused children and their families,* ed. P. Mrazek and H. Kempe. Oxford: Pergamon Press.

———. 1981. Group psychotherapy with sexually abused children. In *Sexually abused children and their families,* ed. P. Mrazek and H. Kempe. Oxford: Pergamon Press.

Mulford, R.M. 1958. *Emotional neglect of children.* Denver: American Humane Association, Children's Division.

———. 1972. The role and function of protective services. In *Proceedings of a national symposium on child abuse.* Denver: American Humane Association: Children's Division.

———. 1983. Historical perspective. In *Child abuse and neglect: A guide with case studies for treating the child and family,* ed. N.B. Ebeling and D.A. Hill. Boston: John Wright, PSG.

Munson, P.J. 1980. Protecting battered wives: The availability of legal remedies. *Journal of Sociology and Social Welfare* 7(4): 586–600.

Murdock, C.G. 1970. The abused child and the school system. *American Journal of Public Health* 60(1): 105–9.

Myer, M. 1985. A look at mothers of incest victims. *Journal of Social Work and Human Sexuality* 3: 47–58.

Nagi, S.Z. 1975. Child abuse and neglect programs: A national overview. *Children Today* 4(3).

Nam, C.B., and Powers, M.G. 1965. Variations in socio-economic structure by race, residence, and life cycle. In *Handbook of research design and social measurement,* ed. D. Miller. New York: David McKay.

Nathanson, P. 1983. An overview of legal issues, services, and resources. In *Abuse and maltreatment of the elderly: Causes and interventions,* ed. J.I. Kosberg. Boston: John Wright, PSG.

National Association of Social Work. 1984. Anatomy of a child neglect case, part 3. *NASW News* 29: 16–17.

National Association of Social Work. 1984. Anatomy of a child neglect case, part 4. *NASW News* 29: 12.

National Association of Social Work. 1984. Negligence changed in child abuse cases. *NASW News* 29: 5.

National Association of Social Work. 1985. Abuse widespread among nation's cults. *NASW News* 30: 7–8.

National Association of Social Work. 1985. Legal system flaws on sex abuse targeted by proposed reform law. *NASW News* 30: 4.

National Center on Child Abuse and Neglect. 1981. *Study findings: National study of the incidence and severity of child abuse and neglect.* Department of Health and Human Services. Publication no. 81-30325.

Neidig, P.H. 1984. Women's shelters, men's collectives, and other issues in the field of spouse abuse. *Victimology* 9(3/4): 464–76.

———. 1985. Domestic conflict containment: A spouse-abuse treatment program. *Social Casework* 66(1): 195–204.

Neidig, P.H., and Friedman, D.H. 1984. *Spouse abuse: A treatment program for couples.* Champaign, Ill.: Research Press.

Neidig, P.H.; Friedman, D.H.; and Collins, B.S. 1986. Attitudinal characteristics of males who have engaged in spouse abuse. *Journal of Family Violence* 1(3): 223–34.

Nelson, B.J. 1984. *Making an issue of child abuse: Political agenda setting for social problems.* Chicago: University of Chicago Press.

Nelson, G.K. 1980. Child abuse reporting laws: Actions and uncertainty. *Child Welfare* 59: 203–12.

Nettle, G. 1974. *Explaining crime.* New York: McGraw-Hill.

Newberger, E. 1972. The myth of the battered child syndrome: A compassionate medical view of the protection of children. In *Proceedings of a national symposium on child abuse.* Denver: American Humane Association, Children's Division.

———. 1975. *Interdisciplinary management of child abuse: Problems and progress.* Denver: American Humane Association, Children's Division.

———. 1975. Medical management of child abuse. In *Proceedings of the fourth national symposium on child abuse.* Denver: American Humane Association, Children's Division.

Newberger, E., and Bourne, R. 1980. The medicalization and legalization of child abuse. In *Child abuse: Commission and omission,* ed. J.V. Cook and R.T. Bowles. Toronto: Butterworths.

———. 1985. *Unhappy families: Clinical and research perspectives on family violence.* Littleton, Mass.: PSG.

Nichols, B.B. 1976. The abused wife problem. *Social Casework* 57(1): 27–32.

Nixon, J.; Pearn, J.; Wilkey, I.; and Petrie, G. 1981. Social class and violent child death: An analysis of fatal, nonaccidental injury, murder, and fatal child neglect. *Child Abuse and Neglect* 5: 111–16.

Nurse, S.M. 1964. Familial patterns of parents who abuse their children. *Smith College Studies in Social Work* 35(1): 11–25.

Nyden, P.V. 1972. Reactor's comments. In *Proceedings of a national symposium on child abuse.* Denver: American Humane Association, Children's Division.

Nye, F.I. 1958. Employment status of mothers and marital conflict, permanence, and happiness. *Social Problems* 6(2): 260–67.

———. 1963. The adjustment of adolescent children. In *The employed mother in America,* ed. F.I. Nye and L.W. Hoffman. Chicago: Rand McNally.

———. 1978. Is choice and exchange theory the key? *Journal of Marriage and the Family* 41(May): 219–33.

———. 1979. Choice, exchange, and the family. In *Contemporary theories about the family,* ed. R.B. Wesley. New York: Free Press.

Oakar, M.R., and Miller, C.A. 1983. Federal legislation to protect the elderly. In *Abuse and maltreatment of the elderly: Causes and interventions,* ed. J.I. Kosberg. Boston: John Wright, PSG.

O'Brien, J. 1971. Violence in divorce-prone families. *Journal of Marriage and the Family* 33: 692–98. In *Violence in the family,* ed. S. Steinmetz and M. Straus, 1074. New York: Harper and Row.

O'Brien, S. 1980. *Child abuse, a crying shame.* Provo, Utah: Brigham Young University.

O'Faolain, J., and Martines, L. eds. 1974. *Not in God's image: Women in history.* Glasgow: Fontana/Collins.

Okun, L. 1984. Termination or resumption of cohabitation in women-battering relationships: A statistical study. Paper presented at the Second National Family Violence Research Conference, Durham, N.H..

———. 1986. *Woman abuse.* Albany, N.Y.: Suny.

O'Malley, H. 1979. *Elder abuse: A review of the literature.* Boston: Legal Research and Services for the Elderly.

O'Malley, H.; Segars, H.; Perez, R.; Mitchell, V.; and Knuepel, G.M. 1979. *Elder abuse in Massachusetts.* Boston: Legal Research and Services for the Elderly.

O'Malley, T.A.; Everett, E.D.; O'Malley, H.C.; and Campion, E.W. 1983. Identifying and preventing family-mediated abuse and neglect of elderly persons. *Annals of Internal Medicine* 90(6): 998–1005.

Only lords can change their minds. 1975. *Economist.* 267(3): 22–23.

Oppenlander, N. 1982. Coping or copping out. *Criminology* 20(3): 449–63.

Ordway, D. 1983. Reforming judicial procedures for handling parent-child incest. *Child Welfare* 62(1): 68–75.

Oremland, E.K., and Oremland, 1977. *The sexual and gender development of young children: The role of education.* Cambridge, Mass.: Ballinger.

Ory, M.G. 1985. The burden of care. *Quarterly Journal of the American Society on Aging* 10(1): 14–17.

Ostbloom, N. 1980. A model for conceptualizing child abuse causation and intervention. *Social Casework* 61: 164–72.

Oviatt, B. 1971. After child abuse reporting legislation—what? In *The status of child protection.* Denver: American Humane Association, Children's Division.

Owens, D. 1975. Battered wives: Some social and legal problems. *British Journal of Law and Society* 2(2): 201–11.

Owens, D., and Straus, M.A. 1974. Social structure of violence in childhood and approval of violence as an adult. *Aggressive Behavior* 1:193–211.

Pagelow, M.D. 1977. Secondary battering: Breaking the cycle of domestic violence. In *Domestic Violence.* Washington, D.C.: Government Printing Office.

———. 1979. Research on women battering. In *Stopping wife abuse,* ed. J.B. Fleming. New York: Anchor Books.

———. Factors affecting women's decisions to leave violent relationships. *Journal of Family Violence* 2(4): 391–414.

———. 1981. *Women and crime.* New York: MacMillan.

———. 1981. *Women battering: Victims and their experience.* Beverly Hills, Calif.: Sage Publications.

Pallone, S.R. 1984. *Helping parents who abuse their children: A comprehensive approach for intervention.* Springfield, Ill.: Charles Thomas.

Palmer, S. 1960. *A study of murder.* New York: Crowell.

———. 1972. *The violent society.* New Haven, Conn.: College and University Press.

———. 1974. Family members as murder victims. In *Violence in the family,* ed. S. Steinmetz and M. Straus. New York: Harper and Row.

Parke, R.D., and Collmer, C.W. 1975. Child abuse: An interdisciplinary analysis. In *Review of child development research,* ed. M. Hetheringron. Chicago: University of Chicago Press.

Parker, B., and Schumacher, D.N. 1977. The battered wife and violence in nuclear family of origin: A controlled pilot study. *American Journal of Public Health* 67(8): 760–761.

Parker, S. 1976. The precultural basis of the incest taboo: A biosocial theory. *American Anthropologist* 78(2): 285–305.

———. 1985. The legal background. In *Private violence and public policy: The needs of battered women and the response of the public services,* ed. J. Pahl. Boston: Routledge and Kegan Paul.

Parnas, R.I. 1967. The police response to domestic disturbances. *Wisconsin Law Review* 14: 914–60.

———. 1970. Judicial response to intrafamily violence. *Minnesota Law Review* 54: 545–85.

———. 1973. Prosecutorial and judicial handling of family violence. *Criminal Law Bulletin* 9(6): 733–69.

Pasananick, B. 1971. A child is being beaten. *American Journal of Orthopsychiatry* 41(4): 540–56.

Pasternack, S.A. 1975. *Violence and victims.* Flushing, N.Y.: Spectrum.

Paterson, E.J. 1979. How the legal system responds to battered women. In *Battered women,* ed. D.M. Moore. Beverly Hills, Calif.: Sage Publications.

Paulsen, M.G. 1966. Legal protections against child abuse. *Children* 13(2): 42–48.

Paulsen, M.G., and Blake, P.R. 1969. The physically abused child: A focus on prevention. *Child Welfare* 48(2): 86–95.

Pelton, L.H. 1978. Child abuse and neglect: The myth of classlessness. *American Journal of Orthopsychiatry* 48(5): 608–17.

Penner, G. 1967. *The protective services center.* Denver: American Humane Association, Children's Division.

———. 1975. Multidisciplinary cooperation for protecting children. In *Proceedings of the fourth national symposium on child abuse.* Denver: American Humane Association, Children's Division.

Pennsylvania Department of Aging. 1982. *Elder abuse in Pennsylvania.* Harrisburg: Bureau of Advocacy.

Pepper, C.D. 1983. Frauds against the elderly. In *Abuse and maltreatment of the elderly: Causes and interventions,* ed. J.I. Kosberg. Boston: John Wright, PSG.

Pepper, C.D., and Oakar, M.R. 1981. *Elder abuse: An examination of a hidden problem.* House Select Committee on Aging. Committee Publication no. 97–277.

Peterson, R. 1980. Social class, social learning, and wife abuse. *Social Service Review* 53(2): 390–406.

Pfohl, S.J. 1977. The discovery of child abuse. *Social Problems* 24(3): 310–23.

———. 1980. The discovery of child abuse. In *Child abuse: Commission and omission,* ed. J.V. Cook and R.T. Bowles. Toronto: Butterworths.

Pfouts, F.H. 1978. Violent families: Coping responses of abused wives. *Child Welfare* 57(2): 101–11.

Philbrick, E. 1960. *Treating parental pathology.* Denver: American Humane Association, Children's Division.

Phillips, L.R. 1986. Theoretical explanations of elder abuse: Competing hypotheses and unresolved issues. In *Elder abuse: Conflict in the family,* ed. K.A. Pillemer and R.S. Wolf. Dover, Mass.: Auburn House.

Pierce, L.H. 1984. Race as a factor in the sexual abuse of children. *Social Work Research and Abstracts* 20(1): 9–14.

Pierce, R.L. 1984. Child pornography: A hidden dimension of child abuse. *Child Abuse and Neglect.* 8: 483–92.

Pietrodangelo, D. 1983. Child abuse: Making the public aware. *Public Welfare* 41(1): 31–35.

Pilisuk, M., and Minkler, M. 1980. Life ties of the elderly. *Journal Social Issues* 36(2): 1450–52.

Pillemer, K.A. 1986. Risk factors in elder abuse: Results from a case-control study. In *Elder abuse: Conflict in the family,* ed. K.A. Pillemer, and R.S. Wolf. Dover, Mass.: Auburn House.

Pizzey, E. 1974. *Scream quietly or the neighbors will hear.* Baltimore: Penguin.

Platt, A. 1969. *The child savers.* Chicago: Chicago University Press.

Pleck, E. 1979. Wife beating in nineteenth-century America. *Victimology* 4(1): 60–74.

Plotkin, R.C. 1982. Utility of a measure of aggression in differentiation among abusing parents from other parents who are experiencing familial disturbance. *Journal of Clinical Psychology* 38(4): 607–10.

Pogrevin, L.C. 1974. Do women make men violent? *Ms.* November, 49–50.

Polansky, N.A. 1978. Assessing adequacy of child caring: An urban scale. *Child Welfare* 57(3): 439–49.

———. 1978. Class orientations to child neglect. *Social Work* 23(3): 397–405.

———. 1979. Isolation of the neglectful family. *American Journal of Orthopsychiatry* 49(2): 149–52.

———. 1983. Social distancing of the neglectful family. *Social Service Review* 57(2): 196–208.

Polansky, N.A.; DeSaiz, C.; and Shlomo, S. 1972. *Child neglect: Understanding and reaching the parent.* New York: Child Welfare League of America.

Polansky, N.A.; DeSaiz, C.; Wing, M.L.; and Patton, J.D. 1968. Child neglect in a rural community. *Social Casework* 49(8): 467–74.

Polier, J.W. 1975. Professional abuse of children: Responsibility and the delivery of services. *American Journal of Orthopsychiatry* 45(3): 357–62.

Ponzetti, J.J., Jr. 1982. Violence between couples: Profiling the male abuser. *Personnel and Guidance Journal* 61: 222–24.

Porter, C. 1983. Blame, depression, and coping in battered women. Ph.D. diss., University of British Columbia.

Porter, F.; Blink, L.; and Sgroi, S. 1982. Treatment of the sexually abused child. In *Handbook of clinical intervention in child sexual abuse,* ed. S. Sgroi. Lexington, Mass.: Lexington Books.

Post, R. 1981. Childhood exposure to violence among victims and perpetrators of spouse battering. *Victimology* 6(1): 156–66.

Power, P.W., and Dell Orto, A.E. 1980. Impact of disability/illness on the adult. In *Role of the family in rehabilitation of the physically disabled,* ed. P.W. Power and A.E. Dell Orto. Baltimore: University Park Press.

Prescott, S., and Letko, C. 1977. Battered women: A social psychological perspective. In *Battered women,* ed. M. Roy. New York: Van Nostrand Reinhold.

Pressman, B. 1985. The guidance counselor's role in treating children from violent homes. *School Guidance Worker* 40: 39–43.

Pruitt, D.A. 1985. A parent-aid program inventory. *Journal of Clinical Psychology* 41: 104–11.

Purdy, F. 1981. Practice principles for working with groups of men who batter. *Social Work With Groups* 4(3/4): 111–29.

Quinn, M.J., and Tomita, S.K. 1986. *Elder abuse and neglect.* New York: Springer.

Quinsey, V.L. 1977. The assessment and treatment of child molesters: A review. *Canadian Psychological Review* 18: 204–20.

Radbill, S.X. 1974. A history of child abuse and infanticide. In *Violence in the family,* ed. S.K. Steinmetz and M.A. Straus. New York: Harper and Row.

Randall, O.A. 1965. Some historical developments of social-welfare aspects of aging. *Gerontologist* 5(1): 40–49.

Raphling, D.L.; Carpenter, B.L.; and Davis, A. 1967. Incest: A genealogical study. *Archives of General Psychiatry* 16(4): 505–11.

Rathbone-McCuan, E. 1980. Elderly victims of family violence and neglect. *Social Casework* 5(1): 36–48.

————. 1982. Older women: Endangered but surviving species. *Generations: Quarterly Journal of the Western Gerontological Society* 6(3): 11–12, 50.

Rathbone-McCuan, E., and Hashimi, J. 1982. *Isolated elders: Health and social intervention.* Rockville, Md.: Aspen Systems.

Rathbone-McCuan, E.; Travis, A.; and Voyles, B. 1983. Family intervention: Applying the task-centered approach. In *Abuse and maltreatment of the elderly: Causes and intervention,* ed. J.I. Kosberg. Boston: John Wright, PSG.

Rathbone-McCuan, E., and Voyles, B. 1982. Case detection of abused elderly parents. *American Journal of Psychiatry* 139(1): 189–92.

Rather a wife than a mistress be? 1977. *Economist* 265(12): 23.

Ray, J.A. 1985. Teaching child sexual abuse prevention. *School Social Work Journal* 9: 100.

Ray, M., ed. 1982. *The abusive partner: An analysis of domestic battering.* New York: Van Nostrand Reinhold.

Reed, E. 1975. *Women's evolution from matriarchal clan to patriarchal family.* New York and Toronto: Pathfinder.

Regan, J.J. 1983. Protective services for the elderly: Benefit or threat. In *Abuse and maltreatment of the elderly: Causes and interventions,* ed. J.I. Kosberg. Boston: John Wright, PSG.

Reid, W.J. 1977. Process and outcome in the treatment of family problems. In *Task-centered practice,* ed. W.J. Reid and L. Epstein. New York: Columbia University.

Reinharz, S. 1986. Loving and hating one's elders: Twin themes in legend and literature. In *Elder abuse: Conflict in the family,* ed. K.A. Pillemer and R.S. Wolf. Dover, Mass.: Auburn House.

Renvoize, J. 1978. *A study of family violence.* London: Routledge and Kegan Paul.

Reynolds, R., and Siegle, E. 1959. A study of casework with sadomasochistic marriage partners. *Social Casework* 40(4): 545–51.

Rheinstein, M. 1965. Motivation of intergenerational behavior by norms of law. In *Social structure and the family: Generational relations,* ed. E. Shanas and G.F. Streib. Englewood Cliffs, N.J.: Prentice-Hall.

Richett, D.M. 1979. The sociolegal history of child abuse and neglect: An analysis of the policy of children's rights. *Journal of Sociology and Social Welfare* 6(6): 849–75.

Riemer, S. 1940. A research note on incest. *American Journal of Sociology* 45(4): 565–71.

Roberts, A.R. 1980. *Sheltering battered women: A national study and service guide.* New York: Springer.

Robertson, P. 1974. Home as a nest: Middle-class childhood in nineteenth-century Europe. In *The history of childhood,* ed. L. de Mause. New York: Psychohistory Press.

Robinson, B., and Thurnher, M. 1979. Taking care of aged parents: A family cycle transition. *Gerontologist* 19(6): 586–93.

Robinson, D.C. 1979. Domestic violence—practitioner's viewpoint. *New Law Journal* 129: 251–54.

Rodman, H. 1972. Marital power and the theory of resources in cultural context. *Journal of Comparative Family Studies* 3 (Spring): 50–69.

Rodriquez, A. 1977. Handbook of child abuse to neglect. Flushing, N.Y.: Medical Examiner.

Rokeach, M.; Miller, M.G.; and Snyder, J.A. 1971. The value gap between police and policed. *Journal of Social Issues* 27(2): 155–71.

Rolph, C.H. 1975. Battered wives. *New Statesman* 90: 811–12.

Rooks, E., and King, K. 1973. A study of the marriage role expectations of black adolescents. *Adolescence* 8(31): 317–24.

Rose, M.A. 1976. Problems families face in home care. *American Journal of Nursing* 76(3): 416–18.

Rose, V.M. 1977. Rape as a social problem: A byproduct of the feminist movement. *Social Problems* 25(1): 75–89.

Rosenbaum, A. 1979. Wife abuse: Characteristics of the participants and etiological considerations. *Dissertation Abstracts International* 40: 1383.

Rosenbaum, A., and O'Leary, K.D. 1981. Marital violence: Characteristics of abusive couples. *Journal of Consulting and Clinical Psychology* 41: 63–71.

Rosenburg, M.S. 1983. Abusive mothers' perceptions of the children's behavior. *Journal of Counseling and Clinical Psychology* 51: 674–82.

Rosenfeld, A.A. 1977. Sexual misuse and the family. *Victimology* 2(1): 226–35.

———. 1979. Incidence of a history of incest among eighteen female psychiatric patients. *American Journal of Psychiatry* 136(6): 791–95.

Rosenfeld, A.; Nadelson, C.; and Krieger, M. 1979. Fantasy and reality in patients' reports of incest. *Journal of Clinical Psychiatry* 40: 159–64.

Rosenthal, M., and Louis, J.A. 1981. The law's evolving role in child abuse and neglect. In *The social context of child abuse,* ed. L.H. Pelton. New York: Human Sciences.

Rounsaville, B.J. 1978. Battered wives: Barriers to identification and treatment. *American Journal of Orthopsychiatry* 48(3): 487–94.

———. 1978. Theories in marital violence: Evidence from a study of battered women. *Victimology* 3(1/2): 11–31.

Rounsaville, B.; Lifton, N.; Bieber, M. 1979. The natural history of a psychotherapy group for battered wives. *Psychiatry* 42(1): 63–78.

Rounsaville, B., and Weissman, M.M. 1977. Battered women: A medical problem requiring detection. *International Journal of Psychiatry in Medicine* 8(2): 191–202.

Roy, M. 1977. A current survey of 150 cases. In *Battered women,* ed. M. Roy. New York: Van Nostrand Reinhold.

———, ed. 1977. *Battered women.* New York: Van Nostrand Reinhold.

———, ed. 1982. *The abusive partner: Analysis of domestic battering.* New York: Van Nostrand Reinhold.

Rubin, J. 1966. The need for intervention. *Public Welfare* 24(3): 230–35.

Rush, F. 1980. *The best-kept secret: Sexual abuse of children.* New York: McGraw-Hill.

Russell, D.E. 1980. The prevalence and impact of marital rape in San Francisco. Paper presented at the American Sociological Association Annual Meeting, October 1980, New York.

———. 1980. *The secret trauma: Incest in the lives of girls and women.* New York: Basic Books.

———. 1984. *Sexual exploitation: Rape, child sexual abuse, and workplace harassment.* Beverly Hills, Calif.: Sage Publications.

Rust, J.O., and Phillips, J. 1984. College students' perceptions of spouse abuse and conjugal power. *College Student Journal* 18: 376–79.

Sack, W.H. 1985. The single-parent family and abusive child punishment. *American Journal of Orthopsychiatry* 55(2): 252–59.

Sagarin, E. 1977. Incest: Problems of definition and frequency. *Journal of Sex Research* 13: 126–35.

Salend, E.; Kane, R.A.; Satz, M.; and Pynoos, J. 1984. Elder abuse reporting: Limitations of statutes. *Gerontologist* 24(1): 61–69.

Salter, A.C. 1985. Treating abusive parents. *Child Welfare* 64(2): 327–41.

Sanford, J.R.A. 1975. Tolerance of debility in elderly dependents by supporters at home: Its significance for hospital practice. *British Medical Journal* 3: 471–73.

Sanford, L.T. 1980. *Silent children: A book for parents about the prevention of child abuse.* New York: Doubleday.

Sarafino, E. 1979. Estimates of sexual offense against children. *Child Welfare* 58(1): 127–33.

Sattin, D.B., and Miller, J.K. 1971. The ecology of child abuse within a military community. *American Journal of Orthopsychiatry* 41(4): 675–78.

Saul, L. 1972. Personal and social psychopathology and the primary prevention of violence. *American Journal of Psychiatry* 128(12): 1578–81.

Saunders, D. 1977. Marital violence: Dimensions of the problem and modes of intervention. *Journal of Marriage and Family Counseling* 3(1): 43–55.

———. 1984. Helping husbands who batter. *Social Casework* 65(2): 347–53.

Saunders, D.G., and Size, P.B. 1986. Attitudes about women among police officers, victims, and victim advocates. *Journal of Interpersonal Violence* 1: 25–39.

Saunders, S., ed. 1984. *Violent individuals and families: A handbook.* Springfield, Ill.: Charles C. Thomas.

Saupe, A.S.; William, A.; and Hazlewood, L.R. 1987. *Violent men, violent couples: The dynamics of domestic violence.* Lexington, Mass.: Lexington Books.

Scanzoni, J.H. 1975. *Sex roles, lifestyles, and childbearing: Changing patterns in marriage and the family.* New York: Free Press.

Scanzoni, J., and Fox, J.L. 1980. Sex roles, family, and society: The seventies and beyond. *Journal of Marriage and the Family* 42(2): 743–56.

Schechter, S. 1982. *Women and male violence: The visions and struggles of the battered women's movement.* Boston: South End Press.

Schein, E.H.; Schneier, I.; and Barker, C.H. 1961. *Coercive persuasion.* New York: W.W. Norton.

Schiff, O.F. 1979. *State of Oregon v. Rideout*—can a husband rape his wife? *Medical Trial Technique Quarterly* 9: 174–89.

Schmidt, M.G. 1980. Failing parents, aging children. *Journal of Gerontological Social Work* 2(3): 259–68.

Schorr, A. 1960. *Filial responsibility in the American family.* Washington, D.C.: Government Printing Office.

———. 1980. . . . Thy father and thy mother—a second look at filial responsibility and family policy. Social Security Administration Publication no. 13-11953. Washington, D.C.

Schulman, M. 1979. *A survey of spousal violence against women in Kentucky.* Washington, D.C.: U.S. Department of Justice, Law Enforcement Assistance Administration.

Schultz, L.G. 1960. The wife assaulter: One type observed and treated in a probation agency. *Journal of Social Therapy* 6: 103–11.

———. 1973. The child sex victim. *Child Welfare* 52(1): 147–57.

Schultz, R., and Aderman, D. 1973. Effects of residential change on the temporal distance of death of terminal cancer patients. *Omega: The Journal of Death and Dying* 4: 157–62.

———. 1974. Clinical research and the stages of death and dying. *Omega: The Journal of Death and Dying* 5: 50–57.

Schuyler, M. 1976. Battered wives: An emerging social problem. *Social Work* 21(6): 488–91.

Schwendinger, J.R., and Schwendinger, H. 1974. Rape myths: In legal, theoretical, and everyday practice. *Crime and Social Justice* 1(1): 18–26.

Scott, E.M. 1977. The sexual offender. *International Journal of Offender Therapy and Comparative Criminology* 21: 255–63.

Scott, P.D. 1974. Battered wives. *British Journal of Psychiatry* 125: 433–41.

Scott, W.O. 1984. The use of skill-training procedure in the treatment of a child-abusive parent. *Journal of Behavior Therapy and Experimental Psychology* 15: 329–36.

Scutt, J.A. 1977. Consent in rape: The problem of the marriage contract. *Monash University Law Review* 3 (June): 255–88.

Seaberg, J.R., and Gillespie, D.F. 1978. A national child abuse and neglect data bank: Interreporter reliability. Prepared for University of Washington, School of Social Work, Center for Social Welfare Research. Seattle. Manuscript.

Seemanova, E. 1971. A study of children of incestuous matings. *Human Heredity* 21: 108–28.

Seligman, B.Z. 1929. Incest and descent: Their influence on social organization. *Royal Anthropological Institute of Great Britain* 59(1): 231–72.

———. 1932. The incest barrier: Its role in social organization. *British Journal of Psychology* 22: 250–76.

———. 1950. The problem of incest and exogamy: An restatement. *American Anthropologist* 52: 305–16.

Sengstock, M., and Liang, J. 1982. *Identifying and characterizing elder abuse.* Wayne State University, Institute of Gerontology, Detroit. Manuscript.

Sgroi, S. 1975. Sexual molestation of children: The last frontier in child abuse. *Children Today* 3(1): 18–21.

———. 1982. *Handbook of clinical intervention in child sexual abuse.* Lexington, Mass.: Lexington Books.

Shainess, N. 1977. Psychological aspects of wife battering. In *Battered women,* ed. M. Roy. New York: Van Nostrand Reinhold.

Shamroy, J.A. 1980. A perspective on childhood sexual abuse. *Social Work* 25(1): 128–32.

Shanas, E. 1979. The family as a social-support system in old age. *Gerontologist* 19(1): 169–74.

———. 1979. Social myth as hypothesis: The case of the family relations of old people. *Gerontologist* 19(1): 3–9.

Scheilds, N.M., and Hnneke, C.R. 1983. Attribution processes in violent relationships: Perceptions with violent husbands and their wives. *Journal of Applied Social Psychology* 13: 515–27.

Shengold, L. 1985. The effect of child abuse as seen in adults: George Orwell. *Psychoanalytic Quarterly* 54: 20–45.

Shepher, J. 1971. Mate selection among second-generation kibbutz adolescents and adults: Incest avoidance and negative imprinting. *Archives of Sexual Behavior* 1: 293–307.

Sherman, L.W., and Berk, R.A. 1984. The specific deterrent effects of arrest for domestic assault. *American Sociological Review* 49: 2261–72.

Sholevarm, G.P. 1975. A family therapist looks at the problem of incest. *American Academy of Psychiatry and the Law Bulletin* 3: 25–31.

Shupe, A.; Stacey, A.; and Hazlewood, L.R. 1987. *Violent men, violent couples: The dynamics of domestic violence.* Lexington, Mass.: Lexington Books.

Sigler, R., and Haygood, D. 1988. The criminalization of forced marital intercourse. *Marriage and Family Review* 16(2): 121–30.

Silbert, M.H. and Ayala, M.P. 1981. Sexual child abuse as antecedent to prostitution. *Child Abuse and Neglect* 5: 407–11.

Silver, L.B.; Dublin, C.C.; and Louriex, R.S. 1971. Agency action and interaction in cases of child abuse. *Social Casework* 52(3): 164–71.

Silverstone, B., and Hyman, H.K. 1976. *You and your aging parent.* New York: Pantheon.

Silverton, R. 1982. Social-work perspective on psychosocial dwarfism. *Social Work in Health Care* 7: 1–14.

Simos, B.G. 1973. Adult children and their aging parents. *Social Work* 18(1): 78–85.

Skuse, D. 1984. Extreme deprivation in early childhood. *Journal of Child Psychology and Psychiatry* 25: 523–41.

Slater, M.K. 1959. Ecological factors in the origin of incest. *American Anthropologist* 61(6): 1042–59.

Sloane, P., and Karpinski, E. 1942. Effects of incest on the participants. *American Journal of Orthopsychiatry* 12(6): 666–73.

Smetana, J.G. 1984. Abused, neglected, and nonmaltreated children's conceptions of moral and social-conventional transgressions. *Child Development* 55: 277–87.

Smith, J.E. 1984. Nonaccidential injury to children. 1. A review of behavioral interventions. *Behavior Research and Therapy* 22: 331–48.

———. 1984. Nonaccidental injury to children. 3. Methodological problems of evaluative treatment research. *Behavior Research and Therapy* 22: 367–84.

Smith, R.E.; Keating, J.P.; Hester, R.K.; and Mitchell, H.E. 1976. Role and justice considerations in the attribution of responsibility to a rape victim. *Journal of Research in Personality* 10(3): 346–57.

Smith, S.L. 1984. Significant research findings in the etiology of child abuse. *Social Casework* 65(2): 337–46.

Snell, J.; Rosenwald, R.; and Robey, A. 1964. The wife-beater's wife. *Archives of General Psychiatry* 11: 107–12.

Snyder, D.K. 1981. Predicting disposition following brief resdence at a shelter for battered women. *American Journal of Community Psychology* 9(5): 559–65.

Snyder, D.K. and Fruchtman, L.A. 1981. Differential patterns of wife abuse: A data-based typology. *Journal of Consulting and Clinical Psychology* 49: 878–85.

Soloman, K. 1983. Victimization by health professionals and the psychology response of the elderly. In *Abuse and maltreatment of the elderly: Causes and interventions,* ed. J.I. Kosberg. John Wright, PSG.

Sonkin, D.J., and Durphy, M. 1982. *Learning to live without violence: A handbook for men.* San Francisco: Volcano Press.

Sonkin, D.J.; Martin, D.; and Walker, L.E.A. 1985. *The male batterer.* New York: Springer.

Sontag, A. 1973. Preventing child abuse. *Social Work Today* 4(20): 634–35.

Spark, G.M., and Brody, E.M. 1970. The aged are family members. *Family Process* 9(2): 195–210.

Specktor, P. 1979. *Incest: Confronting the silent crime.* Minneapolis: Minnesota Program for Victims of Sexual Abuse.

Spencer, J. 1978. Father-daughter incest: A clinical view from the corrections field. *Child Welfare* 57(5): 585–87.

Spinetta, J.J., and Rigler, D. 1972. The child-abusing parent: A psychological review. *Psychological Bulletin* 77(4): 296–304.

Sprey, J. 1974. On the management of conflict in families. In *Violence in the family,* ed. S. Steinmetz and M. Straus. New York: Harper and Row.

Stacey, W., and Shupe, A. 1983. *The family secret: Domestic violence in America.* Boston: Beacon Press.

Stack, C.B. 1974. *All our kin: Strategies for survival in a black community.* New York: Harper and Row.

Stafford, F. 1980. A program for families of the mentally impaired elderly. *Gerontologist* 20: 656–60.

Stahly, G.B. 1978. A review of select literature of spousal abuse. *Victimology* 2(3/4): 591–607.

Star, B, 1980. Comparing battered and nonbattered women. *Victimology* 5(1): 32–44.

———. 1982. Characteristics of family violence. In *The many faces of violence,* ed. J.P. Flanzer. Springfield, Ill.: Charles C. Thomas.

———. 1983. *Helping the abuser.* New York: Family Service Association of America.

Star, B.; Clark, C.G.; Goetz, K.M.; and O'Malia, L. 1979. Psychosocial aspects of wifebeating. *Social Casework* 60(4): 479–87.

Star, R.H., ed. 1982. *Child abuse prediction (policy implications).* New York: Ballinger.

Stark, E.; Flitcraft, A.; and Frazier, W. 1979. Medicine and patriarchal violence: The social construction of a "private" event. *International Journal of Health Services* 9(3): 461–93.

Stark, R., and McEvoy, J. 1970. Middle-class violence. *Psychology Today* 4: 52–65.

Stathopoulos. P.A. 1983. Consumer advocacy and abuse of elders in nursing homes. In *Abuse and maltreatment of the elderly: Causes and interventions,* ed. J.I. Kosberg. Boston: John Wright, PSG.

Stearns, P.J. 1986. Old age family conflict: The perspective of the past. In *Elder abuse: Conflict in the family,* ed. K.A. Pillemer and R.S. Wolf. Dover, Mass.: Auburn House.

Steele, B. 1975. *Working with abusive parents.* Washington, D.C.: Department of Health, Education, and Welfare, Office of Human Development, National Center on Child Abuse.

Steele, B., and Pollock, C.B. 1968. A psychiatric study of parents who abuse infants and small children. In *The battered child,* ed. R.E. Helfer and C.H. Kemper. Chicago: University of Chicago Press.

Steiman, L. 1979. Reactivated conflict with parents. In *Aging parents,* ed. P. Ragano. Los Angeles: Percy Andrus Gerontology Center, University of Southern California Press.

Steinmetz, S. 1977. *The cycle of violence: Assertive, aggressive, and abusive family interaction.* 2d ed. New York: Praeger.

———. 1977. The use of force for resolving family conflict: The training ground for abuse. *Family Coordinator* 26(1): 19–26.

———. 1977. Wife beating, husband beating: A comparison of the use of physical violence between spouses to resolve marital fights. In *Battered women,* ed. M. Roy. New York: Harper and Row.

———. 1977–78. The battered husband syndrome. *Victimology* 2(3/4): 499–509.

———. 1978. Battered parents. *Society* 15(15).

———. 1978. The politics of aging, battered parents. *Society* 15(1): 54–55.

———. 1980. Women and violence: Victims and perpetrators. *American Journal of Psychotherapy* 34(2): 334–50.

———. 1981. Elder abuse. *Aging* 7: 6–10.

———. 1983. Dependency, stress, and violence between middle-aged care givers and their elderly parents. In *Abuse and maltreatment of the elderly: Causes and interventions,* ed. J.I. Kosberg. Boston: John Wright, PSG.

Steinmetz, S.K., and Straus, M.A. 1973. The family as a cradle of violence. *Society* 10(1): 50–56.

———. eds. 1974. *Violence in the family.* New York: Harper and Row.

Stephens, D. 1977. Domestic assault: The police response. In *Battered women,* ed. M. Roy. New York: Van Nostrand Reinhold.

Stern, M.J., and Yeyer, L. 1980. Family and couple interaction pattern in cases of father/daughter incest. In *Sexual abuse of children: Selected readings.* Washington, D.C.: Department of Health and Human Services.

Steuer, J. 1983. Abuse of the physically disabled elder. In *Abuse and maltreatment of the elderly: Causes and interventions,* ed. J.I. Kosberg. Boston: John Wright, PSG.

———. 1984. Caring for the care giver. *Gerontological Society* 9(2): 56–57.

Steuer, J., and Austin, E. 1980. Family abuse of the elderly. *Journal of the American Geriatric Society* 28(3): 372–76.

Stewart, M.A., and deBlois, C.S. 1981. Wife abuse among families attending a child psychiatry clinic. *Journal of the American Academy of Child Psychiatry* 20: 845–62.

Stinger-Moore, D. 1984. Beliefs about and experiences with battering women and men in two populations. *Sex Roles* 11: 269–76.

Stoenner, H. 1972. *Plain talk about child abuse.* Denver: American Humane Association, Children's Division.

Storkey, C. 1985. Personal worth, self-esteem, anomia, hostility, and irrational thinking of abusive mothers. *Journal of Clinical Psychology* 41: 414–21.

Straus, M.A. 1973. A general systems-theory approach to the development of a theory of violence between family members. *Social Science Information* 12(1): 105–25.

———. 1974. A cultural and social organization influence on violence between family members. In *Configurations: Biological and cultural factors in sexuality and family life,* ed. R. Price and G. Barrier. Lexington, Mass.: Lexington Books.

———. 1974. Forward. In *The violent home: A study of physical aggression between husbands and wives,* ed. R.J. Gelles. Beverly Hills, Calif.: Sage Publications.

———. 1974. Leveling, civility, and violence in the family. *Journal of Marriage and the Family* 36(1): 13–29.

———. 1975. Husband-wife interaction in nuclear and joint households. In *Explorations in the family and other essays,* ed. D. Narian. Bombay: Thacker.

———. 1976. Sexual inequality, cultural norms, and wife beating. *Victimology* 1(1): 54–76.

———. 1977–78. Wife beating: How common and why? *Victimology* 2(3/4): 443–58.

———. 1978. A sociological perspective on the prevention and treatment of wife beating. In *Battered women,* ed. M. Roy. New York: Harper and Row.

———. 1979. Measuring intrafamily conflict and violence: The conflict tactics scales (CTS). *Journal of Marriage and the Family* 41(1): 75–88.

———. 1979. *A sociological perspective on causes of family violence.* Paper presented at the American Association of the Advancement of Science Conference, Houston, Texas.

———. 1980. Sexual inequality and wife beating. In *The social causes of husband-wife violence,* ed. M.A. Straus and G. Hotaling. Minneapolis: University of Minnesota Press.

———. 1980. Stress and physical child abuse. *Child Abuse and Neglect* 4: 75–88.

Straus, M.A., and Gelles, R.J. 1975. Physical violence in families. In *Families today: A research study on families,* ed. E. Corfman. Washington, D.C.: Government Printing Office.

———. 1985. Societal change and change in family violence from 1975 to 1985 as revealed by two national surveys. *Journal of Marriage and the Family* 48(4): 465–79.

Straus, M.A.; Gelles, R.J.; and Steinmetz, S.K. 1980. *Behind closed doors: Violence in the American family.* Garden City, N.Y.: Anchor.

Straus, M.A., and Hotaling, G., eds. 1980. *The social causes of husband-wife violence.* Minneapolis: University of Minnesota Press.

Streib, G.F., and Beck, R.W. 1980. Older families: A decade review. *Journal of Marriage and the Family* 49(6): 937–56.

Strube, M.J., and Barbour, L.S. 1983. The decision to leave an abusive relationship: Economic dependence and psychological commitment. *Journal of Marriage and the Family* 45: 785–93.

Stuart, I.R. 1984. *Victims of sexual aggression: Treatment of children, women, and men.* New York: Van Nostrand Reinhold.

Sturkie, K. 1983. Structured group treatment of sexually abused children. *Health and Social Work* 8(2): 299–308.

———. 1984. Family therapy of a domestic violence service-delivery system. *Clinical Social Work Journal* 12(1): 78–84.

Subin, H. 1973. *Criminal justice in the metropolitan court.* New York: DaCapo Press.

Subramanian, K. 1985. Reducing child abuse through respite-center intervention. *Child Welfare* 64(4): 501–9.

Suchman, E. 1965. Social factors in medical deprivation. *American Journal of Public Health* 55(12): 1725–33.

Summers, G. 1984. Blaming the victim versus blaming the perpetrator . . . analysis of spouse abuse. *Journal of Social and Clinical Psychology* 2(4): 339–47.

Summit, R. 1983. The child sexual-abuse accommodation syndrome. *Child Abuse and Neglect* 7: 177–93.

Summit, R., and Kryso, J. 1978. Sexual abuse of children: A clinical spectrum. *American Journal of Orthopsychiatry* 48(2): 237–51.

Sundeen, R.A., and Mathieu, J.T. 1976. The urban elderly: Environments of fear. In *Crime and the elderly*, ed. J. Goldsmith and S.S. Goldsmith. Lexington, Mass.: Lexington Books.

Susman, E.J. 1985. Child-rearing patterns in depressed, abusive, and normal mothers. *American Journal of Orthopsychiatry* 55(2): 237–51.

Sussman, A. 1975. *Reporting child abuse and neglect: Guideline for legislation.* Cambridge, Mass.: Ballinger.

Sutton, J. 1977–78. The growth of the British movement for battered women, National Women's Aid Federation, London. *Victimology* 2(3/4): 576–84.

Swan, H.L. 1985. Child sexual abuse prevention: Does it work? *Child Welfare* 64(3): 395–405.

Swan, R.W. 1985. The child as active participant in child abuse. *Clinical Social Work Journal* 13(1): 62–77.

Swanson, L.D. 1961. Role of the police in the protection of children from neglect and abuse. *Federal Probation* 25(1): 43.

Tahourdin, B. 1976. Battered wives: Only a domestic affair. *International Journal of the Offender Therapy and Comparative Criminology* 1(20): 86–88.

Taubman, S. 1984. Incest in context. *Social Work* 29(1): 35–40.

Telch, C.F. 1958. Violent versus nonviolent couples. *Psychiatry* 21(2): 242–48.

Terr, L.C. 1970. A family study of child abuse. *American Journal of Psychiatry* 127(5): 665–71.

Teske, R.H., Jr.; Williams, F.P.; and Dull, R.T. 1980. *Texas crime poll, spring 1980 survey.* Huntsville: Sam Houston State University, Criminal Justice Center.

Test for a battered woman. 1981. *Marriage and divorce today* 7(5): 1.

Thibaut, J.W., and Kelley, H.H. 1958. *The social psychological of groups.* New York: John Wiley and Sons.

Thobaben, M., and Anderson, L. 1985. Reporting elder abuse: It's the law. *American Journal of Nursing* 85(4): 371–74.

Thomas, S.B. 1975. Federal priorities on behalf of neglected and abused children. In *Proceedings of the fourth national symposium on child abuse.* Denver: American Humane Association, Children's Division.

Thorman, G. 1980. *Family violence.* Springfield, Ill.: Charles C. Thomas.

Tidmarsh, M. 1976. Violence in marriage: Sheffield. *Social Work Today* 7(2): 36–38.

Tiermey, K. 1982. The battered-women movement and the creation of the wife-beating problem. *Social Problems* 29(3): 207–20.

Toby, J. 1966. Violence and the masculine ideal: Some qualitative data. In *Patterns of violence,* ed. M.E. Wolfgang. Philadelphia: Annals of the American Academy of Political and Social Science.

Tomita, S. 1982. Detection and treatment of elderly abuse and neglect: A protocol for health-care professionals. *PT and OT in Geriatrics* 2(2): 37–51.

Toper, A., and Aldrich, D. 1981. Incest: Intake and investigation. In *Sexually abused children and families,* ed. P. Mrazek and H. Kempe. Oxford: Pergamon.

Tormes, Y. 1968. *Child victims of incest.* Denver: American Humane Association, Children's Division.

Treas, J. 1977. Family support systems for the aged: Some social and demographic considerations. *Gerontologist* 17(4): 486–91.

Troll, L.E. 1971. The family in later life: A decade review. In *A decade of family research and action,* ed. C.B. Broderick. Minneapolis: National Council on Family Relations.

———. 1971. The family in later life: A decade review. *Journal of Marriage and the Family* 33(2): 263–90.

Truninger, E. 1971. Marital violence: The legal solutions. *Hastings Law Review* 13: 159–76.

Tuszynski, A. 1985. Group treatment that helps abusive and neglectful families. *Social Casework* 66(4): 556–62.

Tuzil, T. 1978. The aging role in helping children and their aged parents. *Social Casework* 59(5): 302–5.

U.S. Bureau of Justice Statistics. 1980. *Intimate victims: A study of violence among friends and relatives.* Washington, D.C.: Government Printing Office.

U.S. Commission on Civil Rights. 1983. *Under the rule of thumb: Battered women and the administration of justice.* Washington, D.C.: Government Printing Office.

U.S. Congress. House. Select Committee on Aging. 1980. *Domestic abuse of the elderly.* 96th Cong. Committee Publication no. 96–259.

U.S. Congress. House. Committee on Aging. 1980. *Elder abuse: The hidden problem.* 96th Cong. Committee Publication no. 96–220.

U.S. Congress. House. Select Committee on Aging. 1981. *Elder abuse: An examination of a hidden problem.* 97th Cong. Committee Publication no. 97–277.

U.S. Department of Health, Education, and Welfare. 1973. *The abused child: Principals and suggested language by legislation on reporting of the physically abused child.* Washington, D.C.: Government Printing Office.

U.S. Department of Health, Education, and Welfare. 1984. *A report to the President and Congress of the United States on the implementation of Public Law 93–247, the Child Abuse Prevention Act.* Washington, D.C.: Government Printing Office.

U.S. Department of Justice. 1984. *Attorney General's Task Force on Family Violence.* Washington, D.C.: Government Printing Office.

Valentine, D. 1985. Abuse and neglect: Identifying and helping school children at risk. *School Social Work Journal* 9: 83–97.

Van den Berghe, P. 1980. Incest and exogamy: A sociobiological reconsideration. *Ethnology and Sociobiology* 1: 151–62.

Vander Mey, B.J., and Neff, R.L. 1966. *Incest as child abuse*. New York: Praeger.

———. 1982. Adult-child incest: A review of research and treatment. *Adolescence* 17(4): 717–35.

———. 1984. Adult-child incest: A sample of substantiated cases. *Family Relations* 33(4): 548–57.

———. 1986. *Incest as child abuse: Research and applications*. New York: Praeger.

Vanfossen, B.F. 1979. Intersexual violence in Monroe County, New York. *Victimology* 4(2): 229–305.

Villamore, E., and Bergman, J., eds. 1981. *Elder abuse and neglect: A guide for practitioners and policy makers*. Prepared for the Oregon Office of Elder Affairs by the National Paralegal Institute, San Francisco, and by Legal Research and Services for the Elderly, Boston.

Wadlington, W. 1983. *Cases and materials on children in the legal system*. Mineola, N.Y.: Foundation Press.

Wagner, R. 1972. The role of the court. In *Proceedings from a national symposium on child abuse*. Denver: American Humane Association, Children's Division.

Waites, E.A. 1978. Female masochism and the enforced restriction on choice. *Victimology* 2(3/4): 535–44.

Wald, M. 1961. *Protective services and emotional neglect*. Denver: American Humane Association, Children's Division.

Walker, J.C. 1983. Protective services for the elderly: Connecticut's experience. In *Abuse and maltreatment of the elderly: Causes and interventions*, ed. J.I. Kosberg. Boston: John Wright, PSG.

Walker, L.E. 1977–78. Battered women and learned helplessness. *Vivtimology* 2(3/4): 525–34.

———. 1979. *The battered women*. New York: Harper and Row.

———. 1984. *The battered women syndrome*. New York: Springer.

Ward, D.; Jackson, M.; and Ward, R. 1969. Crimes of violence by women. In *Crimes of violence*, ed. D. Mulvihill and M. Tumin. Washington, D.C.: Government Printing Office.

Warrior, B. 1976. *Battered lives*. Pittsburg: KNOW.

———. 1977. *Working on wife abuse*. Cambridge, Mass.

Warwick, D.P., and Lininger, C.A. 1975. *The sample survey: Theory and practice*. New York: McGraw-Hill.

Wasserman, S. 1967. The abused parent of the abused child. *Children* 14(5): 175–79.

Watkins, C.R. 1982. *Victims, aggressors, and the family secret: An exploration into family violence*. St. Paul: Minnesota Departmentof Public Welfare.

Watt, J.W. 1985. Protective service teams. *Health and Social Work* 10: 191–98.

Watts, D.L., and Courtois, C.A. 1981. Trends in the treatment of men who commit violence against women. *Personnel and Guidance Journal* 60: 245–49.

Wawzonek, S.J. 1974. The role of the family in disability. *American Archives of Rehabilitation Therapy* 22: 49–57.

Weber, E. 1977. Incest: Sexual abuse begins at home. *Ms.* (September): 64–76.

Weede, E. 1981. Income inequality, average income, and domestic violence. *Conflict Resolution* 25(4): 639–54.

Weinberg, S.K. 1955. *Incest behavior.* New York: Citadel.

Weinberg, P.E., and Smith, P.J. 1966. The disposition of child-neglect cases referred by caseworkers to a juvenile court. *Child Welfare* 45(7): 457–463, 471.

Weiner, C. 1982. *Criminal violence.* Beverly Hills, Calif.: Sage Publications.

Weiss, J.; Rogers, E.; Darwin, M.R.; and Dutton, C.E. 1955. A study of girl sex victims. *Psychiatric Quarterly* 29: 1–27.

Weitzman, J. 1982. Wife beating: A view of the marital dyad. *Social Casework* 63(5): 259–65.

Werts, C.E.; Rocks, D.A.; and Grandy, J. 1974. Confirmatory factor analysis applications. *Multivariate Behavioral Research* 27: 229–39.

Wetzel, L., and Ross, M.A. 1983. Psychological and social ramifications of battering: Observations leading to a counseling methodology for victims of domestic violence. *Personnel and Guidance Journal* 61: 423–28.

White, L.A. 1948. The definition and prohibition of incest *American Anthropologist* 50(3): 416–35.

Whitehurst, R.M. 1971. Violence potential in extramarital sexual response. *Journal of Marriage and the Family* 33(4): 683–91.

———. 1974. Violence in husband-wife interaction. In *Violence in the family,* ed. S. Steinmetz and M. Straus. New York: Harper and Row.

———. 1975. Violently jealous husbands. In *Sexual issues in marriage,* ed. L. Gross. New York: Spectrum.

Wilderson, A.E. 1973. *The rights of children.* Philadelphia: Temple.

Williams, G.J., and Money, J., eds. 1980. *Traumatic abuse and neglect of children at home.* Baltimore: John Hopkins University Press.

Williams, R.D. 1969. The AFDC worker's role in protective services. *Child Welfare* 48(5): 273–78.

Willie, C.V., and Greenblatt, S.L. 1978. Four "classic" studies of power relationships in black families: A review and look to the future. *Journal of Marriage and the Family* 40(4): 691–94.

Wilson, C.F. 1981. Violence against women: An annotated bibliography. Boston: G.K. Hall.

Wilson, J. 1978. *Religion in American society: The effective presence.* Englewood Cliffs, N.J.: Prentice-Hall.

Winship, C., and Mare, R. 1984. Regression models with ordinal variables. *American Sociological Review* 49(5): 512–25.

Wohl, A. 1985. *Silent screams and hidden cries and interpretations of artwork by children from violent homes.* Brunner/Mazel.

Wojtsa, O. 1980. Disturbing truth about wife battering. *Times Higher Educational Supplement* 389: 7.

Wolf, A.P. 1972. Childhood association and sexual attractions: A further test of the Westermack hypothesis. *American Anthropologist* 70(4): 503–15,

Wolf, D.A. 1985. Child-abusive parents: An empirical review and analysis. *Psychological Bulletin* 97(4): 462–82.

Wolf, R.S.; Godkin, M.A.; and Pillemer, K.A. 1984. *Elder abuse and neglect: Final report from three model projects.* Worcester, Mass.: University of Massachusetts Medical Center, Center on Aging, December.

———. 1984. *Working with abused elders: Assessment, advocacy, and intervention.* Worcester, Mass.: University of Massachusetts Medical Center, Center on Aging.

Wolf, R.S.; Strugnell, C.P.; and Godkin, M.A. 1982. *Preliminary findings from three model projects on elderly abuse.* Worcester, Mass.: University of Massachusetts Medical Center, University Center on Aging.

Wolfgang, M.E. 1958. *Patterns in criminal homicide.* New York: John Wiley and Sons.

Wolfgang, M.E., and Ferracuti, F. 1967. *The subculture of violence.* London: Tavistock.

Wolk, R.L., and Reingold, J. 1975. The course of life for older people. *Journal of Personality and Social Psychology* 31: 376–79.

Wollert, R.W. 1982. Self-help group for sexually abusive families. *Prevention in Humane Services* 1: 99–109.

Wolock, I. 1984. Child maltreatment as a social problem: The neglect of neglect. *American Journal of Orthopsychiatry* 54(4): 530–43.

Woods, L. 1978. Litigation on behalf of battered women. *Women's Rights Law Reporter* 5(1): 7–15.

Wooley, S.F. 1974. Battered women: A summary. In *Battered women,* ed. D. Moore. Beverly Hills, Calif.: Sage Publications.

Worden, R.E., and Pollitz, A.A. 1984. Police arrests in domestic disturbances: A further look. *Law and Society Review* 18(1): 105–20.

Wylie, F.M. 1971. Attitudes toward aging and the aged among black Americans: Some historical perspectives. *Aging and Human Development* 2: 66–69.

Yelaja, S.A. 1973. The abused child: A reminder of despair. *Canadian Welfare* 49(2): 8–11.

Yllo, K. 1984. The status of women, marital equality, and violence against wives. *Journal of Family Issues* 5(3): 307–20.

Young, L.R. 1963. The behavior syndromes of parents who neglect and abuse their children. Ph.D. diss., Columbia University, School of Social Work.

———. 1964. *Wednesday's child.* New York: McGraw-Hill.

———. 1981. *Physical child neglect.* Chicago: National Committee for Prevention of Child Abuse.

Youngerman, J.K., and Canino, I.A. 1983. Violent kids, violent parents: Family pharmacotherapy. *American Journal of Orthopsychiatry* 53(1): 152–56.

Zacher, J., and Bard, M. 1971. The prevention of family violence: Dilemmas of community intervention. *Journal of Marriage and the Family* 33(6): 677–82.

Zalba, S.R. 1966. The abused child: A survey of the problem. *Social Work* 11(4): 3–16.

———. 1967. The abused child: 2. A typology for classification and treatment. *Social Work* 12(1): 70–79.

Zarit, S.H. 1979. The organic brain syndrome and family relationships. In *Aging parents,* ed. P. Ragan. Los Angeles: Percy Andrus Gerontology Center, University of Southern California Press.

Zarit, S.; Reever, K.; and Bach-Peterson, J. 1980. Relatives of the impaired elderly: Correlates of feelings of burden. *Gerontologist* 20(4): 649–55.

Zimrin, H. 1984. Child abuse: Encounter between needs and personality traits within the family. *American Journal of Family Therapy* 12(1): 37–47.

Zoomer, O.J. 1983. On the social causes and functions of violence against women. *International Journal of Offender Therapy and Comparative Criminology* 27(2): 52–71.

Index

About the Author

Bob Sigler is an associate professor in the Department of Criminal Justice at the University of Alabama. He is active in teaching, research, and community service. In addition to his interests in domestic abuse, he pursues interests in the use of volunteers, stress, sexual harassment, and alternatives to corrections. He and his colleagues, Ida Johnson and Jody Crowley are presently investigating agency responses to domestic abuse and cross perceptions in elder abuse.